A Story of Jewish Experience in Mississippi

North American Jewish Studies

Series Editor
IRA ROBINSON
(Concordia University)

A Story of Jewish Experience in Mississippi

LEON WALDOFF

Boston
2019

Library of Congress Cataloging-in-Publication Data

Names: Waldoff, Leon, 1935- author.

Title: A story of Jewish life in Mississippi / by Leon Waldoff.

Description: Boston: Academic Studies Press, [2018] |
Series: North American Jewish Studies | Includes bibliographical references.

Identifiers: LCCN 2018048878 (print) | LCCN 2018050196 (ebook) | ISBN 9781618118905 (ebook) | ISBN 9781618118882 (hardcover) | ISBN 9781618118899 (pbk.)

Subjects: LCSH: Jews—Mississippi—Hattiesburg—History—20th century. | Jews, Russian—Mississippi—Hattiesburg—History—20th century. | Hattiesburg (Miss.)—Ethnic relations. | Waldoff, Leon, 1935-

Classification: LCC F350.J5 (ebook) | LCC F350.J5 W35 2018 (print) | DDC 976.2/18004924—dc23

LC record available at https://lccn.loc.gov/2018048878

©Academic Studies Press, 2019
ISBN 9781618118882 (hardback)
ISBN 9781618118905 (electronic)
ISBN 9781618118899 (paperback)

Book design by Kryon Publishing Services (P) Ltd.
www.kryonpublishing.com

Cover design by Ivan Grave

Published by Academic Studies Press
28 Montfern Avenue
Brighton, MA 02135, USA
press@academicstudiespress.com
www.academicstudiespress.com

To the Memory of Paul and Eva Stein Waldoff

Table of Contents

Introduction	vii
Chapter 1: From Russia to Mississippi	1
Chapter 2: A Merchant, After All	26
Chapter 3: Fear in Low Profile: An Incident in the 1930s	53
Chapter 4: Our Home	76
Chapter 5: Surviving the Depression, Finding Acceptance, Anticipating War	97
Chapter 6: Breaking the Silence about Segregation	121
Chapter 7: Fear in High Profile: Terrorism in the 1960s	156
Afterword	185
Endnotes	190
Acknowledgments	204

Introduction

Since leaving Mississippi more than sixty years ago, I've often been asked, "How did your parents from Russia come to settle in Mississippi?" It wasn't a question I heard when growing up there. Our small Jewish community in Hattiesburg of approximately thirty-five families in the 1930s and 1940s consisted almost entirely of immigrants from Russia and Poland and their children born here. The first few arrived around the turn of the century, followed by others well into the 1920s, including my father in 1924. In the 1940s his small department store was one of six clothing stores and one shoe store owned by Jewish merchants on the same side of the street of one city block. For the first eighteen years of my life, my parents' history didn't seem so unusual. I heard the question for the first time during my freshman year at Northwestern. Although it continued to turn up on occasion in the next fifty-plus years, I gave it little thought. But several years after I retired from the University of Illinois in Urbana-Champaign, where I had been an English professor since 1967, my daughter Jessica asked that very question and this time it struck a deeper chord. By then both of my parents had been dead for many years. She had never known my father, who died two years before she was born, and she knew my mother only from brief visits during Jessica's first nine years.

I began answering her by describing how my father's family came here, mentioning how their experience was part of a general pattern in which networks of immigrant relatives helped one another (what historians call chain migration), and then added several of my parents' stories about their early lives in Russia and Mississippi. Jessica said the stories were fascinating. What I heard in my answer, however, was a lot of stumbling and uncertainty, making me realize how little I actually knew about my parents' experiences as young immigrants who had to learn a new language, find a way to make a living, adapt to the laws and customs of segregation in Mississippi, and survive the Great

Depression. Trying to answer Jessica's question proved to be an unsettling and eye-opening moment that would eventually lead me to begin researching my parents' experience as young immigrants and to discover that their story was indeed remarkable.

The first step was deceptively easy. I began to make a record of my parents' memories of experiences and events, as they had been told to me, from their early lives—for example, that my mother's father had been stripped and beaten during a pogrom in Warsaw in 1905, that she had once heard Trotsky speak, and that guards at the Russian border with Romania stuck pitchforks in the hay wagon in which she and other emigrants were hiding as they made their escape out of the Soviet Union in 1921. I also recalled that when I was eight or nine years old she showed me two small pencil drawings her brother Scholym had sent her (which now hang in my sister Fay's home). He had been an artist before Hitler's invasion of the Soviet Union, become a soldier, and been killed at the front in 1942. Although tinged with sorrow, and at times interrupted by an outburst of bitterness against the tsar more than twenty years after he was assassinated, her stories gave me a sense not only of certain deep resentments she still harbored about her life in Russia, but also of the strong bond she felt with the family she had left behind.

My father's memories, by contrast, were rarely about his family and more often about his observations and experiences. When the Germans occupied Kiev in the last year of World War I, he told me, they brought a much-needed sense of order to the city. In recalling how he'd once sold cigarettes on the streets of Kiev, he emphasized that he'd been able to do so with some success until the Bolsheviks came to power and confiscated all the tobacco he had kept stored in a loft until it could be rolled into cigarettes. He told my brother Milton that in his first year as a peddler in Mississippi, walking from one small town to another, he at times had to get off the road and hide in the woods to avoid being robbed. He once surprised me with the story, still amused by it himself, of a man who had come to his store to see what a Jew looked like, believing Jews had horns.

But it was the story my father's sister Rose told a day or two after his funeral in 1962 that stood out above the others: their father had left for America without first informing his wife, in effect abandoning her and their three children, something neither my father nor my mother had ever said a word about. Then, following, my mother's death twelve years later, my sister Fay, my brother Milton, and I found a batch of letters in Russian my father had written to my mother while he was courting her. Once we had them translated, they proved to be a treasure trove. Here was my father in his own voice as a young man of twenty-one on his way to America with his mother, sister, and brother, revealing his thoughts and feelings to my mother and, after they were both here—he in New York, she in Baltimore—telling her of the conflict with his parents over his plan to go to Mississippi. We also found other letters from my mother's family, most of them in Russian, a few in Yiddish, which we added to a small collection of documents and photos. Later I found ship manifests, naturalization papers, and census records that enabled me to establish basic information about dates, ages, name changes, and the like.

Yet there was so much more still unknown to me. My parents' memories and the family letters referred at times to historical events and to the social and economic restrictions under which Jews in Russia lived. I began to see that I needed to know a great deal more if I had any hope of understanding how my parents' early history had shaped their lives before they arrived at Ellis Island. Even though I had grown up in Hattiesburg, I knew little about its history at the time my father went there, and nothing about his experience as a Jewish peddler going from one small town or rural community to another. I also knew very little about the history of our Jewish community, both the years before I was born and the years after I had left Hattiesburg. I realized I had a lot to learn. I began reading memoirs and histories of Jews in Russia, of their experience as immigrants, of Jews in America and in the South, as well as histories of the South, of Mississippi, of peddling, and other related subjects. I also searched through city directories, the Ellis Island website, court records, more than twenty years of the old *Hattiesburg American* on microfilm, and other materials held in archives in Hattiesburg, Jackson, New Orleans, and Cincinnati.

One of my father's stories of a long-forgotten incident in the history of the Jewish community in Hattiesburg proved to be a turning point in my research and helped me to understand the larger story beginning to take shape in my mind. His memory of the incident, mentioned to me only in passing when I was a teenager, and about which I failed to ask any questions, began to haunt me. Chapter 3 is devoted to it. It concerns a young Jewish man—at seventeen, perhaps more boy than man—who with his black accomplice robbed a local gas station in 1931 and was tried and convicted of a murder committed during the robbery. The story of the murder, trial, appeals to the Mississippi Supreme Court, and strange death of this young man in his jail cell, I would come to see, revealed the underlying fear with which Jews in Hattiesburg lived in the 1930s, despite their generally positive but qualified acceptance by the predominant white Gentile majority and their eventual financial success.

The more I pondered this story, the more I began to understand how the concerns in my father's memory of the case and the fear generated in the Jewish community were inseparable from the larger story of Jewish life in Mississippi, a story that reached a climax during the civil rights movement of the 1950s and 1960s.

Two men who played important roles during those years were Rabbi Charles Mantinband of B'nai Israel Congregation in Hattiesburg and my brother-in-law Adolph Ira Botnick (known to everyone as "B") of the Anti-Defamation League. Rabbi Mantinband arrived in the fall of 1951 when I was a junior in high school. At that time, I failed to appreciate how fortunate I was to know him and be able to meet with him to discuss questions I had about Judaism and, more generally, religion, as well as to benefit from the generous concern he showed for me. It was only after beginning the research for this book and reading his correspondence, diaries, and published essays, as well as essays about him, that I learned of the courage and wisdom he displayed during the crucial years of the civil rights movement and saw its significance for the story of Jewish life in Mississippi I was writing. His congregation wanted him to maintain the long tradition in the South of Jewish silence about segregation. As a tiny minority, they feared for their personal safety and financial security. He understood and sympathized with their concerns, but he also saw segregation as "the supreme sin of our day" and a "monstrous" evil, and he felt bound to speak out against it.

A year after he left Hattiesburg in 1963 for a pulpit in Beaumont, Texas, "B," whom Rabbi Mantinband had recommended for a position with the ADL in Atlanta, was promoted to regional director (for Arkansas, Louisiana, and Mississippi) in the spring of 1964 and moved with Fay and their three children to New Orleans. He was suddenly thrust into what would become the most violent years of the civil rights struggle in Mississippi, 1964 to 1968, when the Ku Klux Klan directed a terrorist campaign against Jews, bombing the synagogues in Jackson and Meridian, as well as the home of Rabbi Perry Nussbaum and his wife in Jackson. As a result of his work with local law enforcement officials and the FBI in their efforts to apprehend the perpetrators, "B" himself became a target of the Klan's best-known assassin, Byron De La Beckwith, the man who had shot and killed Medgar Evers in Jackson in 1963. The individual roles of Rabbi Mantinband and "B" form an essential part of the story of Jewish experience in Mississippi in this memoir.

Since much of the memoir is based on events and experiences in Russia and Mississippi either before I was born, while I was young, or after I had left

Mississippi, I've had to rely on various primary materials and historical studies to inform and supplement the basic story I knew from my parents' memories, my own experiences, and the recollections of others. In telling the story, I've made liberal use of quotations from letters, diaries, memoirs, newspapers, histories, and the recollections of family and friends in an effort to be as true as possible to actual events and experiences. My aim has been to let the people who lived the story be heard in their own voices and in that way to bring them to life, to the extent one can, on the printed page. But I sensed early on, and came to feel ever more strongly the deeper I got into the story, that my wanting them to be heard in their own voices came as much from my being haunted by memories of those I had known as it did from the more rational concern for accuracy and truth. I realized it was the increasing recurrence of those memories as I got older and the relationships at the heart of them, still very much alive for me, that was driving me to write the story this book tells.

CHAPTER 1

From Russia to Mississippi

My father saw my mother for the first time in the office of the Hebrew Immigration Aid Society in Bucharest in November 1921. They had heard of each other's family while still in Belaya Tserkov, a small city southwest of Kiev, and would learn during their courtship that their fathers had once known each other in Warsaw. But it was only after she had died and my sister, brother, and I discovered my father's letters to her and had them translated that I learned he had a vivid memory of their meeting and the time they spent together in Bucharest. In a letter he wrote to her five months later in Bremen, a week before his ship would leave for New York, he tells her he's sitting and holding a small picture of her in front of him: "Looking at the eyes, the whole period of our meeting presents itself: the house of Trakhtmanaya, Elizabeth Boulevard, the steps of the butcher, the first days of your move, the fence, your foot . . . everything!"[1] In another letter, he again says he's holding the picture and tells her he's enclosing one of himself on the back of which he's written that his "image" would have to substitute for the "original" "until we meet again."[2] I wish I had the picture of her he mentions, which may have been a duplicate of her passport photo. But I have another from that time in Bucharest in which she's sitting with a woman friend who's smiling and more fully in the light. My mother, with her long black hair falling across her forehead, her head turned towards the camera at a slight angle, leaving her half in light, half in shadow, looks out from the darker side of the photo. Although the pose she adopts may have been suggested by the photographer, and although my father would have seen her in many other settings and circumstances during those four months in Bucharest, he must have seen her often in the striking way she appears here.

They looked back on that time as an especially happy period in their lives. My mother told me they used to take strolls at night with other young emigrants under the light of the streetlamps alongside one of the grand

My mother (right) with a friend in Bucharest in 1921 or 1922.

boulevards of the city, presumably the one my father mentions in his letter, Queen Elizabeth Boulevard. But it was nonetheless his fault that her English wasn't better, she liked to complain, because too often he persuaded her to go out with him when she should have gone to class or spent her time studying. For my father, their first meeting appears to have been one of love at first sight, but for her, with none of her letters from that time to reveal her thoughts and feelings about him, only the fact that she'd saved his letters for five decades, leaving them to be found after her death, I have to assume that it was at some point during their time together in Bucharest when she came to know him and to return the feelings he had for her. In the next three years, however, as I would learn from his letters, there would be long separations, many uncertainties, troubling differences, and postponed meetings until they were married in January of 1925.

She was the fifth of seven children and the third of three daughters. Her oldest brother, Abraham Stolin, had left for America in 1914 and by 1920 had done well enough to be able to offer to bring other members of the immediate family over. But she was the only one interested. A half-century later, and after her death, her youngest brother, Joseph, writing from Kiev, remembered her as "a girl with rosy cheeks and braids almost down to her heels. Willful, energetic, full of the joy of life, stubbornly realistic, she alone of the large family, then, set off on the long journey."[3] Much of what he says about his young sister rings true to me about the woman I knew as my mother. But as much of her character and spirit Joseph was able to capture in so few words, she was a far more complex person than could be conveyed in a couple of sentences. She was extraordinarily capable at any task she took up and she demonstrated remarkable courage in different periods of her life, beginning with the decision to seize

My mother's parents Malka and Moishe Stolin, with sons Lev and Joseph.

the opportunity for a new life in America. One reason she may have been eager to accept her brother Abe's offer and leave Russia, however, was that she hadn't been allowed to continue in school because of a severe case of psoriasis that left parts of her body scaly and her skin broken with sores. With some bitterness, she told me she'd been made to feel like a leper. My father saw the disfiguring effect of the disease and the anguish it caused her during their time together in Bucharest. After they had both been in America for some months but were living in different cities, he in New York, she in Baltimore, he wrote to her about a young woman he saw in night school who suffered from the disease: "By the way, in my class there is a girl who has *that* on her face, not to mention the other parts of her body. She has not been in school for a few days, but will probably come back. Every time I look at her, I cannot listen to the teacher, remembering every time the separate scenes of your suffering seen by me." He thinks this girl's condition is far worse than my mother's and he tries to reassure her: "You cannot imagine, Eva, how you should now enjoy yourself, dance and be happy with life. This girl is thin, as if tortured. One can see by her face that she suffers much from it."[4]

It may have been as a result of her experience with psoriasis that she began training as a nurse, perhaps working as a nurse's assistant, while still in Russia. I have a photograph of her dressed in what appears to be a white uniform. She kept her Russian textbook on skin diseases and I remember from my childhood being both fascinated and repulsed by the full-page color pictures of diseased arms, legs, necks, and other parts of the body disfigured with ugly sores. To persuade her parents to let her leave, she had used not only her wish to go to America but also the need to find a treatment. In one of her father's letters to her while she's still in Bucharest, he urges her to give up her "ideas" and come home: "Eva, you know full well that I was against your trip to America. But on the other hand, I hoped with God's help you would find a health resort so that you can straighten things out. . . . Let God help you . . . and then come home." His pleading then becomes insistent: "Your mother misses you terribly. As you already well know how she can. . . . If I had known earlier that your mother would miss you so terribly and sadly, then I would never have let you go. . . . I hope to God you will recover and come home. In any event, as God grants quickly, do come home."[5] But the psoriasis continued to disturb her. She told my father she often couldn't think of anything else. She may have been afraid that discovery of it in a medical exam would result either in denying her passage then or entry into the United States later. The extent to which she felt disfigured is reflected in the concern my father showed for her in a letter he wrote from

Bremen warning her about the boarding procedures for immigrants. Among East European immigrants, the German route (most commonly through Hamburg or Bremen), in contrast to ports in Holland, Belgium, and France, had for many years become notorious for its "severities," especially the required bath.[6] Familiar with the procedures from his mother's and sister's experiences, he offered advice: "I just this minute remembered that when you have to leave, they will take all the women to common baths and everyone in one room to see the doctor. . . . I suggest the following: stop off before leaving to see Professor Nikola and get a document with a letter, written in German, requesting that you not be taken together with all the women because you don't want the other women to know about it."[7]

She was on her way to Baltimore to live with Abe and his wife Anne. Like other Russian-Jewish men, he may have had more than one reason to emigrate, not only the restrictions on life in the Pale, the pogroms, and reports of opportunities in America, but also, as a young man who had just turned twenty-one in April of 1914, fear of being conscripted into the army. His son Buddy suggested still another reason when I asked him a few years ago about his father's decision to emigrate. He remembered his father's "adventurous spirit," never hesitating to try something new. He'd already sought opportunities in Warsaw and Odessa. In June of 1914 he boarded a ship at Emden, Germany, and arrived in Galveston in July.

Galveston had not been a port of choice for most Jewish immigrants until 1907 and became one then for only a relatively small number. Jacob Schiff, the distinguished German-Jewish banker and philanthropist, had for a number of years been interested in diverting new Jewish immigrants away from New York and the other eastern port cities, Boston, Baltimore, Philadelphia, and Charleston. Because they tended to settle in these cities, especially New York, he feared their steadily increasing numbers would result in greater anti-Semitism. He lobbied successfully for the passage of a bill to establish an immigration station at Galveston and then personally financed the establishment of an office of the Jewish Immigrants' Information Bureau there.[8] How did Abe become one of the relatively few Jewish immigrants to arrive in Galveston? He may have learned about the Galveston Plan from advertisements and literature distributed by the Jewish Emigration Society, which was based in Kiev and actively recruited emigrants. Participants in the plan received funding, along with promises of relocation and employment. To a young man emigrating alone and without the kind of financial help from a relative in the States that in just a few years he would be able to offer members of his family, the funding must have been an added inducement to his adventurous spirit. He would be traveling on the same ship with his and my mother's first cousin, Barney Auerbach (whose mother, Chaia Stolin Auerbach, was the sister of Abe's and my mother's father, Moishe Stolin). They were lucky in their timing, though it wasn't all luck. I've recently learned from my cousin Maurice, Barney's son, that Barney had been warned by his father that war was coming, a fear that may have been based on what he knew of the Balkan wars of 1912–13. Abe and Barney arrived on July 6 with 181 other immigrants, eight days after the assassination of Archduke Franz Ferdinand in Sarajevo. On July 23, fifty-six Jewish immigrants arrived and they were the last to arrive as part of the Galveston Plan. In August, World War I began, and the Galveston Plan was shut down a few months later.[9] Barney had been promised a job by a merchant in Hattiesburg.[10] The job may have been arranged with the help of HIAS, the Industrial Removal Office, or the Jewish Immigrants' Information Bureau in Galveston. Abe's first destination was Nashville, presumably because one of those agencies had found a job for him there. I was able to find an Abraham Stein (single) in the Nashville City Directory for 1915, but not for 1914 or 1916. By 1916 he was in Hattiesburg, probably because he had stayed in touch with Barney. There he would meet Anne Greenberg, marry her, become the owner of a clothing store, and remain there—except for the years 1920 to early 1923 in Baltimore, where they would move to take care of Anne's dying father—until 1932.

A striking irony of the Galveston Plan is that it was conceived and initiated by wealthy German-American Jews such as Schiff who wanted to help their fellow Jews from Eastern Europe seeking an escape from the anti-Semitism of the Old World but who feared that those same Jews would cause an escalation of it in the New. Their fear intensified in proportion to the steadily increasing number of Jewish immigrants arriving and settling in New York or one of the other port cities on the East Coast at the beginning of the twentieth century. Having come here in the previous century, achieved a considerable measure of financial success, fought in the Civil War, and made strides toward assimilation without giving up their Jewish identity, these German-American Jews were embarrassed by their co-religionists from Eastern Europe. What the newcomers needed, they thought, was "more polish, less Polish," something Buddy told me he remembered being said about—as well as to—Jews from Eastern Europe. It was, according to historian Stephen J. Whitfield, among "the standard instructions that *Ostjuden* received."[11] It's not surprising that the new immigrants came to resent the sense of superiority they perceived in the way the German Jews treated them or that they mentioned to their children the resentment they felt. My father was not alone in believing German Jews took a condescending attitude towards other Jews, meaning those from Eastern Europe.

The German-Jewish community's fear of *Ostjuden*, however, was not an unusual experience among ethnic groups. "Intraethnic hostility was by no means uncommon in American history," historian Howard Sachar points out. "Italian and Irish immigrants faced a similarly cool reception from their nativized kinsmen. So had German Jews themselves at the hands of the Sephardic community." What concerned American Jews most about Jewish immigrants from Eastern Europe wasn't their poverty or the extent to which they would need financial help. It was their striking differences in appearance and religious practices, which they feared would stir anti-Semitism and impede the progress toward acceptance and assimilation into American life made by those Jews already here. With "their outlandish garb and exotic Yiddish patois, their often fundamentalist version of religious Orthodoxy, their evident unfamiliarity with hygiene, the newcomers projected a gauche, even terrifying image to their Western fellow Jews." Sachar believes that "the reaction of America's German-Jewish community was one less of snobbery than of plain and simple culture shock." Yet, as he also points out, that same German-Jewish community worked hard to defeat anti-immigration bills in congress. Those that made it to the desks of Presidents Cleveland, Taft, and Wilson were all vetoed and it was the German-Jewish community's efforts that made the difference.[12]

Upon arriving at Ellis Island, my mother's name was changed from Yoheved Stolina to Eva Stein, using the new surname Abe had adopted. Her journey to this country, unlike my father's, was beset with many difficulties. Aside from her parents' objections and the disease she tried to conceal, she encountered problems at the border between the Soviet Union and Romania. I don't know if in 1921 the new Soviet government was continuing to require, as the imperial government had, that emigrants get an exit permit. Under the tsar, the permits had been so difficult to obtain that most emigration, between 75 and 90 percent, was illegal.[13] Needing help in getting a permit may have been the reason my father turned to a friend in the Communist Party when making arrangements to emigrate. But the group my mother was with, she told me, had to pay off guards and cross the border hidden in a wagon covered with hay, only to face more guards on the other side who at times would randomly stick pitchforks into the hay looking for illegal immigrants. Then, after several months in Bucharest when she was seeing my father and learning English, her first application for a visa was rejected. Later, after obtaining a visa, her departure was again delayed, this time by a vindictive official.

CHAPTER 1

Aunt Rose, Grandmother Celia, and Uncle Ben, with Norman and my father Paul behind them, in Bucharest in 1921.

When he asked her about the book she was holding, she handed it to him and said, "You can read. Read it yourself." He told her to step aside and refused to let her proceed. For many years I thought the book was the nursing textbook she had brought with her, but on another occasion when she recalled the encounter with the official, she told my wife Alice it was *Anna Karenina*. As much as I would like to know the title of the book she was reading then, it's her feisty answer that's the most striking feature of the story. Despite minor variations in the story each time she told it, the official's question and her reply remained the constants in it.

When I asked her what happened then, she said the captain of a Turkish ship, an elderly man standing nearby, intervened in her behalf. He offered to take her to Constantinople and from there she could travel to America. That's what she did. The only thing I remember her saying about the captain is that he looked after her and treated her like a daughter. She remained grateful to him. Although she liked to think of herself as a "free-thinking" woman, something my father mentions in one of his letters to her, she tended to look up to certain men in positions of authority like the captain, her doctor, and her lawyer, and the important men in her family—her father, her brother Abe, her husband and the father of her children, and, after he died, Milton. I don't know how long she was on the captain's ship or in Constantinople, but she sailed from there on the *Madonna* and arrived at Ellis Island on September 1, 1922, five months after my father, and went to Baltimore to live with Uncle Abe and Aunt Anne (as I would come to know and remember them). She apparently gave up the idea of becoming a nurse and found work as a seamstress in a coat factory and as a clerk in a clothing store, though I'm not sure which came first.

When my father met her in Bucharest, he was traveling with his mother, sister, and younger brother. His father had emigrated in 1913, but the story of how he left the family remained unknown to Fay, Milton, and me until after our father's death. It was Aunt Rose, my father's sister, who in the days following his funeral in March of 1962 revealed the story to a small group of us sitting in my parents' living room in Hattiesburg. As the co-owner—with whom Aunt Rose didn't say—of a flourmill in Belaya Tserkov, he was often away from home for several days or a week making deliveries and taking orders. One day my grandmother received a postcard from him with a picture of a ship on the front and the following note on the back: "I am on my way to America. When I have saved enough money, I will send for you and the children." Aunt Rose's story was confirmed more than a half-century later by a cousin on my grandmother's side of the family, who left the Soviet Union for Israel in the 1980s and whom I saw several times when he came to the States for graduate study at Northwestern. Our maternal grandmothers were sisters and he had heard the story from both his grandmother and his mother. Whatever my grandfather actually said on that postcard, the story, condensed into the two short sentences Aunt Rose remembered, suggested to me the shock my grandmother must have experienced as she read his words.

He arrived at Ellis Island on December 18, more than eight months before the outbreak of war in August of 1914 and any subsequent interruption in mail service. But he wasn't heard from again for seven years. His failure to contact the family made me wonder how his nine-year absence affected my father. In one of his letters to my mother after she had arrived in the States, while telling her about his family's opposition to his plan of going to Mississippi, he reports that "father says I have lived with him only for 8 months and he did not know me before that time, because he left me when I was still a child."[14] I've often wondered if the check my father sent each year to Father Flannigan's Boys Home (popularized in a 1938 film my father liked, *Boys Town*, with Spencer Tracy playing Father Flannigan) and the sympathy it expressed for orphaned boys were in some way related in his mind to his own experience. He kept one of the thank-you letters from Father Flannigan under the glass top of the desk in his office at the small department store he owned in Hattiesburg, along with pictures of our family and other memorabilia.

In telling the story of how their father left, Aunt Rose also told us he wanted to escape from a clinging mother and a demanding wife, implying he had no intention of staying in touch and eventually sending for his family. But in turning her story over in my mind many years later, and thinking about the first sentence of the postcard, "I am on my way to America," I wondered what knowledge he assumed his wife had and expected her to use in understanding what he was saying to her. What was there in the historical context of the time that would have prepared her to understand that brief, arresting sentence? I found the beginning of an answer in Mary Antin's first memoir when she described Jewish life in her hometown in Russia where, she said, "America was in everybody's mouth. Businessmen talked of it over their accounts; the market women made up their quarrels that they might discuss it from stall to stall; people who had relatives in the famous land went around reading their letters for the enlightenment of less fortunate folks."[15] Her father left Russia for America in 1891 and he and my grandfather were two of more than a million Russian-Jewish men, among them many husbands and fathers, who left their families for America between 1880 and the beginning of World War I, as did great numbers of men from Ireland, Italy, Greece, and other countries, most, presumably, with the intention of coming back for their families or sending for them after gaining a foothold somewhere, as Mary Antin's father did three years after settling in Boston.

While I knew that for Russian Jews anti-Semitism was a major consideration in the decision to emigrate, I knew little about the extent of it and the effects it had on individual lives that spurred mass emigration until I began to read about the severity of the restrictions—or disabilities, as they were also known—and desperate economic conditions in the Pale of Settlement under which most Jews were forced to live. Following the assassination of Tsar Alexander II in 1881, Alexander III had imposed the old restrictions on Jews with a new force, as well as some additional ones, creating an "atmosphere of aggressive Orthodoxy and Russification" that became a spur to emigrate.[16] The restrictions were economically disabling. In addition to those on where Jews could live, there were others on the businesses and trades they could engage in, the number admitted to schools and universities, the number admitted to the bar, and the kind of medical practice Jewish physicians were allowed to have (private only, and no government appointments). There were also restrictions on religious organizations and on travel. These anti-Semitic policies resulted in the impoverishment of the Jewish population, forcing half of the people in many communities to depend on charity. Restrictions on educational opportunities were a special source of anxiety. The last two tsars, Alexander III (1881–1894) and Nicholas II (1894–1918), wanted to deprive Jews of any hope of improving their economic and social conditions. Based on claims that Jewish students were eager to join with revolutionary workers in opposing government policies, quotas were imposed of 10 percent on secondary schools and universities within the Pale, 5 percent outside the Pale, 3 percent in St. Petersburg and Moscow, then reduced to 7, 3, and 2 percent, respectively. While some exceptions were made, enabling a number of Jews to gain admission above the norm, the quotas remained in place until the end of the Romanov dynasty in 1917. A Jewish newspaper at the time called the quotas on higher education "the silent, invisible pogrom."[17]

Although the fear of being conscripted into the imperial army was no longer a concern for my grandfather, it would have been one for Abe, who turned twenty-one two months before he left Russia in June of 1914. That fear, I learned, had a special place in Russian-Jewish memory, going back to the early nineteenth century during the reign of Nicholas I when Jewish males between eighteen and twenty-five could be drafted for a twenty-five-year period of service. If enough conscripts from that age group could not be found, boys as young as twelve could be substituted, and sometimes boys as young as eight were taken. Harsh physical and other punishments were then used in attempts to convert them to Christianity. The practice of seizing minors ended in 1856 and the term of service was reduced in 1874 from twenty-five years to six, but the practice had created a "traumatic memory" that "remained a notable source of anxiety in Russian-Jewish life for generations thereafter."[18]

But it was the increasing number of actual pogroms in the early years of the twentieth century that became the main spur to emigrate. It was then that the word "pogrom" entered the English language from the Russian. From 1903 to 1906 there were brutal pogroms in Ukraine, where most of Russia's Jews lived, beginning in Kishinev and spreading throughout the Pale of Settlement, including major cities such as Kiev and Odessa, but also many smaller cities such as Belaya Tserkov in 1905. Sholom Aleichem and his family were living in Kiev at the time. Out of concern for their safety he moved them from their apartment in a building known to be largely inhabited by Jews to a nearby hotel. His thirteen-year-old daughter, Maroussia, who would later become her father's biographer, remembered a scene in the street she observed from the windows of their hotel. After hearing "loud shouts and shrill cries," she and her brothers and sisters ran from our beds to the windows . . . and looked down on a scene of brutality and murder—a gang of hoodlums beating a poor young Jew with heavy sticks; blood was running over the face of the young man, who was vainly shrieking for aid. A policeman stood nearby, casually looking on and not moving a finger. Our mother quickly pulled the shade down, sent us back to bed and ordered us never again to go near the windows. But what we had seen was enough to give us nightmares for weeks to come.

The pogrom lasted three days and nights. "It was a harrowing experience for my father," Maroussia remembered, and "it forced his decision to leave the country." The policeman who stood nearby and did nothing is representative of the attitude of many local authorities who "often did little to prevent pogroms and on occasion . . . encouraged them."[19]

None of this is to dismiss Aunt Rose's explanation of the family tensions involved in her father's decision to leave, and leave the way he did. But knowing the historical context provided me with a better understanding of how the conditions of Jewish life in Russia must have figured in his decision. If it wasn't the main spur behind his decision, it was certainly the best justification he could have had for leaving his family, and one that he could have expected to be readily understood, as well as made more acceptable by the postcard's second sentence, "When I have saved enough money, I will send for you and the children."

My father had just celebrated his bar mitzvah when his father left. Like other Jewish boys, he would have attended a heder (elementary school) in Belaya Tserkov (White Church). Although a small city, it had a substantial Jewish population—around 20,000 in 1897, roughly 35 percent of the general population—with a diverse ethnic make-up reflected in the different spellings of its name: Biala Czerkiew (Polish), Belaya Tserkov (Russian), and Bila Tserkva (Ukrainian). It had eighteen synagogues and, though my father may have had some secular schooling, for him and the great majority of Jewish boys heder was the only formal schooling they would have. I remember him complaining that he hadn't had an opportunity to get an education. After his father left, he had to go to work. Whatever education he had, he told me more than once, had been at "the school of hard knocks," meaning experience, of course, but perhaps with an ironic reference to the *melameds* who rapped their students' knuckles or heads if they didn't know their lessons, and sometimes even if they did. In these elementary schools, which were typically a single room in the home of the teacher, boys learned to read Hebrew and studied the Old Testament, though how much knowledge and understanding they acquired, even in subjects of this very limited curriculum, has been questioned. The philosopher Solomon Maimon recalled in his *Autobiography*, written at the end of the eighteenth century, that there was no Hebrew dictionary, that grammar was not taught, that passages from the Bible had to be translated into and discussed in Yiddish (again, with no dictionary), and that the teachers were ignorant. "The pupil thus acquires just as little knowledge of the language, as of the contents, of the Bible."[20] Although improvements were made in the nineteenth and early twentieth centuries, with the Russian language being added to the curriculum in a few schools, the system was not very different in the years my father was a student. Yet, despite the inadequacies of the system and the fact that my father had to give up the idea of any further education and go to work at an early age, he not only knew Hebrew and Yiddish but also Russian, the language in which his letters to my mother were written.

After his father left, his mother and the three children—Paul, Rose, and Ben—went to live with her sister and husband in Kiev and their son Norman. Although there were restrictions on Jews living in major cities, Kiev and Odessa had large Jewish populations. Among the many Jews who lived in Kiev without a permit or right of residence were Sholom Aleichem and his family from 1898 to 1905. By 1910 Kiev's Jewish population had grown to 50,000. But in 1911, Jews in Kiev had a terrifying scare when Mendel Beilis was accused of a ritual murder of a thirteen-year-old boy, the "ritual" part of the charge being based on the myth that Jews need Christian blood to prepare unleavened bread for Passover (leaving unexplained how Jews in Muslim countries manage without it) or to cure certain ailments or to use for other supposed purposes.[21] It became a sensational case widely covered in European newspapers in part because Émile Zola and other prominent writers came to the defense of Beilis. It had been only a little more than a decade since Zola had written his famous "J'Accuse" in defense of Alfred Dreyfus. Beilis was eventually acquitted, but the jurors nonetheless found that "a ritual murder" had been committed, in effect saying, as one Jewish newspaper observed in a caption to a cartoon, "Beilis innocent, but the Jews guilty as usual."[22] This case must have figured in the minds of the many Jews who were thinking of emigrating, as Beilis himself did in 1913 (the year my grandfather left), first to Palestine, then to New York.

One of my father's memories from the years he lived in Kiev was of the German occupation during World War I from January to November of 1918. I found a confirmation of what he told me—that the Germans brought a sense of order to life there—in a report written by a HIAS representative, Isidore Hershfeld, a forty-six-year-old lawyer from New York who toured territories occupied by the German Army. In his report he said the condition of Jews under German control was "indescribably better than under Russia" and that "no distinction on religious grounds" was made in the treatment of the population.[23] But following the signing of the armistice in November of 1918, the exit of the Germans, and the subsequent civil war in Russia, anti-Semitism in Ukraine was encouraged and intensified by White Army propaganda claiming not only that Jews had been the dominant force behind the Bolshevik Revolution in 1917, a claim made believable for some by the prominence of Trotsky (Bronstein), Kamenev (Rosenfeld), and Zinoviev (Apfelbaum) in the Soviet leadership, but also that all Jews were Bolsheviks. In the years 1919–20, there were 1,200 pogroms in Ukraine.

Although I never heard my father speak of the pogroms, he had to have been aware of them. In 1919, during periods when the White Army occupied Kiev, homes and businesses were pillaged, members of a Jewish defense unit killed, women raped, and both men and women murdered. In Belaya Tserkov, "about 850 Jews were massacred . . . by Ukrainian troops, bands of peasants, and soldiers of the White Army."[24] My mother not only spoke of the pogroms but told me that once when she was a child in Warsaw, where her family lived for a time in the early 1900s (when it was still part of Russia), her father was accosted by a group of men on a winter night and stripped and beaten. But I had made no effort to learn more about them until I began researching my parents' history.

The scope and cruelty of them, even after the Holocaust, still has the power to shock. Between 1919 and 1921, there were more than 2,000 pogroms, leaving 500,000 Jews homeless and 130,000 dead.[25] In Isaac Babel's *1920 Diary*, published more than sixty years after his arrest during Stalin's purges in the 1930s and execution in 1940, he describes in vivid detail the brutality and sadism of the pogroms. In Zhytomyr, eighty miles west of Kiev (and fifty from Belaya Tserkov), with a population of 68,000 people, of whom 39 percent were Jews, he reports having seen the Poles and then the Red Cossacks do the following: "they cut off beards, that's usual, cut out tongues, wails heard all over the square. They set fire to 6 houses . . . they machine-gunned those who tried to rescue people. The yardman into whose arms a mother dropped a child from a burning window, was bayoneted."[26] Farther west, near the Polish border, Babel records what he saw after the Polish Cossacks had been there the day before. "A pogrom. The family of David Zys, in people's homes, a naked, barely breathing prophet of an old man, an old woman butchered, a child with fingers chopped off . . . a mother sitting over her sabered son, an old woman twisted up like a pretzel, four people in one hovel . . . just lying there in their blood."[27] In one of his short stories, Babel has his central character, Benya Krik, ask, "wasn't it a mistake on the part of God to settle Jews in Russia, for them to be tormented worse than in Hell?"[28]

My parents were living in two of the cities, Belaya Tserkov and Kiev, where pogroms occurred, and not far from other cities whose pogroms Babel described, though no harm came to them. When Alice and I were in Leningrad in 1990, however, we met one of my mother's cousins, Peter Gorelick, and it was from his memoir that I would later learn something my mother had never mentioned but had to have known: that one of her uncles, Abram Litvak, was killed in the 1919 pogrom in Belaya Tserkov by members of the Ukrainian armed forces.[29] In the same year, her paternal grandfather, Samuel Stolin, died at the age of 103 in Belaya Tserkov either from having his beard set on fire in one family story or being hanged in another, presumably by Ukrainian forces but possibly by Polish or Red Cossacks.

It was in 1920, according to Aunt Rose, that the family in Kiev reestablished contact with their missing husband and father in New York. He was invited to a Friday night dinner at the home of a relative in the Bronx and shown a Yiddish newspaper, possibly Abraham Cahan's *Forverts* (*The Jewish Daily Forward*), in which his name appeared in a list of husbands who had left Europe before the war. In *World of Our Fathers: The Journey of the East Europeans to America and the Life They Found and Made*, Irving Howe explains that "for years the *Forward* ran a feature, 'Gallery of Missing Husbands,' that contained photographs of men who had deserted and pleas that they get in touch with their families."[30] Aunt Rose didn't mention a photograph in the story she told a day or two after my father's funeral, but in the version of it she told my daughter Jessica more than twenty years later she said my father had arranged for their father's name to be included in such a list, along with the address where the family could be reached. Having seen an announcement of a lecture to be given in Kiev by a professor from New York, my father went up to him after the lecture and asked if he would contact a newspaper when he returned—perhaps mentioning the *Forward*, which many Russian Jews knew about—and place a notice inquiring about his father. Not knowing the name had been changed, he must have given the professor the name by which he knew his father, Nuchem Volodarsky. Once reunited, he offered the explanation to his family that after the war he had hired a man who represented himself as a detective to do a search. The man insisted on being paid in advance and after a few months returned to tell my grandfather that his wife and children were dead. I've often wondered with what degree of astonished belief or disbelief his wife and children, particularly my father, received this explanation.

My parents were fortunate to arrive here in 1922, my father in April, my mother in September. In May of that year President Harding signed a bill radically reducing the percentages of immigrants from Italy and Eastern Europe.[31] Two years later the Johnson-Reed Immigration Act signed by President Coolidge added further restrictions on the percentages from Eastern Europe. "The National Origins Act of 1924," as it was also known, was, writes historian Hasia Diner, "a major moment in the history of the Jewish people."[32] With further restrictions added in 1929, it virtually closed the door to them, making it extremely difficult during the 1930s for Jews fleeing Nazi Germany to come here.

Although my father was now living in New York and my mother in Baltimore, and the distance between them was just a few hours by train, they saw each other only once in her first seven months here—from September 1922 through March 1923. He wrote almost every day and urged her to do the same. She saved his letters, but either he didn't save hers or they were lost. As a result, my telling of the story of their courtship over the next few months is necessarily through his letters. When he's responding to something she's written, however, her thoughts and feelings are represented or can be discerned. The letters reveal troubling uncertainties in their relationship and his parents' objections to his plan to go to Mississippi, but also his coming to a new understanding of himself and her and their eventual engagement.

In his letters, he at times shows a certain hesitation in pursuing her, as well as some evasiveness in the reasons he gives for not coming to Baltimore to see her. He's often unsure of their relationship, and not without reason. She wrote less often than he did and seemed less forthcoming than he expected her to be. In December, he learns from her that she's been to New York twice, but hadn't arranged to see him. He's disappointed but writes that he won't ask anything further "as you have special interests that I have no right to ask about."[33] He urges her to tell him more about her life in Baltimore and to visit him in New York but doesn't immediately suggest going to visit her. He twice mentions that he's had to go to Philadelphia to see relatives there. When she asks him to come to Baltimore, he explains that he doesn't have time. He has to work in his father's fruit store every day of the week, including Sunday until two in the afternoon, and attend school in the evening. But he writes her almost every day, sometimes a half hour before school, at other times late at night. In two other December letters, he continues to talk about their seeing each other in New York or Baltimore but proposes nothing definite.

By early January and continuing to early March, as my father's letters reveal, their hesitation and uncertainty reach a turning point in the relationship. On January 10, he writes in response to her last letter, saying it was

> a completely, completely unhappy letter, which affected me so, that today I did not go to school, but wandered along the streets. On the way, I wandered into the library and here I am writing this letter. This cannot be the end already. Will we not see each other anymore? I implore you, Eva, come this Sunday [January 14] on the six o'clock train. I will be forever grateful to you.... It seems that I never asked you for anything, but now I am asking and begging you, entreating you.[34]

But the trip gets postponed until the following Sunday. For some time, she's been upset, though she doesn't say why, and has been thinking about leaving Baltimore. In December, she had written two unhappy letters and now in January she's still thinking about leaving, possibly to return to Belaya Tserkov.

But she agrees to come to New York. "Remember, Eva, don't forget to find out which station your train will be arriving at here," he writes, "and let me know beforehand. New York is very big ... and it is hard to meet ... without knowing the decided place." He's excited about seeing her, but at the same time fears that the anticipation and waiting will make "this week ... worse than the whole year."[35] Then on January 17, not hearing from her, he writes again, wondering if she will actually come ("I would like very much to see you. But whether you would like to ...") and scolding her for not writing ("you are a careless, naughty child, and for that reason I close this letter in the middle"). But he ends with the expectation of seeing her on Sunday: "Be well, and until our meeting on the 21st of January."[36]

But they didn't meet after all, even though she had taken a train to New York that Sunday. He had gone to the train station to meet her and in his letter the next day he tells her: "I stood by the railing and looked for you. Then I worked my way down and in no way could find you. Then after this I turned home." There he found a telegram from her telling him of a change in her plans. It had arrived Sunday morning after he had left home. His parents said they thought he was at the library, but they had made no effort to contact him there. He doesn't believe them and makes it clear to them that they should "feel sorry ... about the lack of notice to me by phone for the arrival of the telegram."[37] He suspects that they didn't phone him in order to prevent him from seeing her.

My mother was convinced all her life that her mother-in-law had been opposed to her. She enjoyed telling me the story of how my grandmother had wanted him to become a doctor. But after finding temporary work with a tailor, my mother said, he pierced his finger with the needle of a sewing machine on the first day and fainted at the sight of his own blood.

In the same letter, he continues to think about the missed opportunity to meet. It's been a year since they've seen each other. "Yesterday, while riding on the train, I thought: this is the first day in a year that any nice thing happened, but its finish was much too soon. . . . I had to turn back and I remained hurt as the train flew like a bullet further and further and I didn't want to know my thoughts and desires; people sat in a circle and laughed, while I thought they were laughing at me."[38] He now promises her, with a resolve inspired by his parents' opposition, that he will "absolutely" come to Baltimore.

The long-awaited reunion is next scheduled for the following Sunday, January 28, but the week before proves to be crucial in his relationship with her, as well as with his family. It's a week of great stress for him, though also one in which he learns a great deal about himself. "Glorious Eva," he begins the letter of Tuesday, January 23,

> So, all right! I am writing you a second letter already, while from you there has not been one. But you know well "I am good." You are probably already making fun of this, as how is it possible for an *egoist* to be good. For this I love you, that it became clear to me what I am like.[39]

It's not clear from his letter that she'd actually called him an "egoist," but something she said in one of her letters must have had the effect of holding up a mirror to him, enabling him to see himself in a way he hadn't before. Now, two days after she had come to New York and returned to Baltimore without his having seen her, he feels himself drawn closer to her and at the same time senses a growing distance between himself and his family.

> My dear, from the moment you left, no one has seen a smile on my face and even more [they] think that I am angry for the lack of notification . . . about your arrival [on Sunday]. Let them think what they want. They are not asking me and I am therefore not saying anything to them. . . . Last night I didn't go to school again and I went to bed at around nine o'clock, so that I overheard them talking [among] themselves. . . . They in no way understand why I am in such a gloomy, confusing mood.[40]

Then he explains that his feelings for her have caused his changes in mood: "In reality, the day was absolutely not peaceful from the moment of your departure." After almost a year of not seeing her, and the recent weeks of urging her to come New York, he's now left with only a painful memory of the missed telegram and their failure to meet. "How much suffering and health love demands," he writes, "and at the same time how wonderful it is! So, for a few wonderful hours on Sundays, I am ready to suffer a few weeks." But he's still not certain when he will go to Baltimore. "I definitely will be at your place in the soonest time, but when I do not know."[41] On the next day, Wednesday, January 24, he promises to be there on Sunday, but only "if there will be an excursion train . . . I will try to come." Then, in a surprising turn in his thoughts, he tells her, "I was very happy to read that you also have not been able to fall asleep. It is some . . . [auspicious sign] and evidence we were made for each other." About his family he says, "These are not people of our time. They will find out when I tell them that I am going to you, to my life."[42]

Whatever her previous thoughts had been about his behavior—his repeated postponements of coming to see her in Baltimore and his apparent egoism—she must have been deeply moved by these two letters and what they revealed about his feelings for her. After recounting in the first letter his ride back on the train (the disappointment and "hurt" he felt and his thought that the other passengers were laughing at him) and then promising to come to Baltimore, he invokes in the second letter the notion that fate meant them for each other and that he is choosing her over his family—"I am going to you, to my life." It's not surprising that she saved his letters, but these two, more than any of the others, suggest how much they meant to her and why she saved them.

Although they did meet in Baltimore on that Sunday, January 28, reunited for the first time in almost a year, two days later he writes little about his visit or what they did together. He mentions accompanying her to the clothing store where she works, but says nothing about the store, where it is, or what exactly she does there. He seems only to have seen and remembered her. "I am recalling our conversations in the store where you work, so I see that you are such a clever girl. If there had been not I but another person sitting with his eyes closed, then he would have said that this is not a woman's head, but rather that of an intelligent man, and if this is a woman then it had been disguised. I can now repeat my words of old, that you are young and even daring, that is, a clever girl. . . . Bravo clever girl."[43] In their conversations in Bucharest and in her letters since then she had represented herself as a "free-thinking" person and a "modern woman."[44] His comments about her now suggest he has these self-representations in mind, though his compliment, made in virtually the same breath, that intelligence is a male faculty ("this is not a woman's head, but rather that of an intelligent man") reflects an attitude toward women not uncommon in the patriarchal culture of their time, and one that recurs often in his letters. She was a strong-willed person, as her brother Joseph remembered and as her response to the Romanian official's question about the book she was carrying—"You can read. Read it yourself"—seem to support. Perceptive and strong-willed though she was, however, I doubt she gave much thought in this instance to my father's remarks. His praise of her intelligence, as well as his admiration for her youth and daring, must have made the more lasting impression.

After returning to New York, his thoughts continue to be about her: "Yesterday when I got off the train in the evening at eleven o'clock at night, I felt more life on the streets and I felt happier.... [But] there was a strong frost and the snow crackled so under my feet [and] there was no one to walk with—you probably were already asleep."[45] Then, after another day has passed, he writes: "Someone there is [who is] suffering because of you....There was a time when it was the reverse: you loved me more and suffered greatly, and I only sympathized, but I couldn't feel this and it was not by my will. I wanted to make it easier for you, but the suffering one was you, and now my dear, the reverse: I am suffering and strongly suffering already a few months."[46] His earlier sympathy, he seems to say, was something thought more than felt. Now, in his own suffering, he has come to a new understanding of his love for her. This moment is similar to the earlier one of nearly a week ago when he asked how it is possible for an egoist to be good and then told her he loved her because in their relationship it had become clearer to him what he was really like. He's articulating—for himself, perhaps, as much as for her—how the relationship and the suffering it has involved have changed him.

Much of what he's experiencing now is due to the conflict he finds himself in when he comes home, where, he says, "everyone was waiting up for me.... There was a whole storm in conversation about the departure for Mississippi. The storm still continues and there is absolutely no talking to them." While he was in Baltimore Uncle Abe and Aunt Anne must have described the opportunities in Hattiesburg and told him of their decision to return there. Now, in his discussions with his family, though he has not yet made a firm decision, the possibility that he might go to Mississippi has alarmed them. Mississippi, from what they may have heard of it, and so far away, may have seemed an American Siberia. "They repeat over and over again one thing: that everything is possible only in New York.

In this respect, they have all the strength. I still have yet to succeed in speaking with them definitely and clearly.... Everyone goes about sad and gloomy, and when I am not around, then they talk about it. But I walk about and cannot talk with anyone. I am all disordered and don't know myself how I can write now." He had already anticipated his parents' objections and had told my mother about them in Baltimore. In their objections, his parents' concerns are "the same ones that I told you [about] when we were going to the station yesterday."[47]

> That Sunday evening when I returned from you ... they asked about the Baltimore idea. I explained to them about the Mississippi one. Without even asking my opinion on this they immediately rejected it and began to worry: "What does it mean?"—the only son to whom they now can talk and whose advice they seek, and at this point they do not have anybody but me. Father says that I have lived with him only for 8 months and he did not know me before that time, because he left me when I was still a child and now this means that I am leaving them and going where? Is New York too small for settling? Besides, the travel expenses [to Mississippi] are too great. Who can allow to spend 140 dollars for a visit? ... It will take me not less than a year to get settled even if I am alone, and after that the worry of taking care of a family gives a person—whether he wants it or not—a fervor to earn more money, as it is needed greatly. All this means that they can only hope to see me in a few years and only in the case that I would be able to settle down well enough to be able to spend several hundred dollars for a two-week visit. According to them, this is absurd, especially noting that I am "still green." For New York, their answer is that I should settle down here and only then come to the second period of my life. They will help me in every way they can.... They are always worrying that one fine day I would come up to them and tell them that I am leaving, which would be a great blow for them. So as a warning they started crying and yelling and threatening me that they would not help me in anything.[48]

He tries to reassure my mother that "they do not have anything against you, dear, so do not take anything personally," but in virtually the same breath he reports his parents have said—presumably in response to the possibility (either mentioned by him or imagined by them) that my mother might move to New York after her brother and sister-in-law return to Mississippi—that "in New York a young girl needs a lot of money and if it is impossible to find a job the expenses would be tremendous."[49] Then he adds, "And summer is not a good season for us. Understand?"

I doubt my mother found either his report of what his parents said or his seeming defense of them reassuring. Her brother is moving back to Mississippi, leaving her alone in Baltimore. "God only knows what lies in store for us," she writes my father (and he now repeats).[50] He is deeply divided, caught between his obligations to his parents and his love for her. Did the thought occur to him of how ironic it was for his father to say to him that he had left "when I was still a child" while now objecting to his leaving the family to make his own way in the world? He tries to reassure himself and her by resolving to show independence and determination: "I now see that only the sick man feels his pains and only he himself must cure them and only he himself must overcome them." At the same time, however, he says to her, "if my friends from Kiev were here, they would say, in surprise, the following: so, Petya [for Peter] do you have such a weak will? They would not have understood it—for if I had thought up something, I would have done it immediately." The fault must lie elsewhere: "America breaks everyone's thoughts and will, and always trips one in various actions. Believe me, my darling, that it was not for nothing that in one of my letters to you I wanted to send America to a certain place."[51] My father could at times be overbearing or insensitive, yet there was something gentle in his nature that made him shy away from swearing and even apologize when a profanity slipped out—"You should excuse me for the expression," he would say—though it was nothing more shocking than, as he implies here to my mother, an innocuous "Hell."

The tension between them increased during the first weeks of February. She tripped and fell and could not go to work for several days. He writes hoping "everything will be fine," but advises her that she needs "someone to walk with, to grab onto if you fall." In an attempt at humor, he attributes the fall to her desire to be independent: "But since you want to play the man, this is an embarrassing thing for you to ask for, so you fell. The next time, *do not be shy*. Why should anyone be shy? In any case, Eva, you want to actively do this, then what? You will be the man. I am forced to make way for you and we'll see how much a woman can do."[52] Either this or something else he said was not received well and she writes back a letter that he says hurt him. Now he attempts to give advice: "Ah, my dear, how sometimes in a minute of an inner flare up of temper, one cannot account for oneself and spills everything on paper. But, you know, spoken words can always be denied or forgotten, but a letter presents in itself something completely different. Paper always remains an eternal memory of words."[53] But suddenly his thoughts take a different turn: "I empathize with you, as with someone ill, for this is a definite symptom of illness." Aware he may have touched a raw nerve, he tries to redirect his thoughts in the next sentence: "However, let us leave this subject, for it is better not to entangle ourselves in it, or it will be difficult to disentangle ourselves from it." But he's unable to leave the subject alone. "My sweet, poor Eva, how difficult it is to you in your life. At first one illness [psoriasis], and then another. During the first one, in a difficult moment of your life, you visited the doctor and received injections, and now you have injections on paper, but the injection is not given to you, but to me, and it hurts me." Then he changes course again: "But it hurts pleasantly as the pain is sweet to me and dear to my heart, but you will not know of this now, but only later."[54] In the remainder of the letter he continues to give advice—"Never spill your hidden thoughts on paper," as he himself has just done, "without at first knowing what the matter is"—and concludes by returning to a thought in his letter of two days ago in which he had equated her independence with attempting to be a man. "Now, my man," he addresses her, "or my second half, I am finishing my letter, for it is too long [and] it will bore you, and the dosage is a teaspoon, as you know. But it is fine, Eva, as you are now Petya, and I am . . . Eva. We switched roles." Then he switches back: "I always remain not Petya, but your Paul," meaning, I suppose, that she can continue to be Petya in the playful little fiction he's just written, but he remains the Paul he's always been for her.[55]

Her independent spirit has unsettled him. Yet she's not so independent that she rejects him. On the contrary, she apparently fears he will reject her. "Am I going to rebuff you?" he writes. "This question is a bit naïve, yet I will still answer you: no, I will not rebuff you. I will wait for you. I wish that Sunday would come sooner, but I know that if it did, it would fly away sooner. This is the trouble. There is so much heaviness on my soul, but . . . Shall I stop writing? Yes! . . . This is not me writing and my mind absolutely does not serve me. This is why I will stop this. Tomorrow I will write more. It's freezing outside."[56] But he is fearful that she is rejecting him and on the very next day he writes his shortest letter of their correspondence to complain that "I did not receive anything from you today" and to say "I am afraid that my letters bore you, so I should make them shorter. Isn't that so, Eva?"[57] Then, in what appears to be his next letter, undated but written in late February, he pleads with her:

> Eva, understand that I absolutely want to see you. . . . How quiet and peaceful everything was, and suddenly one line [from you] and everything was

so chaotic in my soul, that I cannot even explain it. I know that my studies this week will go down the drain. I will not be able to pay attention to them. It is possible that next week will be even worse, so tell me at least this Friday that you will be there, so that I can pay attention for the remainder of the week. . . . Lastly, I will tell you openly that if you were in New York twice without letting me know, then I don't know what you could think if you were in my place. I am ending this letter by pleading again.[58]

A few days later he falls ill with what he calls "American grippe" and writes her only after he's recovered, reporting that he slept for two weeks and still feels weak. By this time Uncle Abe and Aunt Anne have returned to Hattiesburg and she's alone in Baltimore.

After his recovery, he continues to write her about visiting him in New York. On March 12, he writes that he is supposed to go to Philadelphia next Sunday but that he will cancel the trip if she wants to come to New York, and he mentions that there is an excursion train she could take. "I ask you, Eva, answer this now, as my life must go on." She doesn't come and he goes to Philadelphia that Sunday and writes her on March 20 that he "had a very good and happy time there." In the meantime, she invites him to Baltimore, but he writes back that "to my regret, I cannot go, as now, just before the holidays, I have work to do in all respects." Then he adds that he "will have to go to Philadelphia in a few weeks," with no explanation of why he can go there but not come to Baltimore. Still, he is hoping she will come to New York on Sunday. She has sent him a photo and he writes to her,

> What a difference there is between now and last year [in Bucharest] at the exact same time. Then you were thoughtful, in a bad mood, and unhappy with the future . . . [and worrying about] the nearing of the departure and your bad state of health which did not show a promising future. And now the Eva in front of me, even though it is on the picture, is smiling straight into my eyes and before this time I did not see you smiling this way even on a photograph. How I would like to take that mouth into mine, your lips, and bite them, as in time gone by.[59]

This letter, written on March 23, is the last of the dated letters. Most of the rest, few in number, are impossible to date with any certainty from the content alone, and not consequential. But my parents must have continued to correspond, and may even have seen each other, between March 23, 1923, the day of the last dated letter, and the day of their marriage, January 4, 1925, though I have no letters from that time. But two short letters in September 1923 from my mother's father, one to her and one to my father, indicate that by then the relationship had evolved into an understanding, if not a formal engagement. In the one to his daughter he writes, "I received your letters and I had much satisfaction from them. Especially the one from Paul!" In the one to my father he expresses gratitude "for the attention to us and for your photograph." By this time, my father had learned from his father Nathan that he had once met Moishe in Warsaw, where the Stolin family was living for a brief time around the turn of the century. Now in my father's letter to his future father-in-law, he may have introduced himself as the son of the man he had met in Warsaw. I don't know if, in writing the letter and including a photograph, he went through the formality of asking for my mother's hand in marriage, but if he did his future father-in-law's reply, thanking him for "the attention to us," could have been taken by my father as a "yes."

CHAPTER 2

A Merchant, After All

When my father arrived in Hattiesburg in January of 1924, he may have stayed initially with Aunt Anne and Uncle Abe. They had moved back after her father died because, Buddy told me, Uncle Abe's business in Baltimore wasn't doing well. It was a large city with a substantial Jewish population (well over 40,000 then) and a rich religious and cultural life, but also a long-established and more competitive business environment than the one in Hattiesburg where he'd had so much success in only five years. Now back, Uncle Abe opened a store on Front Street called "The Leader" near several other clothing stores, the National Bank of Commerce, and the five-story Hotel Hattiesburg.

The town had been founded in 1882, but few people outside of Mississippi would have heard of it, especially Jewish immigrants in New York or one of the other port cities in the East. Although seventeen years had passed since the end of the Civil War, the Confederacy was nonetheless a part of its birthright. Captain William Harris Hardy, a Confederate veteran who had fought in the Army of Tennessee, most notably against General Sherman during his campaign in Georgia, chose it as the site for the town and it became the seat of Forrest County.[1] The county also had a strong tie to the Confederacy, having been named after Confederate General Nathan Bedford Forrest, who was a brilliant military strategist, though he was remembered by General Grant as the officer responsible for the massacre of black Union soldiers at Fort Pillow, Tennessee, and was as an early member of the Ku Klux Klan.[2] One of the first things my father would have seen after arriving in Hattiesburg was the tall white marble column on the lawn beside the Forrest County Courthouse. At the top stands a Confederate soldier, his rifle at his side. The monument was erected in 1910 and is similar to countless others in small towns and cities across the South.

My father and other Jews who moved to Hattiesburg would quickly learn, if they didn't already know, that "the War between the States" remained the most important historical period in the political and social consciousness of

Main Street in Hattiesburg in the early twentieth century.

people in the South. That consciousness has recently been challenged, as it has often been since the civil rights movement of the 1950s and 1960s, by the removal of Confederate monuments in several cities in the South. In May of 2017, Mayor Mitch Landrieu of New Orleans had the statues of Jefferson Davis and General Robert E. Lee, removed, as well as the one of General P. G. T. Beauregard, whose order to open fire on Fort Sumter marked the beginning of the Civil War. The erection of these and other similar monuments in the South after Reconstruction and into the early twentieth century would have seemed to most people then, I believe, to be simply a tribute to those who fought heroically for the Confederacy. That's the way I saw the one in Hattiesburg and those in New Orleans when I was a teenager. Now, however, the motive for erecting them decades after the Civil War, is being understood very differently. As Mayor Landrieu has explained, "the statues were not honoring history" but helping to "distort history, putting forth a myth of Southern chivalry, the gallant 'Lost Cause,' to distract from the terror tactics that deprived African Americans of [their] fundamental rights from the Reconstruction years through [the] Jim Crow [era] until the civil rights movement and the federal court decisions of the 1960s." They were "symbols of white supremacy."[3]

But in the 1930s, of course, few white people in Hattiesburg would have thought that or accepted it. The monument next to the courthouse had been erected, according to the inscription on it, "Through the devotion and untiring efforts of the Hattiesburg Chapter No. 422 of the United Daughters of the Confederacy." Over a hundred Confederate veterans lived in Forrest County and notices about their pensions and monthly meetings were still being run in the *Hattiesburg American* like the following one from August of 1933: "Confederate veterans pensions for the current month are now available at the chancery clerk's office."[4]

Captain Hardy chose the site for the town as the junction of a future railroad to serve the lumber industry he foresaw being developed in South Mississippi. A line would run between Meridian and New Orleans, another between Jackson and Gulfport, and eventually others running to Natchez, Brookhaven, and Mobile. He named the town after his second wife, Hattie. Within just a few years he also founded Laurel and Gulfport.[5] A bronze bust of him was unveiled in Gulfport in 1929 and, according to the story in the *Hattiesburg American*, was "the work of Count Leo Tolstoy, Jr., the son of the famous Russian author." It was "mounted on a pedestal of granite hewn from Stone mountain" bearing these words: "Lawyer, Statesman, Confederate Soldier, Builder of Railroads, Pioneer in development of the resources of South Mississippi, Founder of the cities of Gulfport and Hattiesburg. A dreamer whose dreams came true." The reporter for the paper imagines him having the dream "as he sat in the shade of a spreading oak on the bank of Gordon's Creek, where now stands the City Hall of Hattiesburg."[6]

The railroads Hardy brought to the region resulted in the start-up of numerous sawmills and, adjacent to them, camps where the men who worked in the lumber industry lived. It was now that the cutting down and processing of the longleaf yellow pine trees in the virgin forest covering most of south Mississippi really began. By 1904 the J. J. Newman Lumber Company, based in Hattiesburg, had become the largest of the mills in the southern part of the state, with total holdings of 400,000 acres and its mills at their peak producing 200,000,000 board feet annually, with most of that harvest being sent by railroad to Gulfport and then shipped overseas.[7] Among the numerous lumber mills operating in Hattiesburg at that time was one called the Brookhaven Lumber and Manufacturing Company, owned by the Dreyfus family. Maurice Dreyfus, who had founded the company in 1881, moved it to Hattiesburg in 1900 and operated it successfully until 1923, when it was reorganized and renamed the Hattiesburg Saw Mill Company. Four years later, having exhausted the timber supply on the thousands of acres of land the company owned and leaving millions of stumps in the ground, Dreyfus and his three sons converted their lumber business into a naval stores manufacturing company,

Dixie Pine Products. In an article I found in the May 1931 issue of *Illinois Central Magazine* entitled "Old Stumps Yield New Wealth," Maurice's son T. F. Dreyfus, president of the company, explained the reason for the conversion by posing a long, illuminating question: "What could be more logical, after cutting down the pine trees until all timber available . . . was exhausted, than to go back and pull out the pine stumps and remove the top wood from the land, and by means of machinery and apparatus extract the turpentine, rosin and pine oil, thereby becoming a part of the naval stores industry, one of the oldest known to man; for is it not recorded in the Bible that Noah 'pitched' the Ark?"[8] It was in the home of the Dreyfus family that a small number of Jews gathered in 1900 or 1901 to hold the first religious services of what would eventually become B'nai Israel Congregation.

In several photographs from that time, the dirt streets crowded with horses and buggies suggest a thriving frontier town. With the onset of World War I in 1914, the increased demand for lumber, the entry of the United States into the war in 1917, and the construction of Camp Shelby twelve miles south, the city's economic growth was intensified and extended. But by 1920 its "two-decade boom" had ended.[9] In 1900 the population had been 4,175; by 1920 it had more than tripled to 13,270.[10] By the time my father arrived, although the boom was over, the city continued to grow and in 1930 the population reached 18,601, with a small Jewish community of around 150.[11]

For my father, going to Hattiesburg involved not only breaking away from his family but also changing his ideas about both himself and this country. In the fall of 1922, after being in America for six months, his plan was to continue working in his father's small fruit store in the Bronx and then in January to enroll in a two-year program to earn a high school diploma. His mother still hoped he would become a doctor. "Why am I studying?" he wrote to my mother. "I want to have a profession in my hands wherever I go. I do not want to work in a factory and give my strength to a machine and capital."[12] He must have learned that many Jewish immigrants had become factory workers, making up three-quarters of all factory laborers in New York's garment industry, and that many others earned their livelihoods as carpenters, painters, and plumbers.[13] In saying he doesn't want to give his "strength to machine and capital," my father is echoing a Marxist notion—capitalism exploits factory workers—that he must have heard often in the three years he lived under Soviet rule and perhaps had seen recently in some leftist Jewish newspapers in New York. It's now, in the same letter, that he says, still holding out for a profession, "being a merchant is not for me."[14]

During most of his first year his attitude toward America remained ambivalent. After only ten days, he writes to my mother in Bucharest that he hopes she will get here soon, "for it is time to see this 'golden country' to which everyone wants to come. Here people don't live. Instead they are slaves of gold and if you will not be this way, then one would die from hunger," though he acknowledges that because of his father and his work in the store, "I am fine."[15] He frequently complains about how little time he has to himself: "Such is America and the New York life where people don't have even a minute and are continually running, hurrying, rushing as here every minute has meaning."[16] New York is a city "in which all of life—noise, din, chaos, hurly-burly, turmoil exists . . . and everyone is in a hurry."[17] While he says he likes New York "very much in comparison with the other American cities" (referring, presumably, to Philadelphia, the only other one he mentions having seen), living there makes him complain that "America squeezes out all of the moral and physical strengths of a person and makes him a living machine, and here you will find very few people who know how to lead life."[18]

Yet his growing criticisms of other immigrants who complain seem to signal a change of mind. He reports to my mother that he recently ran across several old acquaintances from Belaya Tserkov at a Yiddish theater and had little sympathy for their nostalgia for the old country. Of his fellow "White Churchers" he says, "either America cries over them or the reverse." Of the many "greens" he met, "barely one percent say that they are satisfied with America, but why I do not know." Then, apparently recalling the good times in Bucharest (when he didn't have to work, had met my mother in the HIAS office, and had gone strolling along Elizabeth Boulevard with her), he wondered, "Did Romania spoil them?"[19] Still, he himself feels lost. "In my whole life I didn't lose as much spiritual and moral health as I have in this America after such a short time."[20] In another letter he would write, "Believe me, my darling, that it was not for nothing that in one of my letters to you I wanted to send America to a certain place [Hell], as it caused too much mental suffering."[21] But he's skeptical of the good reports from his friends in Kiev about life in the new Soviet Union. He says they write "now it is so wonderful to live there, that one does not need anything better. Life in Kiev became like it was in 1913. Well, go ahead and believe them, when they are not familiar with life here."[22] By March of 1923, after being here for almost a year, he's no longer ambivalent. When he sees an old friend who has unexpectedly shown up, he writes to my mother: "By the way, Isaac Abrutzky came to New York from Palestine. Life is so good there that he had to come here."[23]

After Uncle Abe moved back to Hattiesburg, my father kept asking my mother what news she had from him, and would soon follow him there. Why did he give up the idea of studying for a profession? Perhaps not knowing the language well and needing to take courses at night for two years just to finish high school, he realized it would take many years of study combined with work to earn a professional degree. He may also have heard it was difficult for Jews to get into a university, though in fact many immigrant Jews got into and succeeded at CCNY. He had carried much of the burden for his family in the absence of his father. He wouldn't have seen much future in continuing to live with his family and working in his father's fruit store. Whatever his feelings toward his father were, the responsibility he'd had in Russia after his father's departure would have increased his desire for independence and made him chafe at the restraints the family was now trying to put on him. At twenty-two and in love, the prospect of years of work and study without being able to get married must have seemed to go against everything he had imagined for himself. In Uncle Abe he would have seen a model of the kind of independence and success he wanted, showing him that an immigrant with no trade, no money, scant formal education, and little knowledge of his new country or its language could become the owner of a store—a merchant, after all!—and support a family in a few short years. In making his decision, he would have remembered seeing countless Jewish peddlers with pushcarts not only in New York but also in Russia. Even his father, despite his opposition to the plan, would have been a model in the back of his mind, for he had gone from town to town taking orders and delivering flour and, when he felt the time had come, hadn't hesitated to leave home.

In going to Hattiesburg to become a peddler my father was a latecomer, preceded in the early and middle decades of the nineteenth century by Jewish immigrants who had made their way to various small towns in Mississippi. They had come mainly from Bavaria, Prussia, and other German states prior to the formation of a unified Germany in 1871, as well as from Alsace-Lorraine and the Austro-Hungarian Empire. They, too, had been preceded in the eighteenth century, not in Mississippi but in New England and the Middle Atlantic states. In *The Forgotten Pioneer* Harry Golden makes a case for the peddler as an important figure in American history, exemplified by a few prominent merchants, manufacturers, and investment bankers who had begun as peddlers: Benjamin Altman, Adam Gimbel, Marshall Field, Lazarus Straus, Levi Strauss, Joseph Seligman, Heinrich Lehman, and Soloman Loeb. But the peddler was also an important figure in world history. "Untold numbers of Jews emigrated from some back-home place, landed and spent some time in the big city, be it in

New York or Dublin, Baltimore or Havana," writes historian Hasia Diner, "and later . . . moved on to more remote, less-settled areas to do their peddling."[24] What made the South particularly attractive to young Jews who landed in New York or one of the other port cities in the East was its "persistent agrarianism, its fairly small commercial class, and its lag in industrial and urban development as compared with other American regions."[25]

Many of the first Jewish immigrants who went to Mississippi as peddlers soon became merchants in one of the towns in the Delta, where cotton had become the basis of the state's mainly agricultural economy. By the end of the nineteenth century there were small but thriving Jewish communities scattered throughout the Delta in Canton, Clarksdale, Cleveland, Greenville, Greenwood, Vicksburg, and Yazoo City, as well as in other parts of the state in Brookhaven, Columbus, Jackson, Meridian, and Natchez. Hattiesburg itself was something of a latecomer, having been founded late in the nineteenth century and having, in contrast to most of the antebellum towns, an economy based on lumber mills and railroads.

What my father would have seen when he started walking on a road leading out of Hattiesburg in 1924 was a rural patchwork of segregated communities and neighborhoods of farming and working families, scattered here and there among tiny towns of a few hundred people. He wasn't the first Jewish peddler they had seen or bought goods from, but they were a first for him. A beginning peddler usually bought merchandise on credit from a local merchant, often a relative such as Uncle Abe, who himself had been a peddler. My father carried his merchandise in a pack on his back and a suitcase in one hand. His potential customers were white and black farmers and workers and their wives. The backpack would have weighed between fifty and seventy-five pounds. What was in it? Probably a very limited selection of dresses, blouses, gowns, underwear, pants, shirts, ties, shoes, sox, belts, suspenders, piece goods, patterns, thread, and needles, all of which Uncle Abe had in his store and advertised in the *Hattiesburg American*, as I learned from reading the newspaper on microfilm for those years. Although a few Jewish peddlers in the South were murdered in the nineteenth century, that danger was much less likely by the 1920s. On the other hand, the experience of Hassan Mohamed, a Lebanese peddler, sounds too good to be representative. Soon after landing in New York in 1911 he headed for the Delta, took merchandise on credit from a Clarksdale storekeeper, and started walking on the country roads. He had little knowledge of English or of American currency and so relied on the honesty of his customers. His widow remembered that "they'd buy whatever they bought out of the suitcase, [and] they would make the change. . . . He didn't think anybody beat him out of any money."[26] My father's experience may have been closer to that of peddlers who, for the most part, felt welcomed by both blacks and whites but who nonetheless had to guard against being robbed or attacked by dogs as he walked the roads from one town or community to another. Milton recalls his saying that at times he had to get off the road and hide in the woods until he felt it was safe to continue.

Since many of my father's customers were blacks, I've wondered what they thought when they saw a Jewish peddler. Their attitudes would have been shaped in part by anti-Semitism in myth and folklore, as well as by the New Testament, where Jews are held responsible for the crucifixion of Christ, beginning what became centuries of "ideological anti-Semitism" in church dogma.[27] An example appears in Richard Wright's autobiography, *Black Boy*. Wright grew up in Arkansas and Mississippi and recalled that in the early 1930s "All of us black people who lived in the neighborhood hated Jews, not because they exploited us, but because we had been taught at home and in Sunday school that Jews were 'Christ killers.'" Wright and his boyhood friends would "run to the Jew's store and shout,"

> Bloody Christ killers
> Never trust a Jew
> Bloody Christ killers,
> What won't a Jew do?

"To hold an attitude of antagonism or distrust toward Jews," he says, "was bred in us from childhood; it was not merely racial prejudice, it was part of our cultural heritage."[28]

However strong this anti-Semitic cultural heritage was, it was reinforced by feelings of mistrust and resentment due to Wright's and other blacks' perception that Jews were a part of the white supremacist system holding blacks down. Wright says they didn't hate Jews "because they exploited us," but he remembers them as part of the system that exploited blacks. At the age of sixteen, while in high school in Jackson, he learns of an opportunity to work at a black movie house taking tickets. The Jewish proprietor tells him, "I'll be honest with you if you'll be honest with me. . . . All tickets will pass through your hands. There can be no stealing unless you steal."[29] Although Wright promises to be honest, he has already decided to go along with a procedure for stealing that his fellow black workers had worked out and were using. When the owner wasn't present, they would resell the same tickets several times and pocket the extra payments. Wright desperately wanted money to leave Jackson for Memphis and eventually to escape the white system of oppression of blacks in the South. The Jew as Christ-killer was now less a consideration than the Jew as a white man who, like other white Southerners, was an economic exploiter of blacks. "He was white, and I could never do to him what he and his kind had done to me," he says of the Jewish proprietor. "I felt that things were rigged in his favor and any action I took to circumvent his scheme of life was justified."[30] Although he hesitates because he fears being caught, sent to prison, and put in a chain gang, he asks himself "Was my life not already a kind of chain gang?" He decides to go along with his fellow workers in cheating the proprietor and soon escapes to Memphis and then to Chicago.[31] Wright saw Jews as members of the white race (and this may be the reason he said his distrust of Jews was "racial," though it was not his only reason for distrust). I don't know how representative his views were of the black population in Mississippi at that time. In *Black Boy (American Hunger)* and his novel *Native Son* he was expressing a rage he had observed in himself and other blacks against the injustices and cruelties they were being made to suffer in silence.

On the other hand, blacks in Mississippi and other southern states tended to distinguish Jews from other whites and to see them in a more positive light (as Wright himself eventually did, first making the Jewish defense lawyer Boris Max in *Native Son* a sympathetic figure who understands the history and suffering of black people in this country, then, three years after the publication of the novel, marrying a Jewish woman with whom he would live the rest of his life). In their dealings with Jewish peddlers and merchants they found they were not subjected to the humiliations they had to endure from other whites, something the anthropologist John Dollard discovered in 1935 when he spent five months in the Delta studying the class structure of one town, Indianola. Jews typically owned most of the clothing stores in small towns in Mississippi and they treated their black customers with respect. "In the older white stores, when a Negro went in, the owner would say to him, 'Well, *boy*, what do you want?' even if the Negro in question were eighty years old. The Jews, on the contrary . . . treated Negroes with courtesy . . . and found some way of avoiding the 'Mr.' and 'Mrs.' question, such as by saying 'What can I do for you?'"[32]

In addition, blacks were able to feel a sense of identification with Jews because of a shared history of slavery and persecution. At times their preachers focused the Sunday sermon on the slavery of the ancient Hebrews and their exodus from Egypt, as Martin Luther King, Jr., did in his last speech in

Memphis when he said, "I've been to the mountaintop," "I've seen the promised land," and then, with some presentiment, "I may not get there with you." Many admired the emphasis Jews placed on marriage, family, and home, as well as on frugality and hard work. Blacks also knew that Jews were still kept out of certain hotels and most country clubs. In 1913, they had seen an innocent Jew—Leo Frank of Atlanta—convicted of rape and murder of a thirteen-year-old white girl and two years later taken from jail and lynched. In the 1920s they saw the old, much-diminished Klan reorganize itself into a new force with increased membership and influence. Aaron Henry, a pharmacist who owned a drug store in Clarksdale and in the 1960s would become president of the NAACP in Mississippi, observed that, though Jews went to white schools and had access to other public facilities, they weren't "fully accepted by the whites" and they "had had their share of suffering and didn't want any part of the persecution of Negroes." Despite whatever ambivalence and residual mistrust blacks may have felt from exposure to anti-Semitic myth and folklore and seeing Jews go along with the white supremacist system of segregation, they still felt that Jews were the only whites in the South who treated them with "compassion and respect."[33]

It was this complex racial environment that my father entered when he moved to Hattiesburg to become a peddler, going from one farmhouse to another, one rural community to another. Where would he stay overnight after walking too far to make it back to Hattiesburg before sunset? Peddlers were often able to stay at a farmhouse as a paying guest and perhaps my father did that on occasion. In the nineteenth century, some Jewish peddlers stayed with black farmers. I don't know if any were doing that in the 1920s. My father would probably have been able to stay with two of Aunt Anne's sisters, one of whom, Selma, had a store in Sumrall, a few miles northwest of Hattiesburg, and another, Goldie, had one in Richton, a few miles east. Or perhaps he was able to stay with another Jewish storekeeper in one of the small towns.

A far more difficult problem was that of learning local customs regarding race. He had to be sensitive to the prejudices of whites and the feelings of blacks while trying to communicate in a language still strange to him as he had first heard it in the Bronx, often mixed with Yiddish words and inflections, now sounding so different in the slower speech, pronunciation, and idioms of the rural South, and even more strange in the different southern dialects spoken by whites and blacks. In Russia, he had lived under the tsarist government's anti-Semitic policies, with specific restrictions against Jews, as well as periodic outbreaks of violence in pogroms. But now he found himself on the other side, a part of the white population that reserved the most important civil rights for itself, beginning with the vote, and imposed severe economic, educational, and social restrictions on blacks, enforced, if necessary, by threats or a rope. Did it trouble him now to be on the other side? While I never heard him say anything critical of black people or express racial prejudice or act in any way that indicated prejudice, I don't think he gave much thought to segregation or the moral issues it posed. In this he was like most Jewish immigrants in the South. He took things as he found them. His focus was on making a living and achieving financial independence and security. He was preoccupied with succeeding at peddling and making a place for himself in a new country that, after almost two years, he still hardly knew. Young, single, and in love, he was eager to earn enough money to return to New York and marry my mother.

In writing the last few sentences about my father's response to segregation, my thoughts turned to David Cohn, the best-known Jewish Mississippian in the first half of the twentieth century. A son of Polish immigrants who owned a clothing store in Greenville, he gave considerable thought to the social and moral issues posed by segregation. After going to Virginia for a bachelor's and to Yale for a law degree, he returned to the South, worked briefly and successfully in business in New Orleans, and then returned to Greenville and began writing articles for the *Atlantic Monthly* and other journals, eventually coming to be known as an authority on the South and its racial problems and in the 1950s serving as an advisor to Adlai Stevenson and Senator J. William Fulbright. Despite his firsthand knowledge of the Delta and its people, reflected in his 1935 book *God Shakes Creation* (the title taken from a black preacher's metaphor for the sudden growth and flowering in the spring), however, as well as his sympathetic understanding of the plight of the Negro, Cohn's book became a defense of segregation and the social and economic dominance of the white man. He thought the amelioration of the blacks' condition should be entrusted to the *noblesse oblige* of the aristocratic planters of the Delta.

If a man of Cohn's education and liberal sympathies could hold such a view, I wondered, how different could I expect the views of my parents and of other Jewish immigrants in Mississippi to be? They had far less knowledge of the history of the relationship between blacks and whites in the South, as well as of the political and economic forces that had shaped that history, and had given nothing like the serious thought to them that he had. What my father, Uncle Abe, and other Jews in Hattiesburg observed and heard on the streets, read in the newspapers, saw in stores, restaurants, and offices, at the schools, on baseball and football fields, on buses and trains, in the courts, and eventually heard on the radio was the wide acceptance of segregation and its numerous customs, reinforced in every election campaign by white supremacists like James K. Vardaman and Theodore Bilbo, prominent political figures in Mississippi in the first four decades of the twentieth century. In their speeches, these and other politicians openly preached white supremacy and set a tone for public discourse that seemed to license the use of threats and violence to preserve "our way of life." My father and his generation of immigrant Jews—some, like him, not yet citizens—would not have presumed to challenge the state's laws and customs, even if they had had a strong interest in the moral, social, and political issues posed by segregation. Most had come from a political culture in Eastern Europe, especially Russia, where equality and justice had never existed for them. Although their experience as Jews would have made them more sympathetic than most in the native white population, they "remained torn," in the words of historian Eric L. Goldstein, "between their empathy for blacks and their aspirations for full acceptance in white America."[34]

Among the many customs of segregation my father had to deal with during that first year of peddling, and had probably first heard about from Uncle Abe, was the reluctance of white customers to buy a dress or shirt or other article of clothing that a black customer had tried on. I wondered how he dealt with the custom. Did he honor it by showing different merchandise to whites? Or did he require black customers to buy without trying on and without the possibility of an exchange or refund? Whatever the rules were, blacks would have known them better than he did and he must have learned a great deal from observing them. Many blacks welcomed the Jewish peddler not only because he treated them with courtesy but also because he provided a certain degree of freedom in shopping. They didn't have to stand waiting until all white customers had been helped to get the attention of a clerk and they didn't have to put up with his frequently intimidating presence and the glaring eyes of other whites.

In stores, the custom that blacks couldn't try on clothes went back a long way. Dave Pearlman, a Jewish immigrant from Lithuania who in the 1880s had joined a cousin in Americus, Georgia, as a peddler and later as a partner in a dry goods store, found that if he let blacks try on clothes he would be criticized and even threatened by white customers. "Dave," one of them said, "how come you lettin' this here nigger tryin' on clothes fittin' only for white folks? Better throw them out when he's finished. Can't tell what's on them now."[35] The custom was still firmly in place in the late 1940s and early 1950s, something vividly recalled by Myrlie Evers, widow of slain civil rights activist and field secretary of the NAACP Medgar Evers. "Shopping for clothes in the white stores on Capitol

Street [in Jackson] could be a degrading experience," she wrote. "Many of the clothing stores would not permit Negroes to try on clothes, either in the stores or at home." As she was about to try on a hat, a white clerk rushed over to say, "You can't try that on. . . . You people always have such greasy hair you ruin the hats."[36] But the reasons given could be quite different. Endesha Ida Mae Holland remembers that in Greenwood "colored gals weren't allowed to take clothes into fitting rooms, lest we steal them."[37] Muriel Tillinghast, who had grown up in Washington, D. C., where she had only rarely encountered the "racism of the Deep South," went to Mississippi as a civil rights worker with other college students during Freedom Summer of 1964. But she knew from once having visited Florida "not to even touch the clothes in a department store, and *never* to try them on."[38] The exceptions were stores that catered primarily or exclusively to blacks. Cohen Brothers on Capitol Street in Jackson, for example, not only allowed blacks to try on clothes; it was, in the words of Edward Cohen, "the only white-owned business with an integrated rest room and water fountain."[39]

Although I started working in my father's store on Saturdays and occasional weekday afternoons during this time, beginning in 1947 when I was twelve and continuing well into the 1950s when home from college, I wasn't aware that blacks couldn't try on clothes. As strange as this may seem (and still does to me), I learned of that custom just a few years ago while reading Rabbi Arthur Hertzberg's memoir, *A Jew in America*, where he says that merchants in his congregation in Nashville in the 1940s "adhered to the southern custom that Blacks had to buy clothes without trying them on. Some of the owners explained to me that they had no choice. Jews were a small, tolerated minority in an essentially anti-Semitic region, and it was wisest, and safest, to keep one's head down."[40] This custom and other forms of discrimination, I've learned, were not limited to the South. Some department stores in the North refused to serve blacks; others served them but refused to let them try on clothes; most refused to hire blacks except for menial jobs. Dr. Gilbert Mason of Biloxi remembers from his time as a medical student at Howard University and going shopping in the nation's capital that "department stores in Washington would not serve blacks," though there were exceptions and Julius Garfinkel & Co. allowed him to purchase an umbrella for his fiancé.[41] Another form of discrimination they experienced was at the "Bronx Slave Market," where black girls and women stood at the corners of 167th Street and Jerome Avenue, or at Simpson Street and Winchester Avenue, waiting to find one-day jobs at the homes of Jewish women at exploitative rates of thirty or thirty-five cents an hour.[42]

Closer to home, the secretary of the Mobile branch of the NAACP, L. L. LeFlore, wrote to the president of the L. L. Hammel Dry Goods Company, Barney Strauss, in 1938 to protest the store's refusal to provide "restroom and comfort facilities for colored women and children who shop in your store." Strauss wrote back that it was not the custom in the South to provide such facilities for colored people. But for LeFlore it was not just an issue of civil rights. In his letter he drove home the point that it was above all a moral issue that Jews should understand: "We are bewildered that a member of one oppressed group, because of favorable geographical and other conditions, would be unsympathetic and recalcitrant in regard to the rights of another persecuted minority."[43] Mobile was a city that, more than a decade before LeFlore wrote his letter, had had a Jew, Leon Schwarz, serve as county commissioner, sheriff of Mobile county, and mayor. In 1929, he had come to Hattiesburg to speak at a B'nai B'rith meeting, probably at the suggestion of T. F. Dreyfus. They had been buddies in the Spanish-American War. Hattiesburg's Mayor W. S. F. Tatum was also at the meeting.[44] A number of large cities in the South have elected Jews to be mayors, Sam Massell of Atlanta being a well-known example. But Jews have also been elected mayors in small cities in Mississippi, including Brookhaven, Greenville, Meridian, Natchez, Vicksburg, and Yazoo City.

Before E. J. "Mutt" Evans became mayor of Durham, North Carolina, he had earned the respect of blacks not only by helping to build a Negro hospital but also by providing a lunch counter and a restroom for them in his downtown store, Evans United. "Through the turbulent 1950s when the Supreme Court jolted the South into responsibility and changed all the rules of living," his son Eli Evans wrote, Evans "played the role of peacemaker, presiding over transition years until blacks would demand concessions as a human right and whites would yield as an economic and political necessity." But he also took important initial steps on his own. He hired the first black policeman and fireman, moved blacks into supervisory positions in City Hall, and persuaded the City Council to set up an Urban Renewal Authority to build low-cost housing for the poor of both races.[45]

But Evans and a few others were exceptions. Most Jews in the South, especially in the 1930s, simply by living there and going along with the system of segregation and discrimination, could not escape being viewed with some suspicion by the black community and accused of being, in the words of L. L. LeFlore, "unsympathetic and recalcitrant in regards to the rights of another persecuted minority." Yet the pressure felt by the storekeepers in Rabbi Hertzberg's congregation was very real, as it was in other cities and towns throughout the South. As real as it was for a Jewish community the size of his, nearly 3,000 strong, the pressure was even greater for Jews in Mississippi, where there was no city the size of Nashville and no Jewish community of more than 380 people. In Hattiesburg in 1950 it was 184.[46]

I have no memory of my father or anyone else telling me of the custom regarding try-on rooms, and when I asked Fay and Milton, they didn't either. We also have no memory of seeing black customers go into one of the two tiny try-on rooms, though we remember that they tried on shoes and sat in the same single row of chairs with white customers, though not immediately next to each other. How can I explain this? Is it an example of selective amnesia? Was it OK to try on shoes, but not clothes? And in our store, but not other stores? I don't know. Stella Suberman says of her father's store in Tennessee in the 1930s, "Of course, like all shoe departments in the South, it was for white trade only. Negroes tried on shoes from atop a crate in the back alley and tested them on a strip of rug laid down there."[47] So far as I know, there were no published rules or signs "For Whites Only" with regard to try-on rooms, as there were for public restrooms and water fountains at the courthouse and train and bus stations.

Adherence to some customs could therefore vary in different Southern states, different parts of each state, different towns, even in different stores in the same town. Especially important was the fact that many of the customs of segregation were taken for granted and not discussed much, if at all (at least in the white community). Whites often relied on blacks' knowledge of them and silent submission to them, beginning with addressing whites as "Mr." or "Mrs." or "Miss" without expecting that courtesy to be returned either in oral or written communication (such as newspapers or public announcements). They knew not to offer to shake the hand of a white or come to the front door of a white home. Lossie Glenn, who came to our house six days a week for the first eleven years of my life, always came to the back door, though only now as I write have I thought of it in this context. It's here, in the silent, habitual, adherence to the customs of segregation by both blacks and whites that I see at least a partial explanation of why I failed to see that blacks were not allowed to try on clothes before buying. I think I was so blinded by the segregationist culture in which we lived, despite my increasing awareness of its injustices as I grew older and my going to Northwestern where I had black classmates and friends, that I still remained unaware of many of the daily humiliations that blacks were subjected to, even though the custom of not trying on clothes was being practiced in my father's store, as it must have been in most stores in Hattiesburg. Most of these customs persisted into the 1960s. Of course, in individual relationships the rules could be modified or disregarded, particularly the one about shaking hands. Many black maids worked for white families for so many years that they came to be treated like a member of the family (or so it has seemed to many white families).

One public place in Hattiesburg where a potentially scandalous break in the observance of these customs occurred was in the black business district, which lay several blocks north of the white business district on Mobile Street where my father had a clothing store in the 1930s, and on the other side of two sets of railroad tracks. In it were a number of black-owned businesses, including a hotel, restaurants, a filling station, two barber shops, a theater, two funeral homes, doctors' and dentists' offices, a grocery store, a drug store, and several dry cleaners.[48] I don't know if any of these businesses had white customers, but on Saturday nights other businesses in the district attracted a few whites. In a 1937 story about Hattiesburg's "Harlem," the newspaper characterized the nightlife of blacks by focusing on "bootleg joints" and "negro bawdy houses" mixed in among the stores and shops. On a typical Saturday night from nine o'clock till well past midnight the streets and sidewalks were filled with people, mostly blacks, but also a few whites, all seeking food, drink, and entertainment. A reporter for the newspaper walked through the district one Saturday night and observed through a window "white youths dancing with negro women" and decided he would enter "to watch a mad whirl of sensuous movements."

> Negro women, left by themselves, "danced" with their bodies alone. In emotional hilarity they snatched their skirts above their knees and jerk[e]d their hips in motion with the music while their feet remained glued to the same spot. Three white boys tussled over a sizzling negro lass.... She tore loose, skipped into a corner for a solo wriggle, and stuck out her tongue at the three frustrated youths. A white boy and a light-skinned 'gal' swayed in tight embrace to the strains of the bellowing nickelodeon. His lips touched hers, they clamped, and the two waggled on in a passionate kiss until the record was finished.[49]

But in general, the well-known customs of segregation were followed to a greater or lesser extent, depending on the part of the state one was in, the part of the city or small town where the store was located, the kinds of merchandise the store sold, and the social, economic, and racial class that made up its customer base. Practices in some stores—the smaller, less prominent ones (in contrast to Pizitz's in Birmingham and Montgomery, Rich's in Atlanta, Godchaux's

Paul and Eva after the wedding, dressed for travel.

in New Orleans)—would have been more relaxed, depending on the size of the town's or city's black population, its proportion of the total population, the racial mix of the store's customers, and the location of the store. Evans United in Durham had both an integrated lunch counter and restrooms, but it was, as Eli Evans acknowledged, "a poor people's store and we catered to the Negro trade."⁵⁰ In an extensive remodeling and expansion in 1939, London's in Hattiesburg, a large farm products, grocery, and clothing store on Mobile Street founded by Jewish immigrant Jacob London in 1915, provided four separate restrooms "for white women, white men, negro women, and negro men."⁵¹

Following custom, the janitor in my father's store, Herbert Evans, called me "Mr. Leon" and I called him "Herbert," although he was in his early sixties and I was twelve when I started working in the store. At some point—I can't say exactly when, but while I was still a teenager—I realized this was wrong. We often worked together in the receiving room. The store didn't have an elevator and so the two of us often carried heavy cases of shoes and other goods up two flights of old, foot-worn wooden stairs to the second floor that served as a warehouse. When we took a break in the tiny receiving room at the rear of the store, surrounded by boxes of clothes and shoes, I asked him about his family, his early life in Enterprise (south of Meridian), and the kind of farming he had done before moving to Hattiesburg. He held an important position in his Baptist Church and served as one of its representatives at regional meetings in cities like Birmingham and Atlanta. He was a short, thin, gray-haired man with a wiry build of surprising strength. He moved quietly through the store as he did his job. I never heard my father or any of the clerks utter a word of criticism of him. But occasionally while he cleaned the four mirrors on the square post encasing the supporting beam at the front of the store near the sidewalk, a white businessman walking by would greet him with the remark "Now, Herbert, you know you can't wipe that black spot out." A seemingly friendly attempt at humor, the remark indicated (though I didn't understand this at the time) that the white businessman saw only the blackness of Herbert Evans, making the man himself as a fellow human being invisible, like the nameless title character of Ralph Ellison's *Invisible Man*. It was part of the custom of addressing black men in a condescending way, depriving them of their status as men. "It is not for nothing," Myrlie Evers explained, "that Negro men have for so long been called 'boy' throughout the South, [and] that they have been denied the title, 'Mister.' It is part of the same deliberate plot that has forced Negro men to step off the sidewalk, to bow and tip their hats, to address all white men as 'Sir,' in the manner of boys to superiors."⁵²

Stepping off the sidewalk to let whites pass was a custom Harry Golden hadn't heard of before he moved to North Carolina in 1941. Because he was an immigrant, he was struck not only by surprise but also by the cruel irony of it. "Negroes, whose parents [and their ancestors] had been in this country for two and sometimes three hundred years," in contrast to recent immigrants like himself, "stepped off the sidewalk and tipped their hat," as they were expected to do.[53] Although this custom had disappeared by the time I started working in the store, I learned of it from our family dentist, Dr. Ed Busby, who told me it had been strictly observed when he was a young man in the 1920s and 1930s. Aaron Henry remembered that in the 1930s and 1940s in Clarksdale he became "used to getting cussed out and verbally abused" if he didn't observe the custom. "All we had to do was walk down the street and not get off the narrow sidewalk to let a white pass. Particularly if you happened to bump up against one, he would turn around and start bellowing, 'You black nigger son of a bitch, get off the street,'" not just the sidewalk.[54] I have no memory of the custom being observed, perhaps because in Hattiesburg the custom began to fall away during World War II and after the war was no longer honored. In the store, we didn't address black customers as "Mr." or "Mrs." and since we didn't have charge accounts in those days the issue of courtesy titles for address labels didn't turn up. Although my father's treatment of Herbert Evans was, I believe, perceived by Herbert himself as better than merely civil or courteous, he was once disappointed when my father refused to give him the raise of five dollars a week he'd asked for. I happened to overhear their brief conversation. I've never understood why my father refused. He once referred to someone in our Jewish community as so tight with his money he could pinch the head off a nickel, yet he himself was so concerned with being financially secure (partly because of his experiences in Russia after his father had left the family and later in Hattiesburg during the Great Depression), that his first response to a request for money was often "No," though he could usually be brought around, at least by his children, after a second or third request. I don't know if Herbert asked again, or if my father later changed his mind, but Herbert continued to work at the store until he retired, when his son Sam took his place and continued after my father died and Milton became the owner. When Sam died, his son came to work there, as did other blacks in the years during and after the civil rights movement and after desegregation in public places had become more widely accepted. At some point, Milton appointed a black as manager of the men's department.

My father must have been fairly successful as a peddler. After one year, he had saved enough money to return to New York and marry my mother. I assume that during that year he continued to write her regularly. It's possible she came to Hattiesburg for a brief visit, staying with Aunt Anne and Uncle Abe. But no letters from that year have survived and I remember her making only one remark about the wedding: that it was paid for in large part with money she had saved while working in Baltimore and was now used in a more lavish way than she and my father could afford, all to please her future mother-in-law. She gave me her copy of the wedding invitation and, so far as I know, it's the only one that has survived. It's written in English on one side and Yiddish (in transliteration, using Hebrew lettering) on the other. The wedding was on January 4, 1925, in the Bronx. Aunt Anne and Uncle Abe were not able to attend. They had two small children to take care of and a store to run, and the train trip would have taken most of two days each way. So my mother was married with no one from her family present.

In one of two wedding pictures, my parents are standing in a formal-wedding pose, my mother in front holding a large bouquet of roses covering much of her wedding dress, my father a little behind her and just to her left, with his left arm reaching around her waist in front. I don't know if the wedding dress is one she bought, borrowed, or rented, or one she herself made. On her visa, she had listed "dressmaker" as her occupation, and a superb seamstress she was. She made a tuxedo for me when I was four years old to wear as the ring-bearer in cousin Sarah Stein's wedding in 1939. In the second picture, the pose is still rather formal, but they appear to be dressed for travel. My father always owned a heavy overcoat like the one he's wearing here, mainly for buying trips to Chicago and New York, winters in Mississippi rarely requiring one. I wonder if the photographer suggested to my mother that she hold the gloves in the stylish way she does or if she decided to do so on her own.

When they arrived in Hattiesburg, she told me, they had only five dollars. After a few months of living in a room at the YMCA, they rented an apartment in a house on Bay Street in one of the best parts of town and next to the large home of Dr. T. E. Ross, who would become our family's doctor (to be succeeded by Dr. T. E. Ross, Jr. and, many years later, Dr. T. E. Ross, III). Fay was born in June of 1926 and it was either that year or the next that Norman, having immigrated in 1922 and lived in New York, came to Hattiesburg to join my father in business. I suppose it was partly out of a sense of indebtedness (going back to the years when my grandmother and the three children had moved in with Norman's family in Kiev), but also out of his friendship with Norman that my father suggested to him that he come to Hattiesburg.

Norman rented a room in a boarding house on Main Street, but in a few years, he moved in with my parents, beginning a stay that would last seventeen years. My mother told me his surname was Stempel, not Volodarsky, but when I checked the Ellis Island website he was listed on the ship's manifest as a Volodarsky and—to my surprise—as my grandfather's brother (rather than, say, his son or nephew), even though he was more than twenty years younger. Perhaps my grandfather, as his sponsor, or Norman himself had been advised it was necessary or advantageous for him to be listed as a brother. But during the years Norman and my father were in business together and Norman was living with us, he became known as my father's brother, with the name of one of their two stores—"Waldoff Brothers"—spelled out in black one-inch squares on the white-tile floor of the entranceway between the sidewalk and the front doors. It was not uncommon for business partners who were related to each other to represent themselves as brothers in the name of a business, perhaps with the idea that a family-run business would attract customers. In this instance, however, though family history justified the representation, tensions in both the partnership and the family would eventually result in a permanent break, something also not uncommon. But that lay many years in the future.

I'm not sure exactly when my father ceased peddling and opened a store. He may have resumed peddling after returning to Hattiesburg in January 1925, but by July 1926 he had a store called Mobile Street Bargain House. The City Directory for 1927 shows that both Norman and Uncle Ben worked at this store and lived together at 1007 Main Street. By 1929 my father had moved the store, now called "Waldoff's," to a better location on Mobile Street. He must have been in a confident, expansionist mood, buoyed by his success and the great optimism of the Twenties that was now reaching its peak. Several plans for the downtown business district that had been in the works for a while were announced as finalized. S. H. Kress signed a fifty-year lease for a new building to be constructed on Main Street and F. W. Woolworth would be opening a store at the other end of the same block, on the opposite side of the street. On West Front Street, The Davidson Company was completing its new building and would open its doors in November.

Topping all the new construction in downtown was the nine-story Forrest Hotel on West Pine Street, which opened in September of 1929, becoming the tallest building and best hotel in the city. Aunt Anne's sister Selma and her husband Ira Beck opened a women's ready-to-wear shop in it, with the main entrance on West Pine Street, and another from the hotel lobby. They advertised the store as offering "Exclusiveness without Extravagance." Immediately east of the hotel, the J. C. Penney Company moved into a remodeled building (owned by two members of the Jewish community, Harry Botnick and Sam Eisman). Just south of the hotel the new Saenger Theater opened in November. "Both these buildings," said Max Mabel, manager of the Forrest Hotel (and another member), "mark the beginning of a new era in the Hub City," and it was believed that both would attract many business travelers.[55] Like many of the movie houses of that era, the Saenger was palatial in design, though of course not on the scale of the grand ones in cities such as New Orleans and Atlanta. The foyer was carpeted in dark blue, as were the stairs leading to the balcony. "As one enters the main auditorium," the paper reported, "there is an impression of vastness." The short balcony, extending about thirty feet over the rear seats on the ground floor, contributed to that impression. As one walked down the aisle in the darkened theater and got beyond the balcony close overhead and looked up, suddenly the vaulted ceiling came into view, fifty-five feet high, along with the many dimmed lights of the huge chandelier ten feet high and eight feet across. The chandelier, the paper noted, "was suspended by a special crane concealed in the attic which will lower the huge fixture for cleaning and changing globes."[56] The Saenger also had a stage and dressing rooms, making it possible for the movie house to be used also for performances by local or visiting dramatic and dance groups.

It was in the confident national mood of the 1920s that my father opened a store in Picayune, Mississippi, a small town with a population of around 5,000 and halfway between Hattiesburg and New Orleans, and one he had probably become familiar with during his time as a peddler. In opening another store he may have had in mind the example of Frank Rubenstein, another Russian-Jewish immigrant who had come to Hattiesburg in 1906, begun as a peddler, and opened his first store, followed by others in small towns, often with members of his family. Eventually he had stores in Atlanta, Birmingham, Dallas, El Paso, Houston, San Antonio, and other cities in the South (with various names, including Rubenstein's, Franklin's, and The Diana Shop). My father's store in Picayune was located in a new downtown shopping center, completed in 1928, which had several other stores and offices, as well as a movie house called the Ideal Theatre. Uncle Ben, twenty-one and still single, became the manager. The theater served as a magnet, drawing people to the downtown and to the stores in the shopping center. But a fire started in the early morning hours of October 21, 1929, eight days before Black Tuesday and the crash on Wall Street. It spread quickly and my father's store was one of those that suffered severe damage.

The *Picayune Item* reported in the next day's paper that the fire had started in the Ideal Theatre. A number of the stores were not covered by fire insurance and, though the paper didn't list either the ones with insurance or the ones without, my father's store was one of those without. The cost of fire insurance was very high, in part because of "a lack of water pressure and fire equipment of any kind," as David Stockstill has pointed out in his article about the fire in *The Picayune Item: Keepsake Edition* (January 2, 2000), and in part because the State Insurance Commission had introduced higher rates in January 1927.

But the Commission issued an order on September 12 of 1929, five weeks before the fire, reducing rates effective October 1.[57] I wonder if my father knew this. He probably learned of the fire, which had started around 3:30 a. m., by a phone call from Uncle Ben, but later that day would have seen the headline in the *Hattiesburg American*: "FIRE HITS PICAYUNE BUSINESS SECTION." "Waldorf [sic] Dry Goods Store" was listed with other businesses ruined by the fire. The loss was a devastating setback for my father. How much sharper the pain of regret must have been each time he recalled that he'd missed an opportunity to buy fire insurance at the reduced rates just three weeks before, either because he hadn't known it was possible or had decided against it. The immediate problem he faced now was paying off debts. Many of the goods and fixtures in the store would not yet have been paid for. There would also have been his concern for Uncle Ben, who had moved to Picayune to be the manager. The long-term problem was whether he would be able to stay in business.

A month later in Hattiesburg, on a Saturday night at eleven o'clock, a fire started on the second floor of Wakeland Furniture Company on Mobile Street and spread quickly to the Fokakis Building, home to John Fokakis' fruit stand, Signoff's Shoe Repair Shop, Dixie Café, and Waldoff Brothers. All except the fruit stand were severely damaged. The newspaper's report that "most of Hattiesburg" was aroused by the fire may have been exaggerated (the city at that time had around 20,000 people), but the paper does convey the scale of the fire by its description ("the tumult and spectacular sight") and by pointing out that "guests at Hotel Hattiesburg, across the street, were driven from their rooms by the intense heat." The paper goes on to say that "the extent of the loss in those stores, most of which was caused by water damage, had not been determined today." Then, it notes, "The Waldoff brothers have been having unusually bad luck with fires lately. While operating a store in Picayune recently, their entire stock of merchandise was destroyed by fire."[58] I wonder what my father thought of the phrasing and tone of these two sentences, as well as the failure to mention that in neither case did the fire start in his store.

I was a teenager when I first heard the notion that a Jew who owned a failing store could always sell it to the insurance company. It was told to me as a Jewish joke, using irony to mock the notion. But after learning of the two fires in my father's stores I wanted to know something about the history of the notion, even though I felt certain there was no truth to it regarding my father. I was surprised to learn that Mark Twain seemed to accept it as true when he wrote in his 1899 essay "Concerning the Jews" that, among other forms of dishonest dealings, "the Jew" has "a reputation for . . . burning himself out to get the insurance." Although Twain's comments about Jews are usually favorable, in this instance he leaves the impression that Jews set fire to failing stores and his reputation as America's most widely read author must have seemed to authenticate the notion.[59] It persisted well into the twentieth century and was dramatized in a silent film entitled *Cohen's Fire Sale*, which was produced by the Edison Company in 1907. The owner of a millinery shop, who is caricatured as a stereotypical Jew with "a large nose, black hair, and gesticulating mannerisms," sets fire to his store, collects the insurance, and a few days later places an ad in the paper, "Entire Stock Below Cost."[60] In her 1930 autobiography, *Crusade for Justice*, Ida B. Wells refers to "stories about Jews burning down their stores to get their insurance."[61] Wells may have heard the stories in Chicago, where she had been living for two decades (and had become an important black leader with an international reputation for opposing lynching and advocating full citizenship for blacks), or she may have heard them as a young girl growing up in north Mississippi, near Tupelo, or perhaps in both. I don't know if the stories she'd heard had any basis in fact or were just examples of another anti-Semitic libel, but her distinguished reputation would have given them credibility with many people. In England, where Wells had traveled and lectured in the 1890s, she may have heard some people refer to Jews as "firebugs" willing to "burn down buildings to get insurance" and to fire-engines as "Jewish wedding-bells."[62]

In the week after the second fire, my father placed an ad in the paper that a fire sale would be held at the Batson Street store, starting December 5: "All the stock from our store at Picayune and from our store here must be closed out in 30 days. . . . Most of this stock is undamaged by either fire or water. . . . The whole $15,000 stock must go."[63] On January 17, 1930, he was still advertising the fire sale (which would continue for the next four weeks), but now he indicated the stock had been covered by fire insurance: "This stock [from the Mobile Street store] has been adjusted by insurance people and left to be sold regardless of cost." Had he all along had fire insurance for this store because the necessary water pressure and fire-fighting equipment were available in Hattiesburg, making the insurance more affordable? Or had he decided immediately after the Picayune fire to buy insurance? Another surprising thing about the ad is its invitation to "ask us about the new Ford to be given away on July 3."[64] Why a Ford rather than, say, a Chevrolet? More than once I heard him say he wouldn't buy a Ford because of Henry Ford's anti-Semitism. Perhaps he came to that decision only later, in the 1930s, when anti-Semitism was on the rise and Ford and Lindbergh were the two most prominent figures making it seem respectable, though Ford's anti-Semitism had been well-known since the early 1920s when he ran a long series of articles on Jews over a two-year period in the *Dearborn Independent*. Or perhaps my father's exclusive focus was staying in business and trying to turn the devastating loss from the two fires into an opportunity.

The worst effects of the Depression in Hattiesburg weren't felt immediately. No doubt the presence of Mississippi Woman's College and State Teachers College made a difference, providing steady employment during the economic downturn, as institutions of higher learning usually do. Also important was the continuing operation throughout the decade of the J. J. Newman Lumber Company, as well as several industrial plants processing the stumps of yellow pine trees for naval stores and other purposes (turpentine, rosin, pitch tar, and pine oil) such as Dixie Pine Products Company, Gordon Van Tine Company, Gulf States Creosoting Company, and Hercules Powder Company. But eventually at least one bank and a number of businesses would fail. The bank was Commercial National on Front Street. It failed in June 1931 and was put into receivership, and two years later depositors were still waiting for a liquidation of the affairs of the bank. Some months before its failure my father became concerned about two hundred dollars he had in a savings account there. Milton recalls his saying he was advised by someone, perhaps a lawyer or an accountant, to go to the bank and get a loan for the exact amount. If the bank failed, the loan obligation would be canceled by the loss of his savings. That's what he did. But he and Uncle Abe were not so fortunate with some properties they had bought on the west side of town, near State Teachers College (later to become Mississippi Southern College, then University of Southern Mississippi). They couldn't afford to pay the taxes on them and in March 1932 my mother and Aunt Anne, the titled owners, were listed in the *Hattiesburg American* (along with hundreds of others on long lists in tiny print covering several pages) under the heading "City Tax Collector's Sale of Delinquent Tax Lands."

It was now that the test came of the adventurous spirit Buddy remembered Uncle Abe possessed, particularly his willingness to keep trying new things. When his store on Front Street failed in 1928, he opened a shoe store that also failed. Then he opened a dry goods store that Aunt Anne ran while he took a job as a traveling salesman for a dress company.[65] He used to leave early on Monday morning for Laurel, Jackson, and Meridian, Buddy told me, and then, by the middle of the week, make his way south to Gulfport and Mobile. Once, on returning at the end of the week, he told Aunt Anne that every time he went to Mobile he found more merchants there ready to buy merchandise than in the other cities and, as his grandson Jere Friedman says in his family history, they "re-ordered sooner" and he thought it "would be a better place to do business."[66] So they drove down to Mobile, taking Sarah and Buddy (now fifteen and twelve) with them. One of the first places he took them to was a delicatessen. When Aunt Anne walked in and saw all the food in the display cases and took in the aromas of Jewish cooking, "That was it," Buddy told me. "What kind of capital did Pop have to move to Mobile and go in business? He was able to borrow $500 on his life insurance and another $500 from a bank, and with the $1,000 he opened a store on Dauphin Street in 1932."

The largest department store in Hattiesburg to fail was The Davidson Company. Founded in 1906, it had moved into its own newly constructed three-story building on Front Street opposite the new Saenger Theater in November of 1929, costing what was then the enormous sum of $125,000. For the grand opening, the owners announced that the Davidson Company was now an associate store of Marshall Field & Company, enabling it to take advantage of the buying power, brand names, and style contacts of the famous Chicago store. "What Sterling means in silver, Packard and Cadillac in automobiles," the *Hattiesburg American*'s reporter wrote, "Field means in ready-to-wear clothing, furniture, art goods, etc."[67] Bronze plaques on the inside and outside of the building identified Davidson's with Marshall Field. With 36,000 square feet of floor space, the store boasted that "14,500 persons could stand shoulder to shoulder without being crowded." In addition to the usual departments (men's and women's clothing, shoes, piece goods), the store also sold furniture, draperies, rugs, bedding, towels, jewelry, and candy. It had a soda fountain and a luncheonette on the ground floor, and a free parking garage in the basement, from which one could take an elevator up to the store. There was also a service station in the garage offering 24-hour service.

The store styled itself "The House of Courtesy." It appears to have been the finest department store in the city, perhaps even in the state (as the paper claimed), "and one of the most modern in the South." In February of 1930, three months after the opening and four after the crash on Wall Street, W. H. Nevins, one of the founders of the company, advised other businessmen "who insist on howling about poor times" that they "are merely hurting themselves." He went on to say, "It's poor business and poor psychology to be talking pessimistically, particularly when there is no foundation for pessimism. Our business last year was good, and we expect to enjoy even better conditions this year. And one reason I believe we will do more business is the fact that we are in a receptive frame of mind."[68] But the Davidson Company closed its doors for good in 1934. A few months later the manager and one of the owners became partners in a new store called The Mullinix / Davidson Co., diagonally across Main Street from Fine-Bros.-Matison, but four years later they closed this one, too.

    My father didn't go bankrupt, but he remained in debt for the next few years and until he had paid back his vendors and the bank. Although he had been advised by his lawyer to take bankruptcy, he refused. When I asked him once how he had managed to survive the Depression without going bankrupt, he told me he used to take out only enough money to live on from each week's sales and put the rest back into merchandise for the store (actually two stores for all but two or three of those years). It was important not to miss a sale. More than thirty years later, and after he had died, Milton told me, he was remembered by the president of the First National Bank, his lawyer, and others for the way he eventually paid off every cent he owed, even though during those years, as he told me once, he went to the store in the morning and by the end of the day had sold only a single fifty-cent item.

CHAPTER 3

Fear in Low Profile: An Incident in the 1930s

When I was a teenager my father told me about an incident in Hattiesburg in the early 1930s that caused the Jewish community to live in a state of more than ordinary anxiety for over a year and a half. "A Jewish boy robbed a filling station and killed the man who ran it," he said. "His name was Wexler and his girl friend, Bessie Buchalter, was with him at the time. After he was convicted and sentenced to death, one of the elders in the congregation went to the jail to convince him to stop eating." My father may have remembered more, though after nearly two decades some details would naturally have slipped away and errors slipped in. In fact, two of the first things I learned in researching the incident were that Wexler had a black accomplice and that Bessie Buchalter was not with Wexler at the time. My father's omission of the accomplice and inclusion of Bessie, I would come to see, reflected the emphasis his memory placed on the three Jews who played important roles in the incident and its outcome, as well as on the vulnerability that he and other Jews in Hattiesburg felt then. More than once he told me my behavior had to be above reproach, a standard held up to Jewish children everywhere. "It was dinned into Jewish children," John Gross wrote about his growing up in London, "that they were liable to be judged by the worst among them rather than the best, and that if they got into trouble they would bring shame on the community as well as themselves"[1] This concern had become second nature to Jews in the South. It meant keeping a low profile, particularly regarding our more liberal views on racial issues, but including any activity that might put the Jewish community at risk, a concern shared by Jews in apartheid South Africa, who also tried to keep a low profile, though their phrase for it, as journalist Roger Cohen remembers, was "to stay below the parapet."[2]

I remembered Bessie Buchalter as the daughter of Leon and Jennie Buchalter, friends of my parents (though of course I didn't know her then, the robbery having taken place four years before I was born). But who was Wexler? And why did one of the elders go to the jail and suggest self-starvation? I learned from Milton that he had been told by our father pretty much the same thing I had. From Buddy I learned that once, when he was eleven, he saw Wexler brandish a knife while talking to him and several other boys. Buddy had an excellent memory and was a good storyteller and now, in recalling the incident, he dramatized his surprise by suddenly flinching, as if Wexler was at that moment flashing his knife before the two of us. What he was remembering after more than seventy years was something unpredictable and reckless in Wexler's character. After our conversation, I knew I wanted to research the incident and find out what had happened to Wexler. Not knowing how to find the case, however, and having only Wexler's name, I asked a young lawyer, Aili Monahan, the daughter of friends, if she could find it, and she did. She gave me the case number for the appeal to the Mississippi Supreme Court and with that information I was able to find coverage of the incident in the *Hattiesburg American*, beginning with the robbery and murder. Behind the facts I hoped to find an answer to the question of its significance for my father and the Jewish community.

Wexler wasn't initially implicated in the robbery, which took place on Wednesday night, December 9, 1931, around 7:45. It was a young black man who robbed a Standard Oil filling station and in the course of the robbery killed the white manager, J. L. Odom. When he went into the station he told Odom to stick up his hands, but, as he would recall at the trial, Odom "didn't do no way like putting his hands up and . . . [started] coming toward me, and I told him to go back, and I shot him."[3] The robber took the money and checks in the cash register, amounting to around twenty-seven dollars, and returned to the car where his accomplice was waiting. They divided the money and headed toward Laurel for another robbery, but on the way the young black man got drunk and the plan was abandoned. In the meantime, Odom, using his left hand to hold his abdomen where the bullet had entered, went out to the street to seek help, was taken to Methodist Hospital, and died the following day.

On Friday, the police arrested two black men. By 8:30 that night a large crowd had gathered around the county jail and the officers on guard duty expressed "fear of a mob attack." On Saturday, Sheriff Joe B. Gray asked "citizens" to "assist and not hinder officers in their investigation." Aware of the spread of rumors that the police had caught the man who had killed Odom, Sheriff Gray feared an attempt to lynch him might be made. In Poplarville in 1918, in Tylertown and Quitman in 1920, and in Clarksdale in 1925 black defendants charged with murdering whites were taken from jail—or, in one instance, a courtroom—and lynched, two before they could be tried, one after he had been convicted and sentenced, and one after he had been acquitted.[4] Sheriff Gray had read a report just two days before on the front page of the *Hattiesburg American* about a lynching in Lewisburg, West Virginia. A mob of sixty men had invaded the jail at two o'clock in the morning and overwhelmed the jailer. They took two young black men who had been arrested in connection with the killing of two white men, strung them up from the cross arms of a telephone pole, and fired shots into their bodies.

Sheriff Gray now used the paper to make a statement:

> I want to ask the public . . . not to interfere as the crowd did last night. If I had the guilty man under arrest, I certainly would not leave him in the Forrest county jail realizing the feeling here as a result of Mr. Odom's death. . . . The gathering near the jail last night was most uncalled for and was a result of unfounded rumors that we had the 'lone wolf.'[5]

Because the *Hattiesburg American* didn't have a Sunday edition, it had to wait till Monday to report in its headline: "HOLD-UP AND KILLING OF ODOM BELIEVED SOLVED."[6] Immediately below in bold italics ran the lines "White Man and Negro Held in Connection with Bold Crime Here." On the previous Saturday afternoon, three days after the holdup and shooting, a young black man, Andrew Prince, had been arrested along with a friend, James Johnson. Prince had something of a reputation in the nightlife of the black section of town and was known by two other names, "Peanut" and the "Lone Wolf." The officers who arrested him and his friend did so on the pretext of suspecting them of stealing automobile tires. In the course of questioning, Johnson revealed that on the day after the shooting Prince had told him "I got one last night, but I hated to do it." Johnson believed Prince was referring to the shooting of Odom. He also told the police that Prince, who was illiterate, had asked him to read the newspaper's account to him. Sheriff Gray used Johnson's testimony to get a confession from Prince and the paper quotes Prince as saying, "De light is de truf, and I am agoin' to tell de truf," and it was then that he named Wexler as his accomplice.[7] After Prince had confessed, he was secretly driven to an undisclosed city, placed in jail, and his confession taken down in writing.

Sheriff Gray continued to fear a lynching. In the years 1889 to 1945, Mississippi ranked first in lynchings and, as historian Neil R. McMillen points out, "first in virtually every category—the most total lynchings, the most multiple lynchings, the most per capita, the most female victims, the most victims taken from police custody . . . the most public support for vigilantism."[8] In February of 1930, a man from Worth, Mississippi, wrote to the sheriff of Florence, Arizona, to volunteer his services in the hanging of a woman sentenced to death for killing a rancher. He offered to do the work for twenty dollars less than anyone else. "I haven't had much experience in legal hangings," he acknowledged, "but have participated in several private lynchings."[9] On more than one occasion the paper had run editorials against lynching and in September of 1930 it called attention not only to the lynching of a black man in Georgia, but also to the failure of law enforcement officials to prevent it.[10] The South has a history of some law enforcement officers cooperating with lynchers or even joining them, as happened in the 1964 lynching of the three civil rights workers, Chaney, Goodman, and Schwerner in Philadelphia, Mississippi.

On Sunday morning, with Prince safely away, the police went to arrest Wexler. He lived with his mother, his brother, his sister, and his brother-in-law, Sam Rubenstein. The police found him still in bed. He denied knowing Prince, as well as having any connection to the crimes. But under his pillow the police found four new pistol cartridges (".32-caliber, steel jacket") that they concluded tallied "in minute detail with the hull of the automatic bullet found on the filling station floor."[11] They also found two pistols and ammunition for them in clothing hanging in Wexler's closet, one of the pistols being a .32-caliber Smith and Wesson revolver, the other a .25 automatic. When asked who owned the guns, neither brother claimed them. But evidence continued to mount up. A cash register stolen from a store in Hattiesburg was found in Rubenstein's store in nearby Sumrall, along with other stolen merchandise. Wexler continued to deny knowing Prince and being involved in the crime, but when he was included in a lineup of prisoners, Prince walked over and placed a hand on him and said "'Dis is Mister Paul." Both were charged with first-degree murder. Rubenstein was accused of receiving and handling stolen goods, but released on $1,000 bond signed by two members of the Jewish community, Sam Adler and Sam Eisman.

In January, when Wexler appeared in court for a motion for change of venue, the paper described him as "boyish in appearance . . . solemn, but apparently unperturbed . . . dressed in gray trousers and black sweater, the small youth sat perfectly still throughout the proceedings."[12] He was eighteen years old. At the arraignment, he "smiled nonchalantly as he was being escorted into the courtroom . . . and appeared unworried throughout." But his appearance of confidence changed quickly and he became silent, never testifying. The prosecution characterized him as "the master mind" of the robberies and

Forrest County Courthouse (with Confederate Monument) where Prince and Wexler were tried.

Prince as "a black automaton" under his control, characterizations based on stereotypes of the Jew as the smart exploiter and the black as an unthinking follower.[13]

Because Prince had confessed, he was tried first in order to help the prosecution build its case against Wexler. The first day was devoted to the selection of jurors and the testimony of a few witnesses who helped establish the facts of what had happened on the night of December 9. On the second day, his confession was read aloud in court. Immediately afterwards, following his lawyers' instructions, he pleaded not guilty. Since a confession alone could not warrant a conviction, as the judge mentioned in comments to the defense, Prince's lawyers wanted to create doubt about it in the courtroom and the paper appears to honor their effort by repeatedly referring to Prince's "purported confession."

Nonetheless, his confession was indisputable. In it he acknowledged that he had shot Odom and described in some detail how it had happened. Upon entering the station, gun in hand and wearing a cap and goggles, he said "Hands up," but Odom was "coming toward me and I was inching off from him."

He "didn't do no way like putting his hands up" and he kept "coming towards me."[14] Prince said Odom was "patting his hands" while coming towards him. Whatever Odom meant to convey by his actions, he must have frightened Prince. "I said 'stick them up,' and he come patting his hands and went to hollering and I shot him. The way I shot that man—you know how an automatic is—first time I had an automatic."[15] Because Prince didn't disavow his confession, his lawyers sought to characterize him as a pawn manipulated by Wexler. They emphasized that he was illiterate and that Wexler was the one responsible for what they had done together, "a white man—a master mind . . . found behind all such crimes." Unable to overcome the weight of evidence against Prince, the defense called no witnesses. At the end of the second day, the jury took just six minutes to reach a verdict. The sentence was made mandatory by the verdict. Judge Pack asked Prince if he had anything to say before being sentenced. "I'm just sorry I done it, that's all."[16]

Judge Pack had been elected circuit judge in 1929, having once served temporarily on the Mississippi Supreme Court following the death of one of its members. The *Hattiesburg American* had strongly endorsed his candidacy. In the second of two editorials about him, the paper said he was an "able and high-minded citizen" who would "restore the dignity and prestige of the court."[17] It was something Judge Pack must have felt was needed, for by the end of his first month on the bench he had held four men in contempt of court for failing to appear for jury duty, fined them twenty-five dollars each for not "send[ing] legal excuses for failure to appear," and allowed their names to be printed in the paper.[18] He was an active member of his Baptist Church and occasionally gave talks at other local churches. In his address to the graduates of Hattiesburg High School in May of 1930 (among whom were two from the Jewish community, Sam and Esther Kelsey), he concluded by saying that "a fixed, unshakable faith in Jesus Christ is a positive requirement for complete success."[19]

After Prince said he was sorry, "the kindly voiced judge pronounced the solemn words that alone broke the strained silence: '[You are to be] hanged by the neck until you are dead, dead, dead.'"[20] Why "the kindly voiced" judge repeated the word "dead" isn't explained. Was it a practice in Mississippi to use such repetition in cases where the death penalty was imposed? If so, for what purpose? Or was it an expression of the judge's personal feelings, held under judicial restraint throughout the trial but now leading him to express his moral outrage at the murder of Odom and to act as the community's agent of retribution in the last minutes of the trial? Prince responded by saying "Thank you, Judge, thank you," repeated several times, as if he had picked up something in the tone and rhythm of the judge's words, and was responding to the spirit of them, whatever that was, and sounding genuine in his humility and deference before the man who had just sentenced him to die.

The trial of Wexler began the next day. In the previous week, however, Wexler's lawyers had filed a motion for a change of venue. Since the death of Odom, they argued, feelings in Hattiesburg and throughout Forrest County had run so high that it would be impossible for Wexler to receive a fair and impartial trial. (Although a similar motion could have been made for Prince, his lawyers hadn't filed one, probably because it seemed futile in the case of a black man who had already confessed to killing a white man.) To counter the defense's argument for a change of venue, the prosecution summoned thirty-nine witnesses willing to testify that they thought Wexler could receive a fair and impartial trial. Among them were two well-known and respected members of the Jewish community, Herman Katz and his son-in-law Marcus London, though they weren't asked to testify. Wexler's lawyers then summoned witnesses to support their claim that Wexler could not receive a fair trial, but no Jews were among them. Presumably no one in the Jewish community thought he could not receive a fair trial, or was willing to come forward and say that he couldn't. The evidence against Wexler was no doubt discussed widely in the Jewish community and many Jews, perhaps most, may have concluded he was guilty.

In their cross-examination of the state's witnesses, Wexler's lawyers repeatedly placed emphasis on the paper's front-page coverage of the case, the widespread "indignation" in the public's mind that they claimed was directed primarily against Wexler, the four or five hundred men who had gathered around the jail after two black men had been arrested, and the removal of Prince and Wexler to a jail outside Forrest County. Yet their arguments that Wexler couldn't receive a fair trial in Hattiesburg were undermined by the state's witnesses, several of whom were prominent citizens: H. O. Hoffman, purchasing agent for the Mississippi Central Railroad, who said he hadn't heard much talk about the case and none about "mob violence"; F. W. Foote, President of the First National Bank, who said the feeling in the community was "more against the crime than the boy"; and Seth Heidelberg, owner of a furniture store, who said what he'd heard about the case had been "in condemnation of the act rather than the prisoner." When former Sheriff (now Deputy Sheriff) Joe Gray testified, he said he had moved Wexler to another jail as a "precaution," but not, as Wexler's lawyers were suggesting, "on account of the sentiment and inflamed condition of the public mind against this boy."[21] Judge Pack ruled against the motion for a change of venue.

On the day of Wexler's trial, the courtroom was filled with more than a thousand spectators. He pleaded not guilty but, on his lawyer's advice, would not testify in his own defense. Although he had all along denied any connection to the crimes or even acquaintance with Prince, the prosecution brought forward several witnesses, both black and white, who corroborated Prince's testimony. They had seen him with Prince on different occasions. Prince's mother and sister said Wexler had come to their home to pick him up around 7:30 on the night of the shooting. His sister said that she, Prince, and a young woman who was a friend of Prince's were playing cards when Wexler came to the house. The young woman, who acknowledged that she and Prince had been "sweethearts in a way," also testified that Wexler had come to the house that night. On the Friday after the shooting, according to Prince's mother, Wexler came to the house at six in the morning to say to Prince, "Boy, I want to tell you, you better be careful, for the police are out looking for you and they want you bad."[22]

The prosecutors' main effort went toward establishing that Wexler was equally responsible for the death of Odom, even though he hadn't pulled the trigger. They showed that the gun Prince had used had been given to him by Wexler, along with instructions on how to use it. "After we left the house that night," Prince testified, "Mister Paul stopped the car and showed me two guns. He asked me which one I wanted. I told him I had never used an automatic before, but he said, 'Peanut, when you push up on this [safety device] and pull the trigger it will shoot, and when this is pushed down it won't shoot,' and he left it up and said 'All you do now is pull the trigger,' and we went on down Hardy Street."[23] Prince said that after shooting Odom, returning to the car with the money, and relating what had happened, Wexler said to him, "Peanut, you had to shoot him, didn't you?"[24]

When T. Webber Wilson, a former congressman and prosecuting attorney in next-door Jones County and now the more aggressive of Wexler's two attorneys, tried during cross-examination to get Prince to admit Wexler didn't tell him to kill Odom, Prince replied, "This is what he said to me—'Peanut, when you go in a place and they don't stick 'em up, you shoot 'em'—that's what he said to me."[25] While Prince repeated versions of this statement several times during the trial, Wilson tried to undermine his testimony by asking questions in a tone designed to rile him ("Don't you know you're lying about that?" "You ain't going to jump on me, are you?" "Still got hell in you, haven't you?"). Although Judge Pack had previously instructed Prince to answer Wilson's questions without additional comment, Prince apparently couldn't resist at one point and said to Wilson "The way you talk to a man—talk to a man like he's a dog." Wilson tried one more time: "And you would like to kill me now if you had a gun, wouldn't you?" But Prince replied "No, sir."[26]

The clinching testimony, however, may not have been Prince's but that of Wexler's fifteen-year-old girl friend, Bessie Buchalter. As a Jewish witness for the prosecution of a Jewish boy, her credibility in the minds of the jury must have seemed beyond doubt. Like many in the Jewish community, she had social ties reaching beyond her family and their Jewish friends and into the white Christian community. The Buchalters not only knew the Odoms, they were friendly with them. The jurors saw Mrs. Odom sitting in the courtroom, often in tears, while they listened to and observed Bessie Buchalter as she gave her testimony. She had known Wexler since August and had often gone riding with him in his green Chevrolet coupe. She had seen him with Prince on two or three occasions when Wexler was planning to drive to Prince's home and asked her if she would like to come along. On the Thursday after the shooting, they happened to meet in front of the post office. She was sitting in her mother's car, waiting for her to return from mailing a letter, when Wexler came up to the car and they began to talk about what had happened.

District Attorney Alexander Currie asked her to state what Wexler said to her about "his knowledge of this shooting."

> BB: Yes, sir, and after I asked him if he knew anything about it, he said "Yes, I know all about it, I was there."
> ...
> AC: Go ahead.
> BB: I asked him to tell me about it and he said he waited in the car, that they went there to rob the place and the negro went in.... The negro went in there and told him to hold his hands up and he wouldn't do it—this is what the negro told him happened—and he wouldn't hold his hands up, he just clapped them like he was going to reach for a gun or was signaling to someone, and then the negro shot him and he came to the car and they left—that's all.[27]

Wexler's other defense attorney, Burkett Collins, used repetition in his questions to emphasize Wexler wasn't present in the gas station for the robbery or the shooting and so shouldn't be held responsible for Mr. Odom's death.

> BC: And he told you that he wasn't present when it happened?"
> BB: No sir, he wasn't present.

BC: That is what Mr. Wexler said, that he wasn't present when it happened?

BB: Yes, sir, and he said if he had known what would be the result, he would never have gone there; he said, "No man's life is worth measly money."[28]

Because he hadn't pulled the trigger, his lawyers argued he should be put in the state penitentiary, not hanged "for something he did not actually do himself." To make a plea for his life was certainly the humane thing to do. Whether or not it was a legally sound and persuasive argument, I don't know. For it to succeed, however, his lawyers apparently felt they had to appeal to the prejudices of the all-white male jury, eleven farmers and one employee of the county road department. They tried to persuade the jury that he shouldn't be hanged on evidence provided largely by a "convicted negro murderer" and other black witnesses. Their hope appears to have been that if he was convicted and sentenced to death the governor might be open to the possibility of commuting the sentence to life imprisonment. This became one of the strategies of the appeals after the trial. Former Governor Bilbo was reported in the *Hattiesburg American* to be "openly adverse to capital punishment" and to have "on numerous occasions . . . commuted the death sentence to life" in prison.[29] In January of 1932, his last month in office, "he freed seventy-three convicts of whom twenty-three were serving sentences for murder, manslaughter, robbery, and other serious crimes."[30] But Governor Sennett Conner, a native of Hattiesburg, had so far not given any indication of his views on commuting death sentences to life imprisonment.

The jury took just one ballot to reach its verdict. Most of the estimated fifteen hundred spectators that day stayed to hear it. Wexler "flushed slightly as the jury walked from its room, and his fingers twitched nervously." The faces of the jurors reflected a distaste of their task. "There were tears in the eyes of at least one juror." When the finding of "guilty as charged" was read, there was no sound in the courtroom. Wexler's mother and brother had twice left in tears, but stayed to hear the verdict. After Judge Pack asked Wexler if he had anything to say and heard him reply "No, sir, not a thing," he spoke the same words used in sentencing Prince—"You are to be hanged by the neck until you are dead, dead, dead." Wexler remained standing, "looking steadily and pleasantly at the man who pronounced his doom, until bailiffs were ordered to take him away." But tears came as he was being led down the back stairs. When he reached the sidewalk and a deputy told him on their way to the automobile that would take him away, "Paul, Bessie said to tell

Hattiesburg American, July 14, 1932. One of numerous articles about Wexler that appeared between December 1931 and April 1933.

you goodbye for her," Wexler answered "'Goodbye,' his voice almost breaking." She had visited him the previous day during a court recess, but was not present when the verdict was read. As the car drove away, he turned around to look through one of its windows at the courthouse, "presumably seeking a glimpse of friends or relatives."[31]

The headline that afternoon, January 29, 1932, was "PAUL WEXLER GIVEN DEATH PENALTY BY JURY." Over the next fourteen months there would be numerous front-page stories about the appeals that Wexler's lawyers would file. In the most important one, they used prosecuting attorney D. W. Holmes' statement at the beginning of the trial that he was "speaking for an enraged citizenry."[32] Judge Pack had sustained their objection to Holmes' statement and they used his decision now as evidence that the motion for a change of venue should have been granted. But they are more explicit than they had been in the pretrial hearing about the potential for prejudice against Wexler as a Jew.

> The organic law of this country does not throw its shield of protection alone around the white Gentile, but that guarantee is equally strong to the Jew. The law knows no distinction. The Constitution and laws of the State of Mississippi guard just as sacredly the rights of the wondering [sic] Jew who has no country, as it does the white Gentile who gave his blood for the existence of the government.[33]

In this well-intentioned attempt to ensure that the laws will extend the same protections against prejudice to their Jewish client that it does to other whites, however, Wexler's lawyers unwittingly include two common notions about Jews based on prejudice. The first, represented in the reference to the legend of "The Wandering Jew," suggests that Jews are aliens, people without a country rather than citizens, and that a Jew's identity can be traced back to a mythical figure who taunted Christ on his way to being crucified and as a result was condemned to wander the earth until the Second Coming. The second is represented in the statement that only "the white Gentile gave blood for the existence of the government." Although the phrasing is ambiguous, a clear implication is that Jews hadn't fought for either the establishment ("existence") or the defense (the continued existence) of the state or country in which they live. Mark Twain repeated this notion in his essay "Concerning the Jews" when he said Jews showed "an unpatriotic disinclination to stand by the flag as a soldier" and advised them to "get up volunteer regiments composed of Jews solely" in order to counter the notion that "you feed on a country but don't like to fight for it" until, after publication of the essay, it was pointed out to him that Jews had served honorably in the Revolutionary War, the War of 1812, the Mexican War, and the Civil War (with some for the Confederacy, others for the Union).[34] But the notion that they hadn't remained a commonly held belief persisting well into the twentieth century, one that my brother-in-law "B" told me he had heard repeated among his fellow soldiers during his service overseas in World War II.

While the attitude of Wexler's lawyers stands in stark contrast to the openly anti-Semitic views of Henry Ford and Father Coughlin, the reference to The Wandering Jew repeats an example of religion-based anti-Semitism that has been part of Western culture for centuries. The perception of Jews as aliens, sometimes as dehumanized beings with horns, remained an experience in the life of Jews, often appearing unexpectedly, as it did one day in the early 1930s when a man came to my father's store to see what a Jew looked like. He stood for a moment in the doorway, then took a few hesitant steps in to get a closer look. He thought Jews had horns. My father was not alone in being the object of such curiosity. When the first Jewish child in Williamson, West Virginia, was born, "people came from all over to see the Jew-baby—expecting horns."[35] In Union City, Tennessee, when a nineteen-year-old boy came into the only Jewish-owned store in the town and saw the owner, he cried out "You won't do atall" because he thought "Jews were *supposed* to have horns. The Bible said so."[36] Where had these people gotten this notion? Probably from family and friends, the notion having been part of an oral tradition that included other myths and folklore, but also, I've learned, from a print tradition that included anti-Semitic tracts, literature, cartoons, and art works. It has been traced back to Christian art of the thirteenth century in which Jews were depicted as the children of Satan. "Jews were delineated with hooves, claws, and horns," writes historian Frederic C. Jaher, "and sometimes as actual devils. . . . Illustrations abounded showing Jews and Satan together as allies, thirsting for blood and poisoning the Savior's wounds. These caricatures would persist through the ages and appear in twentieth-century anti-Semitic propaganda."[37] The attempt to dehumanize Jews is similar to the notion, still circulating in the 1940s, that black men have tails.[38]

Wexler's lawyers' appeal to the Mississippi Supreme Court for a change of venue was based on the argument that he could not receive a fair trial in the same city where the crime had been committed. It was denied. The court found that the state of the public mind in Hattiesburg "was not so much against appellant [Wexler] and Prince, but against the dastardly crime that had been committed."[39] Wexler was then scheduled to hang on July 14. This setback was followed by a plea to Governor Sennett Conner for a commutation of the sentence to life imprisonment. But the plea ran into unexpected opposition from the black community. President J. E. Johnson of the Prentiss Normal and Industrial Institute, a black college, wrote to say that he represents "a committee of one hundred leading negroes of the state . . . [who are] asking the governor, in the event he commutes the sentence of Paul Wexler . . . that he also commute the death sentence of the negro." They don't condone the crime and they do not ask the governor to intervene. But in the event that he does, they ask him "to give the negro the same consideration."[40] It's clear they believed the strategy of Wexler's lawyers in effect put the greater blame on Prince.

At the public hearing on July 11, Mrs. Odom, sitting with her three children directly in front of the governor, also asked him "not to interfere with the judgment of the court" and to "let this boy hang."[41] Wexler's lawyers (now including Simon Rosenthal from Jackson) based their plea for executive clemency on two claims: that Wexler was "mentally sub-normal" and "too young to hang."[42] After the hearing, Governor Conner examined Wexler in his office for an hour in the presence of two ministers and two guards. While the examination was going on, plans for the execution of the two young men continued to go forward in the gallows room at the top of the county courthouse. Two hemp ropes nearly an inch thick and 17½ feet long were being stretched and given a coat of lard "to take the slack out of them," a reporter explained, "so they will pull taut when the body of a man is suspended."[43] On the eve of the next day, July 14, when Wexler and Prince were to be hanged, Governor Conner granted both a fifteen-day stay of execution so that he could look further into Wexler's case.

In its editorial the next day, the *Hattiesburg American* objected to the governor's interference. It began by stating the two-fold purpose of capital punishment: "to fulfill the ancient law of—an eye for an eye and a tooth for a tooth—hence, a life for a life" (a reference to the Old Testament that would not have been lost on the paper's readers, both Christian and Jewish) and "to act as a deterrent to crime." The governor's "interference" was "an affront to the law enforcement agencies of Forrest County, the Forrest County Circuit Court and to the Supreme Court of Mississippi as well as to the whole citizenship of this territory."[44] Governor Conner decided not to interfere and the hangings remained scheduled for Friday, July 29.

But then Wexler's attorneys sought and obtained in a chancery court in Vicksburg a writ of *coram nobis* (a legal order allowing a court to correct an error) that provided a thirty-day stay of execution and an opportunity for Wexler's lawyers to reexamine aspects of the case. Wexler's mother and brother came to Judge Pack's courtroom, where Wexler sat "shaking his head, moaning and at times crying out hysterically." After hearing the arguments regarding the writ and the plea for a sanity hearing, Judge Pack dismissed the writ on the ground that a chancery court "had no authority to restrain or delay any order of a common law court," but granted the request for a sanity hearing and scheduled it for the following Monday.[45]

At the sanity hearing Wexler's lawyers questioned four inmates from the jail in Jackson who had had opportunities to observe his behavior. All said they thought he was insane. They gave as examples his butting his head against the wall of his cell, riding a mop as though it were a horse, tearing his clothes, placing a lighted cigarette in his mouth, and eating "like a dog." One testified that

Wexler had remained in bed for three weeks, had refused to talk to other prisoners, and had become so violent that he had to be put in a cell by himself. According to this witness, Wexler had "refused to bathe and was only cleaned when forcibly put under a shower."[46] In affidavits presented to the court prior to the hearing, a number of individuals who had had opportunities to observe him stated they thought he was deranged. Dr. O. C. Miller of the Baptist Orphanage of Jackson, for example, thought Wexler had "a touch of 'dementia praecox' [early insanity], and also averred that he was a moron."[47] A witness from New Orleans, Mr. J. Silver, testified that he had known Wexler's father, Jules Wexler, and that both Jules and his sister had for a time been confined to a hospital for the insane in Romania.

The defense now called three "alienists" to testify about the sanity of Wexler. This term (from the French *aliéniste*) was widely used in the first three decades of the twentieth century—most famously, perhaps, in the Loeb and Leopold trial in 1924 to describe the psychiatrists whose testimony Clarence Darrow used to support his plea of temporary insanity in his effort to save the two young murderers from execution—to refer to a psychiatrist or other specialist accepted by a court of law as qualified to assess the mental competence of a defendant. Although "alienist" carried in its etymology (from the Latin *alienus*) the sense of being an "other," a foreigner or alien, its use now referred to a specialist in diagnosing and treating individuals who were "other" or "alien" in a psychological or mental sense. But during the hearing on Wexler's sanity that distinction may not always have been clear.

The three specialists Wexler's lawyers called were Dr. J. H. Fox of the Federal Veterans' Bureau in Jackson, Dr. Milton S. Freiman of the LSU School of Medicine, and Dr. O. A. Schmidt of the staff of the East Mississippi Hospital for the Insane in Meridian. They testified that Wexler had *dementia praecox* and one, Dr. Freiman, described it as "a catatonic type" of the disease. Dr. Schmidt called it "a typical hospital type." As an example, Dr. Fox cited Wexler's reaction when H. T. Odom, brother of the slain man, took the witness stand. Wexler had "jumped up and struggled with his wardens who finally had to carry him from the courtroom into the jury room," where he was attended by several physicians, including Dr. Fox, who now said Wexler's reaction in the courtroom was "characteristic of that type of insanity."[48]

The turning point came when the doctors called by the state—all from Hattiesburg, none psychiatrists or experts on mental illness—testified that they thought Wexler was sane. Judge Pack questioned Dr. Harvey T. Mounger about his examination of Wexler following the young man's hysterical outburst in the courtroom on the first day of the hearing. Dr. Mounger replied that "the pulse of Wexler was virtually normal as were the reflexes of his eyes. His heart action was good and he had run no temperature. He was revived within a few minutes. His outburst . . . was due to hysteria brought on by the strain of the proceedings or by shock."[49] Other witnesses for the state also testified that he was sane. Former Sheriff Joe. B. Gray said that throughout the time of his arrest, trial, and conviction he was "perfectly normal in every respect." Sheriff Estus E. Hudson corroborated the testimony of former Sheriff Gray, but noted that Wexler's behavior had changed after the clemency hearing held by Governor Conner in July. The implication in Sheriff Hudson's comment would be made clear in Judge Pack's ruling. Declaring Wexler sane, he stated "that the defendant for the first time had acted in an insane manner following the refusal of the governor to grant him a stay of execution or executive clemency" and that he had "resorted to the only possible avenue of escaping the gallows, that of insanity . . . appear[ing] perfectly sane at the hearing before the governor and up until a few days prior to his scheduled execution last July 29."[50] At the end of the hearing, Judge Pack resentenced him to hang on December 23, 1932.

Now in a final effort, Wexler's lawyers appealed Judge Pack's ruling and were scheduled to appear before the Mississippi Supreme Court on April 24, 1933. Until then, Wexler and Prince were given another stay of execution.

It was probably earlier in the appeals process when, as my father remembered, one of the elders in the Jewish community went to see Wexler and suggested he stop eating. On June 27, 1932, the paper listed four visitors: "his brother, sister, a spiritual advisor and a young girl friend of the prisoner." The girl friend must have been Bessie Buchalter. But who was the "spiritual advisor"? One possibility is Rabbi Herman D. Bloom, whose name has appeared from time to time in brief notices about forthcoming Jewish holidays, but most recently for having signed an affidavit supporting a new motion for a change of venue.[51] Since he had already been named on these occasions, however, it's not clear why he wasn't this time if he was the person referred to as "spiritual advisor." Other possibilities are a relative, a friend of the family, the elder my father mentioned, or another member of the Jewish community. Any of his visitors could have discussed with him his chances in the courts, legal alternatives, and personal choices left to him, including self-starvation. It was one of the elders, however, who, according to my father, suggested to Wexler that he stop eating.

Wexler began accepting only orange juice and cereal in July.[52] By November, a week before the sanity hearing, he wouldn't eat anything.[53] His appetite began to improve in December, but then from January to March he again refused to eat and was force-fed by means of unspecified "artificial methods of feeding." Two county physicians visited him daily, presumably to ensure he would survive to be hanged. During this time he made several attempts to commit suicide, according to Jailer Cooper, by "cutting himself with broken glass and butting his head against the wall of his cell." He continued to refuse to eat or speak to anyone and appeared to be detached from or unaware of his surroundings. In April he started eating again, at one point asking for red beans and rice, a favorite New Orleans dish, saying he was going to let them hang him. "He began to speak rationally," the paper reported, "and his conversations with his attendant [a black trusty experienced in nursing] and with Jailer Cooper disclosed, they say, that he had been conscious and appreciative of his surroundings while apparently in a comatose condition."[54] How could he be said to speak, not to mention "rationally," while comatose? Perhaps what the trusty and Jailer Cooper were observing, and the reporter was trying to convey, was that he was still able to speak, though his mental condition had deteriorated from going without food for so long. Then, on April 14, a little more than a week before the appeal was to be heard by the Supreme Court, he died.

Dr. Leo H. Martin, county physician, said the cause of death was "self-inflicted starvation having for its purpose escape from the gallows." Despite his return to eating, even saying "he wanted to build his strength," according to Dr. Martin, his "self-imposed fast . . . had taken its toll . . . [and] Wexler's organisms . . . suffered collapse from which he was unable to rally."[55]

After his death, Prince pleaded with Jailer Cooper that he be allowed "to see Paul for the last time."

> [Cooper] took Prince to the cell in which Wexler had just died. Prince bowed his head and said with emotion, 'Poor, poor boy.' He stood for a few minutes at the bedside of Wexler and then was led back to his cell where he repeated his oft-made statement that he was prepared to go to the gallows.[56]

Wexler's body was sent to New Orleans early in the morning of April 14 and he was buried beside his father in the afternoon, following the Orthodox tradition of burying the dead in twenty-four hours. Wexler's mother was with her daughter in West Allis, Wisconsin, and was unable to attend the funeral.[57]

On the day before Prince was to be hanged, he sent letters to Governor Conner and Odom's widow that he had dictated to a local attorney who had agreed to help him. To the governor: "I am writing not to ask you to do me no favor, but to thank you for what you have done for me. You are a good governor and I don't hold no ill will against you, and I hope you don't hold nothing against me. Please don't sign no petition to help me, 'cause if God wants me to I am going and if not I will still be here, 'cause God's will going to be done." To Mrs. Odom: "I am writing you this letter to ask you to forgive me for taking your husband's life. If God is ready for me to go next Tuesday I will be ready, and I want to go knowing you forgive me for what I done, and I hope Mr. Odom's little children wont hold nothing against me in their little hearts. I told the court the truth about how it all happened and I feel God done forgive me. I hope your little children will read the Bible and learn the Lord's prayer. Forgive me. This is the last letter from Andrew Prince. X (His mark)."[58] The following day, sixty-three persons, including Mrs. Odom, witnessed the execution.

When the elder went to the jail to see Wexler, even if not designated by the Jewish community to go as its representative, he couldn't have gone simply as an individual. His long-standing role as a prominent figure in the Jewish community implied something more, and he wouldn't have gone without first having discussions of Wexler's chances and alternatives, as well as the possible backlash against the Jewish community, with others in the congregation, including, presumably, Rabbi Bloom. This is what I had inferred. Then, while revising this chapter and still thinking about how to define what I saw as the importance of the case in my father's memory and in the experience of the Jewish community, I was surprised to run across a reference to it in the diary of Rabbi Charles Mantinband, which only a few months before had been donated to the Institute for Southern Jewish Life in Jackson. Alice and I drove to Jackson and spent several days reading the diary. I was especially interested in the years 1951 to early 1963 when I knew him, the first two of those years when I was in high school and afterwards when I was home from college and later for brief visits. He had learned of the Wexler case from a visitor in his last few months in Hattiesburg and characterized what he was told as a "revisiting 30 years back of a murder & how a Jew was saved from the gallows tho alas by suicidal means and maybe rabbinical collusion."[59]

His brief summarizing reference seemed to me to confirm not only what my father had told me about the involvement of the elder in Wexler's self-starvation but also, with the use of the word "collusion," to indicate that he hadn't acted alone and had discussed the matter with others in the Jewish community. But it didn't explain why he and others were so concerned. Was the suggestion of self-starvation made out of an altruistic concern for Wexler, with the purpose of enabling him to escape the gallows, or out of a concern to protect the Jewish community from the scandal of a public execution of a Jew? It may well have seemed impossible to separate the two concerns. Although it was Wexler who had been put on trial, it must at times have seemed to the Jews in Hattiesburg that they, too, were being put on trial. In teaming up with a black in a robbery that had resulted in the murder of a white, he had put the reputation of the entire Jewish community at risk. The prosecutors had called him the "master mind" and Prince his "black automaton." A Jewish boy teaming up with a black in a criminal act would, for a few people, have brought to mind the old saying "A Jew is just a nigger turned inside out," which was still circulating in the 1950s.[60] For others, it would have confirmed their suspicion of an alliance between Jews and blacks that threatened the "Southern way of life," a suspicion supported by the reputation of Julius Rosenwald as the philanthropist who built schools for blacks in the South, of the brothers Joel and Arthur Spingarn as lawyers for the NAACP, and of Sam Leibowitz as the New York lawyer who in 1931 had gone to Alabama to defend the nine black boys accused of rape in the Scottsboro case. Jews in Hattiesburg, having won a degree of acceptance by the white Gentile majority, knew their economic survival and personal security depended on conformity to the South's racial laws. But now Wexler's criminal behavior had aroused their fears and memories of times in Jewish history when the alleged act of one Jew had put all in jeopardy.

Those from Eastern Europe, including my parents and most of the Jewish community at that time, hadn't forgotten the pogroms in Russia and the case of Mendel Beilis in Kiev, who was accused of ritual murder. It hadn't been that long—1913, the same year as the trial of Beilis—since Leo Frank in Atlanta, though innocent, had been convicted of the murder of young Mary Phagan and two years later lynched. Four days before the lynching, the anti-Semitic populist and journalist Tom Watson had warned in a headline of his paper the *Jeffersonian*, effectively inciting those who favored lynching, that "THE NEXT JEW WHO DOES WHAT FRANK DID, IS GOING TO GET EXACTLY THE SAME THING WE GIVE TO NEGRO RAPISTS."[61] Frank was taken at night from the state prison in Milledgeville where he was being held after his sentence had been commuted to life imprisonment by Governor John M. Slaton, driven back to Mary Phagan's birthplace, Marietta, hanged, and his body mutilated. What had happened to him would have served as a pointed reminder to Jews in the South of their vulnerability. The *Hattiesburg News* (precursor of the *American*) had carried the story of Frank's trial from July 29 to August 26, usually on the front page. Following the lynching in the early morning of August 17, 1915, the paper carried two photographs on the same page, one of Frank's dead body hanging from the lynching tree, with members of the lynch mob standing beneath it an hour after his death, the other of the "mob" that had "collected in front of the local undertaker's shop, believing the body had been taken there."[62] "It was after the lynchers had done their work that the spirit of the Roman holiday prevailed," wrote C. Vann Woodward. "A heel was repeatedly ground into the flesh of the dead man's face, and bits of his clothing and of the rope were distributed as souvenirs."[63] The impact was devastating to Jews in the South. "What happened to Frank could have happened to any of them," wrote Leonard Dinnerstein, and for "the next half century they lived in great apprehension."[64]

Four years later in Ellisville, just a few miles up the road from Hattiesburg on the way to Laurel, a gruesome lynching of a black man, John Hartsfield, became a major public event. It had been planned and advertised days in advance. "Sawmills released their employees, farmers brought their families and dogs, and whites jammed interurban trains as several thousand spectators—some with picnics of fried chicken and layer cake—arrived to see a spectacle that Governor Bilbo declared he was 'powerless to prevent.' The afternoon editions of newspapers in Jackson and New Orleans announced the impending event—'3000 WILL BURN NEGRO,' 'JOHN HARTSFIELD WILL BE LYNCHED BY ELLISVILLE MOB AT 5 O'CLOCK THIS AFTERNOON.' ... At the appointed hour the black man was kicked unconscious, hanged from an ancient sycamore tree, and riddled with bullets before his body was engulfed in flames." Some of Ellisville's white citizens described the lynching "as one of the state's 'more orderly' executions."[65]

Another reason to be fearful was the evidence of increasing anti-Semitism in the 1920s and early 1930s. Of the main charges brought against the Jew for much of Western history—Christ killer, economic exploiter, eternal alien, subversive element in Christian civilization, and embodiment of evil—it's not surprising that the most prominent one in the 1930s became economic exploiter. It had been a central feature of a series of articles in the early 1920s entitled *The International Jew* in Henry Ford's widely circulated *Dearborn Independent*, a weekly newspaper that in 1922 had a circulation of 300,000 and in 1924 had increased to 700,000.[66] Though not a national newspaper, its wide circulation was ensured by the subscription policy Ford imposed on Ford dealerships across the country: "Ford salesmen were informed by the home office that . . . every customer should become a regular reader." To avoid a conflict with the home office and the possibility of losing their dealerships, dealers often "spent their own money on complementary subscriptions for friends and acquaintances, Rotary members, local fraternity brothers, Chambers of Commerce, and so on."[67] While it's impossible to know how many people actually read the paper or took the series on Jews seriously, Ford's subscription policy gave him a national voice and anti-Semitism the appearance of respectability.

The series claimed that the theater, liquor, and loan businesses in the United States, as well as the motion picture, sugar, tobacco, meatpacking, jewelry, grain, cotton, and Colorado smelting industries were all controlled by Jews. Most of the "musical purveying done in the country," "magazine authorship," and "news distribution" were also said to be in the hands of Jews. Worst of all, international finance and banking were controlled by Jews. "I know who caused the [First World] war—the German-Jewish bankers," Ford had once exclaimed. "I have the evidence here. Facts!"[68] The series won Hitler's admiration, leading him to cite it in *Mein Kampf* and to award the Grand Cross of the German Eagle to Ford on his seventy-fifth birthday.

As the Depression worsened in the 1930s, Ford's and Hitler's claims about Jews came to seem more believable and, as Dinnerstein points out, "people eagerly blamed Jewish businessmen, who allegedly controlled the money supply, for the economic crisis."[69] It wasn't only anti-Semites, however, who believed Jews controlled the wealth of the country. The pastor of the Assembly of God Church in Hattiesburg, James E. Hamil, for example, wrote an essay for the newspaper in 1936 that appeared under the headline "Jewish Race Is Favored." In it he claimed that the centuries-long persecution of Jews was soon to end because "the program of God to bring Israel back to Palestine" had begun to be fulfilled in 1917 when General Allenby took Jerusalem with English troops and Lord Balfour declared that the British government looked with favor on the establishment of a permanent home for Jews in Palestine. It was also part of God's plan, Rev. Hamil believed, that Jews now "own half of the banking houses in the world. Half of the world's wealth is in Jewish hands. Half of the jewelry stores belong to Jews, and most of the moving picture industry is controlled by Jews."[70]

Claims about Jewish control of the American economy, however, were investigated and refuted in an article entitled "Jews in America," published in *Fortune* magazine in 1936. Jews didn't control or even have a significant presence in the country's major industries—oil, gas, coal, steel, automobile, rubber, railroad, shipbuilding, aviation, banking, tobacco—and the article concluded that there was "no basis whatever for the suggestion that Jews monopolize U. S. business and industry."[71] Only a few industries had a prominent Jewish presence—for example, clothing, scrap iron, and filmmaking. The newspaper and magazine industry only seemed to have one because of the quality and distinction of a few publications, particularly the *New York Times* and the *New Yorker*. Since *Fortune*'s circulation did not compare with that of *Reader's Digest* or *Time* or *Newsweek*, however, the article did not have much potential to reshape opinion. Anti-Semitism neared its peak in 1938, the year Ford received the award from Hitler. Public opinion polls showed that "at least 50 percent of Americans had a low opinion of Jews, 45 percent thought that they were less honest than Gentiles in business, 24 percent thought that they held too many government jobs, and 35 percent believed that the Jews in Europe were largely responsible for the oppression that had been heaped on them."[72]

What I learned from the Wexler case and the research I did to help me understand it in its historical context made me realize that I couldn't hope to understand the life of my parents and of the Jewish community in Hattiesburg without taking into account its fears during the year and a half in the early 1930s when Wexler was repeatedly in the news. Given the many false notions about Jews and explicit expressions of anti-Semitism in the 1920s and 1930s, Jews in the South lived with "a pervasive sense of anxiety."[73] Although a tiny minority, their clothing and other retail businesses gave them a highly visible presence. They were viewed as the "eternal alien," according to W. J. Cash in his classic study *The Mind of the South*, which was written in the 1930s. In Hattiesburg, they had memories of persecution and pogroms, sometimes involving members of one's own family, as was the case with my mother. Although a vestige of another time and place, their fear was nonetheless real. While I don't think it was unremitting or prevented them from feeling generally accepted, it was always present, just below the surface, leaving them with a sense that the acceptance remained conditional. Later in the 1930s, the fear would be raised to the level of an alert by the rhetoric of Father Coughlin, Charles Lindbergh, and *Bundesführer* Fritz Kuhn of the German-American Nazi Party. In the 1950s and 1960s it would ring like an alarm bell when the Ku Klux Klan began a campaign of terror against Jews in the South because of the activities of Jews in the civil rights movement, among them a few courageous Southern rabbis—Charles Mantinband, for one—and young Jewish activists from the North.

After the deaths of Prince and Wexler, their names and what they had done disappeared from the newspaper and began to fade from local memory. Mrs. Wexler, her son Sol, and the Sam Rubensteins had already moved away. Bessie Buchalter married Arthur Frohman, moved to Laurel, raised six children, and lived into her nineties. The elder remained an important figure in the congregation. Members of the Jewish community continued to attend services on Friday nights in the small synagogue on West Pine Street and worked long hours trying to stay in business and survive the Depression. If they remembered the case, they preferred not to discuss it. In the 1950s Maurice Auerbach, home from college, saw a reference to it in the paper and asked his father about it. Barney shook his head, brushed the question aside with a wave of his hand, and walked away.

CHAPTER 4

Our Home

However unrelenting the economic conditions during the Depression seemed to be, there must have been times when my parents, after arriving home from a long day at the store, felt confident that things would get better. Or perhaps it was just that occasionally hope got the better of experience. Milton was born in 1931 and I came along in 1935. Throughout these years our family lived in one rented house after another. The second of these was a small brick house on Eleventh Avenue three blocks from the filling station Wexler and Prince had robbed. My mother must have run it with the characteristic energy and efficiency that I remember seeing later. In 1933, Fay and Milton, seven and two, had to be taken care of, as did Norman when he returned from the hospital after an appendectomy. She had help then, but the responsibility for the home was hers. She also had to find time to work in the store. In those years a steady stream of visitors came through the house. My grandmother usually came in the summer for several weeks, sometimes longer. I learned from the "Seen and Heard" section of the newspaper that in 1933 she arrived at the beginning of July and stayed until the first week of September. Uncle Ben also came and returned the following year with his fiancé, Jean Bakalar, who had been born in Odessa and had studied piano at the city's famous conservatory and who, many years later, after she and Uncle Ben had settled in Hattiesburg, would become a well-known and much sought-after piano teacher in the city. Aunt Rose, not yet married to Uncle Joe, also came for a visit. What my mother recalled about my grandmother's long visits was that she was never at a loss for something or someone to criticize, including her *schmutzige* (dirty) grandsons when she saw us coming into the house from an afternoon spent outside playing.

The visits my mother looked forward to most were from Uncle Abe and Aunt Anne. She was always in her best mood with them and she and my father returned the visits as often as they could. Once, however, she had to stay home and take care of me—ill, though with what I don't remember—while my father, Fay, and Milton went to Mobile. What I do remember is that while taking care of me she complained about missing the chance to see her brother. Although she had shown a certain boldness and independence in leaving her family in Belaya Tserkov to come to America, as well as in refusing to heed the last-minute pleas of her father to return while she was still in Bucharest, she couldn't have known then how long it would be before she would see them again. Her father died in 1928 and her mother in 1940. Her brother Scholym was killed at the front in 1942. The correspondence she kept up with her mother and sisters and the numerous packages she sent them before, during, and after World War II reflected the emotional bond she still felt with the family she had left behind. In a letter from her mother she saved, one of only two, both written in 1938 when, as a widow, her mother was still living in their house in Belaya Tserkov, but now with her second daughter, Klara, her son-in-law, and their son, her mother begins by thanking her and Uncle Abe for the most recent package they had sent. She itemizes and comments on the clothes in the package for her and Klara (coats, dresses, shirts, sweaters, stockings, and several pairs of shoes—"They fit me to a 'T'"). Near the end of the letter, after asking for another coat ("a lightweight one") and a black undershirt ("a good warm one") to be included in the next package, she writes: "I don't have a nice scarf, so please, my dear Chevelleh [an affectionate variation of Yoheved], pick out a nice scarf that you like. I see already that you know what we need." Then Klara says, "there's no sister like Cheved. She even knows everyone's measurements." Here must have been the heart of the letter for my mother, expressing confidence in her memory, taste, and judgment and giving special recognition to her, the youngest of the three daughters. The bond she felt, renewed and strengthened by the letters she received and packages she sent and would continue to send throughout the war and afterwards, was a part of her life I knew nothing about that day when my illness kept her home while the rest of the family went to Mobile.

She and my father must have rejoiced when they learned that Josef Rosenblatt, the world-famous cantor, would be coming to Hattiesburg in January of 1933 to sing in the synagogue. To Jews in this country, particularly those from Eastern Europe, he was a revered figure. In his singing he revived old feelings for the religious life and culture of the *shtetl*, which represented what has been called the golden age of *Yiddishkeit*, and in his life as an Orthodox Jew he seemed to represent an ideal of religious conviction and observance. But to my parents he had a special significance: he had been born in Belaya Tserkov.

Rosenblatt's father had been a cantor there and it's possible that both my mother's and my father's parents had at one time or another heard young Rosenblatt accompany his father in one of the synagogues in the mid-1880s. Once word got around about the cantor's "little assistant," wrote Samuel Rosenblatt in his biography of his father, "the synagogue began to attract a wider clientele. Members of other congregations commenced to attend its services in large numbers." So large were the numbers that on sabbaths and holidays "crowds of people, unable to get into the house of worship, would be standing in the street outside the synagogue to hear the singing through open windows."[1]

In 1917 Rosenblatt toured the United States and gave concerts in many cities to raise money for Jews in Europe after World War I. The next year he was offered an opportunity by the Chicago Opera Association to sing the part of Eleazar in *The Jewess* by Fromental Halévy. He was to receive $1,000 for each performance, plus railroad fares between New York (where he was living) and Chicago. Rosenblatt initially accepted the offer, then changed his mind and persuaded Morris Newman, the president of his congregation in New York, to give the reasons for turning it down. "Our board of trustees agrees with you," Newman said in his letter to Mr. Campanini of the Chicago Opera Association, "that there is no objection to this opera from a Jewish standpoint, but we feel that the Rev. Mr. Rosenblatt's sacred position in the synagogue does not permit him to enter the operatic stage. We have, however, no objections to his singing at concerts, whether sacred or otherwise.... We hope that your future requests will be of a nature that they will meet with the entire approval of our board of trustees." The effect across the country was "electrifying." "From Maine to Florida, from New York to the West Coast the Jewish as well as the non-Jewish press carried the story of the cantor who had refused $1,000 a performance to sing in the opera on purely religious grounds."[2] In the article in the *Hattiesburg American* announcing that he would sing at our synagogue, the paper alludes to his refusal: "Cantor Rosenblatt adheres strictly to the tenets of the Jewish faith. He does not travel on the Sabbath day nor does he make public appearances. He has turned down contracts, offering large sums of money, because they would interfere with the exercise of his beliefs."[3]

His performance in Hattiesburg was one of his last to be given in the United States and it was, as the paper noted in an editorial welcoming him, both "a signal mark for the enterprise of the Jewish people of this city" and "a notable event in the life of Hattiesburg," which was one of only a few small cities included in Rosenblatt's last tour.[4] In a recital just two days before, the *Chattanooga Times* (owned by Adolph Ochs of the *New York Times*) reported that Rosenblatt had sung "his way into the hearts of a large Jewish and Gentile audience."[5] The program in Hattiesburg included traditional songs in Hebrew, as well as a popular number in English, "The Last Rose of Summer." The reviewer's praise was unqualified.

> Before an audience of representative citizens who sat enthralled by the witchery of his art, Cantor Josef Rosenblatt presented a program of Hebrew music last evening at the synagogue of the congregation B'nai Israel on West Pine Street. Marvelous tone coloring, an ability to sing a pianissimo in an unforgettable manner and an engaging presence combine to make Cantor Rosenblatt an outstanding figure in the musical world. He possesses a voice of rare beauty of almost unbelievable range, extending from low C to G altissimo. His remarkable voice control was exemplified in the ease with which he contrasted his tones, from florid passages taken falsetto in almost a whisper to dramatic climaxes of emotional power and intensity. . . . The congregation of B'nai Israel merits congratulations on their enterprise in bringing to Hattiesburg Cantor Rosenblatt whose art will long be remembered by those fortunate enough to have heard him.[6]

While I can't be certain my parents were in the audience that Friday night, it's hard to believe they weren't, or that Uncle Abe and Aunt Anne hadn't driven from Mobile to be there, too. After the performance, my parents, Uncle Abe, and Barney Auerbach, would have gone up to Rosenblatt to introduce themselves. It was an occasion my father would have greatly enjoyed. Although not really a gregarious person, he never hesitated to step forward in a situation in which he felt he had a strong interest, and did so with a natural, robust self-confidence that stands out in my memory of him. I can see him now greeting Rosenblatt and exchanging a few words about the town where he had grown up and young Rosenblatt had first begun to sing in public, even though Rosenblatt had left long before my father was born. By 1889, when little Yossele was seven, the family was forced to leave Russia because Rosenblatt's father was legally a subject of Austria. "It was the avowed policy of the imperial Russian government to find excuses in order to rid itself of its unwanted dependents," Samuel Rosenblatt writes. "Although an unannounced raid on the Rosenblatt apartment one night failed to produce clear evidence of contraband harbored, that did not prevent an ukase from being issued the next morning giving the helpless aliens twenty-four hours to leave the country."[7] Not long after his performance in Hattiesburg, Rosenblatt left for Palestine and died there a few months later.

I doubt my parents went to many other performances. My father enjoyed listening to music on the radio at home, on occasion playing a record of Rosenblatt singing old favorites. Fay remembers his saying that in Russia he used to stand in the snow for hours waiting to buy a ticket at what was called an "opera house" (which may have offered a variety of productions, including plays, classical operas, and other musical performances) and in his first year in this country he wrote to my mother about going to a Yiddish theater in New York. I remember his telling us about musicals he had seen on buying trips to New York, including *Oklahoma* and *South Pacific* shortly after each had opened. In the early 1950s he took Milton and me to see *Pajama Game* when we were all in New York together. On one of his trips to Chicago when I was at Northwestern he took me to a play based on the short story "Bontsche the Silent" by the Yiddish writer I. L. Peretz. For most of the time when I was a child, however, he and my mother were bound to a schedule of long hours at the store. I remember during the war that they sometimes came home late on Saturday nights, the store having remained open till eight or nine o'clock, and only then having a bite to eat. I don't remember if on those nights my mother used her samovar, but I do remember that she would sip her tea with a lump of sugar in her mouth, as she had done in Russia, and my father would sip his tea only after adding a teaspoon of cherry jam. Sometimes they would open a box of Barricini chocolates he had brought back from New York and I remember trying to pick a shape—round for chocolate-covered cherry, square for chocolate-covered caramel—I knew I would like. On Friday nights, we usually went to temple, but on Saturday nights, if they didn't get home from the store too late, they often played poker with two or three couples from the Jewish community, all immigrants from Russia or Poland, though in later years the men came to prefer gin rummy and often played at Barney Auerbach's house.

But if they'd had the interest, time, and money (for tickets as low as a dollar and a half each), there were opportunities to see famous performers brought to Hattiesburg by State Teachers College and Mississippi Woman's College. Among musicians who appeared during the early years of the Depression were Hungarian violinist Joseph Szigeti, who came directly from an appearance at Carnegie Hall; Nathan Milstein, one of the most famous violinists of the twentieth century; Nelson Eddy, the well-known baritone who appeared in numerous films with Jeannette MacDonald; and violinist Stefan Sopkin, first violinist with the Cincinnati Symphony Orchestra. The DeWolf comic opera company presented two Gilbert and Sullivan operettas, *The Mikado* and *H. M. S. Pinafore*, and the Don Cossack Russian Male Chorus sang church music, folk songs of the Ukraine, and Cossack soldier songs. In the 1935–36 season, there were performances by the American Society of Ancient Instruments, violinist Jan Kubelík and his accompanist (and son) Rafael Kubelík (who was also Conductor of the Czech Philharmonic Orchestra), the Vienna Choir Boys (who returned several years by popular request), and harpist Alberto Salvi. In addition to these and other musical performances during the 1930s, audiences saw dramatic performances—for example, Max Montor, the German actor, in readings from Schiller's *Maria Stuart, Don Carlo,* and *Wallenstein* and Judith Anderson in a dramatization of Edith Wharton's *The Old Maid*.

Blackface minstrel shows offered a very different kind of entertainment. They were immensely popular as a form of musical comedy and were performed throughout the country, not just in the South, and not just in the white Christian community. In New York and Chicago, as well as in Atlanta and New Orleans, "members of Jewish clubs and societies . . . regularly staged blackface minstrel shows."[8] Although blackface minstrels continued to be performed well into the twentieth century, they had stiff competition from vaudeville, radio, and film and by the 1930s most were locally produced. The Blackbird Minstrel performed in Hattiesburg in 1934 was sponsored by the Woman's Missionary Society of Main Street Methodist Church and held at the YWCA. In its usual effort to support local events and performances, the paper provided a write-up that served as an advertisement several days before: "It's new! It's clean! It's humorous! It's different! It's peppy! It's full of snappy jokes, lively songs and special features." For its humor, the show would draw on stereotypes of blacks suggested by the list of characters and the addition of "Mr." or "Miss" to them (to suggest social pretentiousness since these courtesy titles were reserved for whites): Mr. George Washington Edison Bell Thomas Jefferson, Mr. Columbus Ohio Bonaparte, Mr. Doolittle Africanus, Mr. Sunshine Shucks, Miss Snowball, Miss Piny White, Miss Hanover Touch-Me-Not, Miss Virginia Butyspot, and Miss Pinky Marshmellow[*sic*].[9]

I remember going to a minstrel show when I was a teenager and seeing the black-faced white men on the stage and hearing the roars of laughter in the white audience surrounding me. I laughed at the puns and jokes and enjoyed the songs, still blind to the racist nature of all the merriment. Al Jolson and Eddie Cantor, as well as other Jewish performers, had made blackface entertainment "one of their specialties." In attempting to explain why, Irving Howe suggested, "perhaps it was no more than shrewd opportunism, an eagerness to give audiences exactly what they seemed to want." But he also thought there was something more to it, an element of "ethnic pastiche," a joining of two peoples "who live in culturally ambivalent situations." When Jewish performers "took over the conventions of ethnic mimicry . . . [they] transformed it into something emotionally richer and more humane. Black became a mask for Jewish expressiveness, with one woe speaking through the voice of another."[10] I find the idea of one woe speaking through another persuasive, especially in an opera such as Gershwin's *Porgy and Bess*, where the characters are not objects of satire. But I wonder if the use of blackface by Jewish performers in minstrel shows and films doesn't also reflect a degree of Jewish insensitivity at that time to the far greater woe of blacks in this country. What would Jews in Germany or Poland have thought, I wonder, about a satirical equivalent of the minstrel show I saw based on stereotypes of Jews? Stella Suberman remembers her father thinking it was "hard to defend Jolson." "Those thick white lips, the coal makeup. Was it not too much? To make fun of people already so *auf tsores*, already so full of woe?"[11]

Readers of the *Hattiesburg American* had an opportunity everyday to see a cartoon at the bottom left corner of the front page that made fun of blacks. It was entitled "Hambone's Meditations" and was the creation of a syndicated white columnist, J. P. Alley, for the Memphis *Commercial Appeal*. Hambone was a poor Negro who appeared in work clothes and a tattered hat, along with a corncob pipe. His sense of humor and folksy wisdom possessed that kernel of truth about human nature needed to make humor and irony work. With a smile on his face, he showed understanding of the pitfalls in social climbing ("Sto'-keepah broke inter high s'ciety heah while back, en he bin broke evuh since!!"). He enjoyed noting the mischief-making character of people ("Ef'n you preaches on sin you hits de devil, but preach on rascality en you's shootin' inter de crowd!!"). At times, he appeared to hold the same stereotype of blacks that whites held, as when he said "De ain' nobody whut kin jes' set down en do nothing ez nach'ul ez a nigguh kin do it!!"). But at other times his comments reflected a certain hopelessness about the chances of a black man ever being able to improve his situation, as when he said, "wen a country nigguh git a job in town he ain' got no mo' sense dan ter jes' work he fool haid off!!"[12]

When the Passion Play from Freiburg, Germany, was advertised in the paper, Jews in Hattiesburg knew it was their turn to be observed in a performance. The Passion Play depicted the trial and crucifixion of Christ. It was staged in the auditorium of State Teachers College in November of 1933, ten months after Hitler had come to power. It had a proven capacity in Germany and Eastern Europe to promote anti-Semitism. In its dramatization of the life of Christ it highlighted the role of Judas as a traitor, implying, or leaving open the easy inference, that a collective, hereditary burden of guilt had fallen on all Jews. The anti-Semitism of Henry Ford, the recent trial and death of Wexler, and the reports of Hitler's persecution of Jews had already aroused anxiety among Hattiesburg's Jews. The staging of the Passion Play couldn't have been reassuring.

Despite the otherwise welcome concert and theatre performances, often by distinguished artists, and the cultural life they represented, Hattiesburg in the 1930s may have seemed to a Jewish visitor from Boston, New York, or Chicago, or even from Atlanta or New Orleans, to be an outpost on the frontiers of civilization. Later, during World War II, when thousands of Jewish soldiers from these and other cities found themselves stationed at Camp Shelby for a brief period of time, they may have suffered culture shock on first seeing our town. They would have been accustomed to being able to choose from a number of Orthodox, Conservative, and Reform synagogues, to seeing neighborhoods where Yiddish was the primary spoken language, and to having access to Jewish community centers, social clubs, restaurants, and delicatessens. Hattiesburg, like most small towns in the South, had only one synagogue and, alas, no delicatessen. In order to get matzoh and Manischewitz wine for Passover or simply old farorites such as challa, pumpernickel bread, kosher salami, pickled herring, and halvah, my parents had to drive to Mobile or New Orleans, although on occasion they were able to buy these and other goods from an elderly local couple who sold them in their home. Even after becoming a Reform congregation in 1935, some members continued to adhere to Orthodox tradition well into the 1950s when Charles Mantinband was our rabbi, something not uncommon then in Jewish communities with only one house of worship. The leader of Orthodox services on the High Holy Days was Sam Eisman, the son of a rabbi and someone highly respected for his knowledge of and commitment to Orthodox tradition. I remember peeking into the reception hall on Rosh Hashanah or Yom Kippur to see the men conducting a separate service entirely in Hebrew. With yarmulkes on their heads and tallises draped over their shoulders, I saw them swaying back and forth while looking down at the prayer books in their hands. Our family attended only the Reform services, where most of the men wore yarmulkes, and only a few also wore tallises. I doubt my parents' families in Russia were Orthodox, at least in any strict sense. My mother's memory of her mother saying "if it's clean, it's kosher" and the pictures of the two families at that time, with most of the men beardless, suggest something less than strict adherence to that tradition. But even if both sets of grandparents had been Orthodox, my parents, like most Jewish immigrants who settled in small towns in the South, would eventually find Orthodox observance difficult to maintain and would

A family dinner in 1941 or 1942 with guests from Camp Shelby, with my father at far left, then (clockwise) Captain and Mrs. Norman Gottlieb, unknown guest, empty chair where the photographer-soldier was sitting, another soldier, Norman, Fay, Milton, my mother, and me.

come to regard it as a feature of Jewish life in the old country they were happy to give up. Orthodox Jews who moved to small towns in the South found they had to keep their stores open on Saturdays. Apart from the purely economic motivation, historian Lee Shai Weissbach has suggested, there may also have been "a desire on the part of small-town Jews to minimize perceptions of Jewish 'otherness.'"[13] They didn't want to be perceived as aliens. Many gave up trying to keep a kosher home. Harry Applebaum, at one time the mayor of Yazoo City, said Reform Judaism is "the only kind of Jewish religion you can have down here and stick to it."[14] Nonetheless, it was still possible in Hattiesburg in the 1950s to keep up a modified commitment to Orthodox tradition.

In his early years in Hattiesburg my father closed the store for two days on Rosh Hashanah and one day on Yom Kippur. When I was in the ninth grade he wouldn't let me travel to Jackson with our junior high school football team because the game that year was scheduled for the same day as Yom Kippur. He tried to assure me that Coach Dement would respect me all the more for holding to religious observance over football. But since Coach Dement knew the decision wasn't mine, whatever respect he might have felt would not have gone to me. Being Jewish was central to my father's sense of who he was, and it was defined not by belief or prayer but by being a member of the congregation, attending Friday night services, respecting the traditions he had been brought up in that he thought were important, and making sure his children did, too. Fay studied Hebrew in preparation for her confirmation, as did Milton and I for our bar mitzvahs.

Passover was the Jewish holiday that made the strongest impression on me. My parents kept to the tradition of holding a service in our home on two successive nights. Given their early experience of living in tsarist Russia and then of emigrating, the story of the bondage of the ancient Hebrews in Egypt and of their exodus told in the Passover service must have had a personal significance and emotional resonance for them that it could not have for those of us born in this country. More than any other Jewish holiday, it seems to me to renew one's sense of Jewish identity through the celebration of a defining event in Jewish history. One of my vivid memories is of my father at the head of the table, dressed in a navy blue suit, seated in an arm-chair with pillows and presiding over the most festive occasion of the year, with ten or twelve people at the table, including several guests, often soldiers stationed at Camp Shelby. It wasn't easy at ages seven or ten or thirteen to sit through a three-hour service read in Hebrew, but I still looked forward to these festive nights. In the late afternoon, I saw my mother running back and forth between the kitchen and the dining room, setting the table with a white linen tablecloth, her Passover china and silverware, stemware etched with a six-pointed star, and a silver goblet for my father.

I'd been taught that the first course included matzoh (unleavened bread), bitter herbs (parsley, celery, and horseradish), haroseth (a paste-like mix of apples, nuts, and wine) to represent the bitter experience of the ancient Hebrews' enslavement in Egypt. "This is the bread of affliction which our ancestors ate in the land of Egypt" were among the first words read from the Haggadah. My role in the service as the youngest male child was to ask the four questions in Hebrew, which I'd studied and memorized but now read aloud and which, with the open-ended first question, "Wherefore is this night distinguished from all other nights?" began the extended narration of the story of the Passover, mostly in Hebrew, and led by my father. Although I enjoyed my role, the service made for a long night and I was very hungry and my eyes were fixed on the gefillte fish almost within reach and the red horseradish that would accompany it. My mother used to buy a large radish several days or a week before Passover, bury it in the ground beside the backdoor steps, then dig it up a day or two before the first night, chop and grind it into a grits-like consistency, and color it a bright red with beet juice. That color, like the brilliant redness of a hat or flower in a Renoir painting, has remained the focal point of my memory of our Passover table. Her horseradish was always strong, sending lightning shocks through one's nostrils and into the brain and often prompting my father to joke that my mother had been angry when she made it. I'm not sure which I liked more, the glass of Manischewitz wine I was allowed to have or the small role I played in asking the four questions that began the service.

What I didn't understand then, however, was that for my parents, as well as for the young soldiers stationed at Camp Shelby who knew they might be sent to Europe, these wartime Passover services had a special meaning. While reading and reciting the narrative of the escape from Egyptian bondage, following the ritual of eating unleavened bread and bitter herbs, and attempting to reenact aspects of the experience of the ancient Hebrews held in slavery, their thoughts and some of the conversation turned to the millions of Jews trapped in Europe. After Hitler's invasion of the Soviet Union in June of 1941, my parents became concerned about members of my mother's family in Moscow and Belaya Tserkov. Stalin, now eager to receive war materiel and financial aid from the United States, permitted greater correspondence between his people and their relatives in the States. My mother's main correspondent during the war was her sister Celia in Moscow, the oldest of her siblings. Their mother had died in 1940, though my mother didn't learn of it right away. Some letters, both to and from the Soviet Union, did not get through because of wartime conditions or Soviet censorship, and, of those that did, some were heavily censored, with lines blacked over to make them unreadable. But enough of the packages of food and clothing my mother sent got through for her nephew, David Vinitsky (Celia's son), to be still grateful to her forty-five years after the war (and sixteen years after her death) when Alice and I sat with him and his family at the dinner table in his apartment in Moscow in 1990 and listened to him describe his and his family's excitement on the day one of those packages arrived. But because of their fear of informers who might report them as spies, David told Fay a few years later, letters were destroyed after they were read, and news of packages from American relatives was kept quiet.

In our home, it was also something of an event when my mother received a letter from Celia or Klara during the war. In one letter, she learned of the death of her brother Scholym in 1942. An artist before the war, he was killed at the front. When a letter arrived, she used to take the small globe from Fay's bedroom, place it on our kitchen table, and then with my father and Norman search for the region or major city in the Soviet Union where she either thought or knew the letter had come from. Small as the globe was, it would have identified only a few major cities and large regions such as Ukraine, the Ural Mountains, and Siberia. In November of that year she received a letter from Celia, who was living then in Kamensk-Uralsky, an important munitions-industry city east of the central Ural Mountains where she and her children would remain for the duration of the war (her husband having long before been sent to Siberia—for reasons that, so far as I know, were never revealed—and then allowed to return, only to die soon afterwards). Klara and her husband also moved to Kamensk-Uralsky to work in a factory. I don't know when they left Belaya Tserkov, but it was none too soon.

Hitler's Sixth Army overran the city in August 1941 in his rush to capture Ukraine, with its rich agricultural resources. German observers and perpetrators left a record of the killings of Jews in photographs, films, and written reports that later became the basis of detailed testimonial evidence in postwar trials. In Belaya Tserkov, between August 8 and August 19, *Einsatzgruppen* shot between 800 and 900 local Jews. Ninety children were being held in a building guarded by Ukrainians, but it soon became their turn. When *SS-Obersturmführer* (First Lieutenant) August Häfner was ordered to execute the children, however, he objected that the men under his command were all young men. "How are we going to answer to them if we make them shoot small children?" After a brief "tug-of-war" between him and his superiors about who would do the shooting, Häfner suggested that the Ukrainian militia shoot the children and there were no objections. After the war, he gave the following statement describing the murder of the children:

> I went out to the woods alone. The Wehrmacht had already dug a grave. The children were brought along in a tractor. I had nothing to do with this technical procedure. The Ukrainians were standing round trembling. The children were . . . lined up along the top of the grave and shot so that they fell into it. The Ukrainians did not aim at any particular part of the body. . . . The wailing was indescribable. I shall never forget the scene throughout my life. I find it hard to bear. I particularly remember a small fair-haired girl who took me by the hand. She too was shot later.[15]

In October, the Germans continued their killing of the Jews of Belaya Tserkov, 6000 in all.[16] No one at our Passover table in 1942 could have known or even imagined what had taken place in Belaya Tserkov or in a ravine called

Babi Yar on the outskirts of nearby Kiev at the end of September (where over 33,000 Jews were murdered) and would continue to take place for the next three and a half years, mostly in Poland and the Soviet Union. It would be only after the war that it became known how far Hitler had gone in carrying out his plan to exterminate the Jews of Europe and then a decade or two more before the word "Holocaust" came to be widely used to describe what had happened. For his part in the murders in Belaya Tserkov, *SS-Obersturmführer* Häfner used the defense of having "followed orders" at his trial in 1965. He was sentenced to eight years in prison.

By the spring of 1944, however, my parents and others at the Passover table had learned something of what had taken place in the territories occupied by the Nazis, and even in Belaya Tserkov, though they didn't tell us children. My mother had received two letters from Klara's husband, Moishe Prylutsky, reporting what he had learned after returning from Kamensk-Uralsky. In the first one, dated January 1, 1944, he wrote, "My three sisters who [had] remained in Kharkov were murdered by the evil hands of the Germans. One sister with an infant whose husband was then in the army and is now wounded in the hospital, another sister with a seven-year-old boy and husband, and the third one who was still unmarried. They also killed my uncle—an invalid 72 years old." He went on to say that "Belaya Tserkov is completely demolished." In the second one, dated January 22, 1944, he wrote that what the Germans did was far worse than had so far been reported: "witnesses of the evil deeds done by the Germans say that what is written in the newspapers about the torture, shootings, murder, and robbery, etc., which the Germans did, especially to the Jews, the elderly, the women and the children, was only a tenth of what actually happened." Attempting to place all this in historical perspective, he concludes,

> We Jews will remember the Germans for a long time. There was not a single city or village that they had been to where a Jew remains. They killed old men, women, and children. Those who did not die were buried in holes in the ground. The corpses were burned. Before the kill they tortured and abused them. The Spanish Inquisition pales in comparison with that which the Germans did to the peaceful Soviet citizens. For all this, history will avenge. The revenge will come, but the dead will not be resurrected.

The house where these Passover services took place, and where we lived from 1940 to 1952, sat on a corner lot just two blocks from Camp School, the grammar school Fay, Milton, and I went to (and Sarah and Buddy before us). It was the first house my parents owned and had been built by Aunt Goldie and Uncle Sam, who had lived there until they moved to Laurel in the early 1930s. It was a long, one-story, four-bedroom house with oak floors and an architectural style reflecting Spanish influence (by way of New Orleans, or perhaps Biloxi or Mobile) in its white stucco facing and the arch over its front doorway. The arch disappeared in a remodeling my parents had to undertake when they discovered termites a year or two after moving in. There were several impressive one- and two-story homes within a few blocks of ours, and at least two that might be called mansions (one owned by a son of the lumber baron and former mayor, W. S. F. Tatum), but most of the houses, including ours, were modest, comfortable, and unremarkable. The front entrance, only rarely used, faced Mamie Street, a name which, like those of its two parallel sister streets, Adeline and Corrine, could have been taken from a popular Victorian songbook of the 1890s. The side entrance faced Seventh Avenue, unpaved and a constant source of dust that drifted in through the open windows in the spring and then in the summer months was sucked in by the attic fan, frustrating my mother's tireless efforts to keep a spotless, white-glove-test-worthy home. During the war years she had a Victory garden in the back yard that I remember mainly for the corn we used to get from it. At the end of the back yard was a small one-room house that Milton and I used as a playhouse. Beside it was a chicken coop from which we used to get eggs, as well as a chicken for Sunday dinner. On Saturday afternoons Lossie Glenn, who had started working for us shortly after I was born, stayed for eleven years, and later returned to help out on holidays and special occasions, would walk into the coop with a coat hanger she had unwound, making it as straight as she could and using its neck as a hook with which to catch a chicken by one of its legs. Emerging from the coop while holding the chicken firmly by its neck, with its eyes and beak visible just below the tightened grip of her fingers, she wrung it fiercely until the body came off, fell to the ground, and ran headless in circles spouting blood until it was exhausted, fell over, and lay still—a memory not easy to put aside the next day at the dinner table.

Of the other Jewish families in our neighborhood, my parents' relationship with the Auerbachs was of course the oldest, going back to Belaya Tserkov, where, I've been told by Maurice Auerbach, my mother's family and Barney Auerbach's family had lived in houses across the street from each other and from where Uncle Abe and Barney departed for America together, traveling to Galveston on the same ship and both eventually settling in Hattiesburg. Barney and his wife, Irene, lived next door to her sister, Dora, and her husband, David Levine, whose father had been the rabbi in Hattiesburg from 1920 until he moved to Knoxville in 1929. The two families now lived only two blocks from us and the Auerbachs would sometimes walk to our house on the second night of Passover to join us for dessert and the singing of Passover songs. They were also frequently at our house, as my parents were at theirs, on Saturday nights for poker, along with Leon and Jenny Buchalter, Isidor and Frieda Cohen, and other friends. On Sunday mornings, my father and a few other Jewish businessmen gathered at Barney's store to continue playing gin for a couple of hours and until they received a call from one of us children waiting at the temple to be picked up after Sunday school. "Last game, boys," Mr. Auerbach would call out while putting the receiver down, only to repeat the same words fifteen minutes later when we had to call again.

He and my father saw each other often, their stores on East Pine Street just two doors from each other. Like my father, he spoke with an accent, though one that was a little heavier, I think, and more often interspersed with Yiddish. Also like my father, and unlike the other card players sitting around our kitchen table, he didn't smoke. On occasion during a game he would get up and go to our refrigerator, find an apple, and take a deep bite out of it, visibly relishing its taste while standing and watching the game and not noticing or perhaps not caring that the second or third bite had spattered his shirt with juice from the apple. He enjoyed playing, but also watching. He died at the age of ninety-three, having lived thirty years longer than my father, and longer than most members of our two families and many of their friends. He and his wife had three children roughly the ages of the three of us, their youngest, Maurice, born a week before me. He's now a retired professor of political science living in New York, but back then he and I used to play cowboys and Indians, usually at his house (also white stucco with Spanish accents in its architectural style), running round and round it chasing each other with cap pistols, and in turn being chased by his dog, Spot. Eventually his grandmother, Mrs. Shor, perhaps concerned about his health (he was skeletally thin), would open the back door and call out to him in Yiddish that it was time for him to come inside. Yiddish remained her primary language, as it was for my grandmother in New York.

My parents, however, had to use only English all day in the store, as well as in all their comings and goings in town to grocery stores, restaurants, and banks, as well as doctors' and lawyers' offices. Even when my father ran into Barney Auerbach or Leon Buchalter on the sidewalk in front of his store or one of theirs, they continued to rely on English, though at times interspersed with a few words of Yiddish. Living—and making a living—in a small town in the South required it. In this way my parents' experience was strikingly different from that of my grandparents and other Jewish immigrants in New York who lived in neighborhoods that were eighty or ninety percent Jewish and could get along speaking Yiddish almost exclusively. My grandfather spoke little English and used Yiddish all day long with his customers in his small fruit store in the Bronx. Sherwin Nuland, recalling his experience of growing up in the Bronx in the 1930s in his memoir *Lost in America*, writes: "We were a family of immigrants, even the two of us born in America. Yiddish was the language of the household, and the worldview of the ghettoized Jews of Russia pervaded the spoken and unspoken teachings transmitted to Harvey [his brother] and me. None of the adults ever learned to read or write any English beyond their own painstaking signatures." His grandmother "spoke no English at all, though she had been living in New York for almost three decades."[17]

Our home in Mississippi was as different from the home of my grandparents and that of Nuland as it was in distance from the Bronx, but Yiddish remained a shared though far more limited constant of Jewish life in it. My parents' use of it in our home—for keeping things from the *Kinder*, as well as for humor, nostalgia for the old country, nuances of thought and feeling that they felt only Yiddish could express, and, in the end, as a natural, reflexive expression of their Jewish identity—remains in my memory as one of the distinguishing features of the Jewish identity and life of our home, though not one so strong that it ever occurred to me to think of myself as an immigrant, as Nuland thought of himself. They also used it occasionally in the car on the way home from the store or on a family outing. When I was a child I sometimes heard them on a trip to Gulfport or Mobile sing an old favorite my father had sung to me at home such as "Oyfn Pripetchik." ("Oyfn pripetchik brent a fayerl / Un in shtub is heys / Un der rebbe lernt kleyne kinderleky / Dem alef-beyz" [In the fireplace burns a fire / And the house is warm / And the rabbi teaches little children / The alphabet].) My niece Wendy, Fay's daughter, now old enough to be eligible for social security, told me recently that she remembers my father taking her on his knee when she was a child and singing it to her. In the song, the *rebbe*'s use of Yiddish to teach the children Hebrew, a common practice for centuries in East European countries, reflects a significant linguistic and cultural duality in Jewish life. While Hebrew was the sacred language of the Torah, the Talmud, and the prayer books used on Friday nights, Rosh Hashanah and Yom Kippur, Bar Mitzvahs and Bat Mitzvahs, Passover, and other holidays, Yiddish was the language of everyday life for East European Jews in small towns in America.[18]

My mother used it more than my father, not because she resisted English but because she spent more time at home, where she naturally recreated many distinctive features of her home in Belaya Tserkov, including the aromas and tastes of foods her mother had cooked and she now served to us with their Yiddish names: *gefilte* fish, *schmaltz* with rye bread, kasha *varnischkes*, carrot *tzimmes*, *Hamentoschen*, and *Mandelbrot*, as well as other dishes such as borscht, roast with kasha, and apple strudel, all stirring such immediate, sensory memories of my mother's cooking that they can at times seem to be more important to my sense of the Jewishness of our home than anything else. The fact that some of the dishes were as much Russian or German as they were Jewish doesn't seem to matter to my stubborn memory. It's possible they may have come to seem even more distinctively Jewish because of the contrast with the many Southern dishes we also relished (fried chicken, baked ham, barbecued beef, black-eyed peas, corn on the cob, lima beans, pecan pie). Although my mother gave up keeping a kosher home, she kept a separate set of dishes for Passover. I remember her reciting the traditional Hebrew prayer on Friday nights before supper, standing over the table while blessing the light of the candles, covering her head with a handkerchief, and moving her hands from over the lighted candles to her face in the traditional manner as she recited the prayer. She gave up the ritual when I was in high school—by then Fay was married and had children of her own and Milton was away at college—and we went to temple less often, but our Jewish identity continued to be reinforced for me by attending Sunday School and going to temple on Jewish holidays, by the comings and goings of my parents' Jewish friends and their similar use of Yiddish (and English spoken with an accent), and by my parents' discussion of articles in the local paper about our rabbi, meetings of the B'nai B'rith and the Temple Sisterhood, and stories about this or that member of the congregation.

But home was also the place where she felt most free to say what she wanted and she naturally turned to Yiddish, the *mama-loschen*, "the mother's tongue" and language of the home. At times, she used it to vent her feelings about someone, referring to him as a *shnorrer* (a moocher or cheapskate), a *meshugener* (a crazy man), or a *momzer* (a bastard or untrustworthy person), and to her as a *kvetch* (a complainer), at other times to dismiss someone as a *schlemiel* (a fool or simpleton) or a *schlimazel* (an unlucky person or loser) or a *nebbish*, and at still other times to express her admiration for someone, saying "He's a *Mensch*." In making a home for herself and our family, and recreating some of the character of her home in Belaya Tserkov, she at times used expressions representing how Jews felt about those in the Gentile majority, referring to them as the *goyim*. "Just as some Gentiles use 'Jew' as a contemptuous synonym for too shrewd, sly bargaining ('He tried to jew the price down')," Leo Rosten explains, "so some Jews use *goy* in a pejorative sense." As an example he uses the saying, "'*A goy blaybt a goy*' ('A Gentile remains a Gentile,' or, less literally, 'What did you expect? Once an anti-Semite, always an anti-Semite')." He goes on to explain that "relentless persecution of Jews, century after century, in nation after nation, left a legacy of bitter sayings" and compares these sayings to Mexicans using "*Gringo*" and Frenchmen using "*Boche*."[19]

In my experience among my Jewish friends in high school and college, however, as well as later among my Jewish colleagues and friends, the term had ceased to be used. We had grown up in a very different environment in which greater acceptance and assimilation of Jews, as well as increased intermarriage, had already made many of the old sayings, especially this one, a thing of the past. We didn't think of ourselves as being so different, or as being treated by others as if we were. Even when my parents and other immigrants in the Jewish community used "*goy*," I think it was already more of an echo of life in Eastern Europe than it was a representation of their life here. In their new homeland, my parents didn't face anything like the old anti-Semitism. On the contrary, they found general acceptance. In everyday life, aside from exclusion from certain clubs, something I never heard them mention and I believe they didn't care about, the worst they were likely to encounter was "Jew" written on the store window (which I saw once on a Saturday morning when I arrived for work) or being called a "damn Jew," as my father was once by a dissatisfied customer and as I was once in grammar school, another time in junior high school, and again in the army, the first two times involving me in fights and the third coming with the threat of being beaten up by a couple of toughs in the same platoon I was in when I told them I would report them to the sergeant major if, as they were planning to do, they beat up a black in our platoon. For me, the important distinction between the sayings my parents sometimes used and the "damn Jew" and other derogatory phrases about Jews we sometimes saw or heard is that the former were used exclusively in the home or in the company of other Jews, and were for their ears only, while the latter were often used openly and aggressively to insult or threaten a Jew and in the presence of others who, the user typically assumed, shared the user's prejudice, as was the case with the two toughs who threatened me in the presence of others in the platoon standing by and watching (but whose presence as witnesses I must have been counting on to keep the toughs from beating me up). These sayings and threats weren't used as often or as widely as "nigger," but I knew they were always out there. While the use of Yiddish sayings about Gentiles has greatly diminished, if not entirely disappeared, anti-Semitism appears to be again on the rise, sometimes disguised as anti-Zionist protests, at other times directed as vandalism against synagogues and Jewish community centers. One of the Jewish centers in Champaign has been vandalized several times in the last two or three years.

What my mother loved most about Yiddish was its treasure of epithets and sayings that could capture the nuance of thought she had in mind and had first heard in her home in Belaya Tserkov. But she also came to have an appreciation for Southern idioms that over the years she'd heard on the lips of neighbors, businessmen, clerks in the store, and customers, as well as the Jewish women she played cards with who had been born in the South and, as the title of the picture-history book *Shalom Y'all* suggests (with its text written by Vicki Reikes Fox, who grew up in Hattiesburg), spoke with a Southern accent. My mother also picked up certain names and epithets from general American usage. In calling me "the absent-minded professor," I suppose she was saying here's a little boy who is disengaged and out of touch, living in a world of his own, a boyish version of a comic stereotype in fiction and film. At times, she created her own epithet. Fay told me the one for her was "the silent symphony." In using it, I suppose, she was mocking her daughter's withdrawal into her own world of playing the flute or being engrossed in one book after another by the time she was twelve or thirteen. Disguised as humor, the epithet may have been used to register a complaint that Fay's silence was shutting her mother out. But I think the use of it also reflects my mother's love of wordplay and her ability to create a striking, memorable phrase that expressed insight into her daughter's character and love of music and books.

In February of 1937 she learned she had ovarian cancer. Although I knew she had become seriously ill shortly after I was born, I've only recently learned more about that period in her life, Milton having provided me with copies of her medical records and Fay telling me what she remembered from having accompanied mother for treatments. She'd had an appendectomy and a difficult, partial hysterectomy the year before. Then, in a routine check-up nine months later, Dr. Ross found a tumor the size of a hen's egg, he said, and advised her to have it removed. Reluctant to undergo surgery again, she asked for a consultation with a doctor in New Orleans she had seen once before. He told her the tumor was very likely malignant and advised her to have it removed as soon as possible. She went back to Dr. Ross for a second operation. After recovering from it, she returned to New Orleans and to the Touro Infirmary for radium treatments. From what I've been able to learn, I gather that a capsule with radium placed at the site was thought to be more effective and to have fewer risks of endangering other nearby organs than a more general treatment of radiation using an external source of penetrating rays.[20]

She took Fay, who had turned eleven that summer, out of school for two weeks to stay with her in a hotel while she was getting the radium treatments. The success would be measured, she was told, by whether or not she survived the next five years. Fearing she might not, Fay told me, she began to look into the possibility of finding and adopting a girl seventeen or eighteen years old in a home for Jewish orphans in New Orleans capable of assuming the responsibilities of taking care of the three of us. She must have reasoned that our father would be too preoccupied with trying to ensure that his business survived the Depression (the only source of income he had) to be also responsible for a girl eleven and boys five and a half and two, as well as for the running of a house. Did she consider the simpler alternative of hiring someone who could assume both responsibilities? By the time of the first operation Lossie Glenn, at age eighteen or nineteen, was still in the first of the eleven years she would work for us. She was highly intelligent and responsible, as her later career proved. After working for a number of years at Rollings Jewelers, she became the director of the black community center in Hattiesburg. Whatever my mother's reasons were for giving up the idea of adopting a girl from the Jewish orphanage, as well as the alternative—if she considered it—of entrusting Lossie with the responsibilities for the house and children, she eventually worked out an arrangement in which, if she died, Fay would remain at home with our father, Milton would go to Aunt Anne and Uncle Abe in Mobile, and I would go to Aunt Anne's sister and brother-in-law Goldie and Sam Percoff in Laurel. Her immediate fear now was that the cancer had spread and the radium treatments would prove ineffective. That fear would haunt her for the next five years.

It was during these and the next few years when, having been forced to think about her own mortality, she learned of the death of her mother in 1940 and brother Scholym in 1942. Her father had died in 1928. She learned in 1944 from Klara's husband, Moishe, about the murders of members of his family by German soldiers. During their first decade in Hattiesburg, she and my father had been focused on making a living and beginning a family. But now, with the possibility that the cancer might return and the news of the deaths in her family, her thoughts took a more reflective turn. She read *The Prophet* by Kahlil Gibran, which was a very popular book in those years, offering up wisdom in a series of aphorisms in short chapters on Giving, Joy and Sorrow, Buying and Selling, Good and Evil, and Death. She also read, or read in, Rabbi Joshua Loth

Liebman's *Peace of Mind*, another popular book at the time that Fay had read and recommended to her. I remember her quoting a few lines to me from the chapter on children in *The Prophet*, but I don't know how much of Rabbi Liebman's book she read, which would have been a far more difficult read because of its use of philosophy and psychoanalysis in discussing religion and the pursuit of peace of mind. I mention these books now because, as I look back on that time in her life and try to gain a better sense of what she was going through, her reading them seems to me to represent a reflective turn in her thoughts, a search for understanding.

CHAPTER 5

Surviving the Depression, Finding Acceptance, Anticipating War

My father's sense of his place as a businessman in Hattiesburg, as well as his place in the Jewish community, would have been measured in his own eyes by the location of his stores on two secondary streets and their relatively small size when compared with those of his older and more established fellow Jewish merchants. I remember seeing the one on Mobile Street when I was a child, but not the one on Batson Street, which Norman ran. Both were in a part of the business district catering primarily to farmers and blue-collar workers and their families, white as well as black. The city's best clothing stores were in the central business district and catered to the more affluent of the white population and were, like Eisman's and Fine Bros.-Matison, on Main Street, along with First National Bank, Citizens Bank, S. H. Kress, Woolworth, Rollings' Jewelers, Sarphie Jewelers, and other stores. Beck's was in the Forrest Hotel and J. C. Penney was next to it on the first block of Pine Street west of Main. The Emporium, Silver the Tailor, The Globe, Louis Tailoring, Diana Shop, and Famous Department Store were on the first block of Pine east of Main. While East Pine Street wasn't the best location, it was next to best.

As I sat in the University of Illinois Library or the Urbana Public Library reading the *Hattiesburg American* on microfilm a few years ago, I saw that during the 1930s a number of stores owned by members of the Jewish community on each street—for example, Fine-Bros-Matison, The Emporium, and the Diana Shop—placed large ads in the paper several times a month, depending on the season. The ads were typically quarter-page, half-page, or full-page, and occasionally two full pages (for anniversary or back-to-school sales). In contrast, my father rarely placed ads in the paper and when he did the ads were tiny, most of them about the size of a one-inch by two-and-a-half-inch ad in the classified section of a newspaper today and listed only a single item (for example, a particular style and brand of dresses, overalls, dress shirts, or shoes). The tiny ads in the back of the paper probably gave the impression to most readers (and certainly to other Jewish storeowners) of a relatively small stock of goods and a limited volume of business. In the paper's coverage of local news he would have occasionally seen the names of Jewish businessmen who served on important committees in the town's civic and business affairs. Although he had been a latecomer as a peddler, and had for a time just before the crash appeared to be prospering as a merchant, he was now struggling financially from the losses suffered in the two fires (and the closing of the store in Picayune) and the debts he was determined to pay off, as well as from the continuing effects of the Depression.

The question in my father's mind from the very beginning of the Depression must have been "How long will it last?" On March 7, 1932 the *Hattiesburg American* ran a brief story with the headline "Old Man Depression Now in State of Coma, Says Doctor in New Bulletin."

> Overcome by the changed atmosphere of Hattiesburg beginning to radiate warmth under the rays of prosperity's returning sunshine, Old Man Depression dug deep into his heap of rags in his lonely, secluded hovel down on the Leaf River bottoms. His condition was desperate and just at press time, the following bulletin was issued by the famous medical expert, Dr. Killem N. Grin: "Depression in critical condition due to prosperitis. Pulse barely discernible. Patient in delirium, believing slump still exists. Temperature subnormal. It gives me great pleasure to report the patient can not survive. Now sinking into coma."

Everyone who read this caricature of the Great Depression as a dying old man must have been as pleased by the diagnosis as his attending physician was. But the old man lived on until 1940. Other stories in the paper revealed the harsh reality many families faced. In June of 1933 the following item appeared in the "Seen and Heard" column: "Anyone having clothing to spare for two boys, 11 and 10 years old, and a girl 13, will do a great service to Mrs. C. J. Morgan, 1012 Edwards Street, she stated today. She desires to have the three children placed in a state school but she needs the clothing to carry out her plan. She is a widow and also has four more children."[1] In November of 1934 a story about blacks close to starvation appeared on the front page with the title "*Memphis Negroes Eating Away Mississippi River Banks of Clay*":

> Memphis police have solved the mystery surrounding a gradual disappearance of two clay deposits on the banks of the Mississippi river. In fact, Police Chief Will D. Lee said today his officers have found negroes, by the dozens, eating the earth away—feasting on it as if it were a great pork chop or a huge brick of ice cream. And what's more startling about the whole thing is that Memphis physicians agree that some medicinal benefit may be derived by the imbibers if they happen to be suffering from anemia or intestinal parasites. "They are loading it by the bucketful, digging it out with picks, knives, and spoons," Chief Lee declared. "There is no law against it and there is no way to stop them." The chief estimated that a ton of clay had been moved from the river banks recently. "Police Capt. Phelan Thompson said one negro informed him that his wife and her sister eat an average of 10 pounds of clay a week and suffer no ill effects."[2]

Some of the suffering, however, wasn't reported in the paper. In May of 1936 an anonymous letter (though now known to have been written by a black man) was sent to President Roosevelt telling him not only that people in Hattiesburg are starving but also that his intentions of helping the poor are not being honored by local administrators:

> Mr. President Sir We are starving in Hattiesburg we poor White's + Negros too[.] i wish you could See the poor hungry an naket half clad's at the relief office an is turned away[.] With tears in their eys Mississippi is made her own laws an don't treat her destuted as her Pres has laid the plans for us to live if the legislators would do as our good Pres has Said. What few days we have here could be happy in our last days both old white + Colard[.] Cencerely looking for our old age pension's an will thank you[.] they has made us Sighn for $3 00 a Month[.] Can't live at that.[3]

The writer may have been one of many sharecroppers cut from the relief rolls in the previous year. Most of the sharecroppers were black. The cut had been ordered not by the federal government but by the state administrator of the federal program. The sharecroppers who had been receiving aid from federal funds would in the future be "forced to rely on the farm owner for further help." In the paper's story, entitled "Employment Gains in Hattiesburg," emphasis is placed on pride in keeping the cost down: "Hattiesburg shared in keeping the cost of relief in the south at a lower figure than any section of the nation."[4]

Instead of stories of hardship and suffering, the paper of course preferred news about increasing employment and economic development. In this way it reflected the hopeful mood of the country created by President Roosevelt when he came to Washington in 1933 and in his first hundred days initiated a series of programs designed to put people back to work. Throughout that year the paper was filled with stories and ads indicating strong support for Roosevelt's policies. The National Recovery Act became the center of attention. Its purpose was to increase employment and wages by limiting the hours of employees and asking employers to raise the pay of their workers. Jewish merchants placed ads in the paper supporting the NRA, often with a picture of Roosevelt in the center of the ad. Pictures of him could also be seen in their stores. My father had one hanging on a supporting beam in the center of his store near the cash register. While not ubiquitous (like pictures of Washington in schoolrooms across the country), they were very common, representing the trust and hope Roosevelt inspired, and can still be seen in movies from the 1930s.

One supporter of the NRA's policies was Ben Beck, owner of the women's clothing store in the Forrest Hotel (previously owned and run by Selma Beck, Aunt Anne's sister, and her husband Ira). In May of 1933 he received a letter from the White House signed by Louis Howe, the president's old friend and political advisor, thanking him for announcing a 10 percent increase in wages for his employees. "My dear Mr. Beck," it began,

> The President asks me to acknowledge the receipt of your letter of May eleventh with enclosed clipping. He is glad to know of the action of your company in the matter of wage increase and wishes me to express his appreciation of your thoughtful kindness in telling him of it.[5]

Beck ran an ad in the paper accompanied by a picture of the president that stated "We Have Accepted President Roosevelt's Program 100%."[6] On the same day, fourteen clothing and jewelry stores ran an ad announcing new shopping hours that followed the NRA code. On the following day fifty-seven representatives of business firms sent the president a telegram: "Complying with your request over radio last night the retail merchants and affiliated interests of Hattiesburg, Mississippi, assembled in meeting tonight voted unanimously to support your blanket code, in the spirit in which you intended it to be supported." Then, at the end of July, sixteen stores, among them Waldoff Bros., ran an ad endorsing the NRA code, along with other ads placed by furniture and grocery stores. In September, a full-page ad appeared asserting "You Should Be Willing To Pay Higher Prices!" and explaining why the seventy businesses listed below the explanation, including most Jewish businesses, again one of them Waldoff's, supported the NRA.

> In factories all over the country deplorable conditions existed before enactment of the National Recovery Act; not in all factories were wages down to the starvation level but in a great many they were. And all factories were in direct competition with the low wage factories. Wages of $3, $4, and $5 a week were common. Millions were thrown out of work. Why were wages so low? Because PRICES were so low most factories could not exist on anything but low wages. Workers preferred a few dollars rather than nothing. Now factories are organizing under NRA codes—increasing wages to a living basis. When you jump wages from $3 a week to $12 or $15 a week it makes a difference in the retail price. Instead of working three or four machines, the workers are restricted so others can work. This is a move to put millions of people back to work. In due time the whole country will benefit. People must be willing to pay reasonable prices to end starvation and unemployment.[7]

Two years later, however, the Supreme Court declared the NRA unconstitutional. I don't know all the reasons economists give for its failure, but I gather that an important one was that it had been dominated by large business interests: "As long as businesses were permitted to raise prices to coincide with (or exceed) mandated wage increases," historian Robert S. McElvaine explains, "there would be no redistribution of income and no stimulation of purchasing power."[8] At that time, however, most businessmen in Hattiesburg remained enthusiastic supporters of both the program and the president. In an editorial on March 2, 1934, the paper predicted that President Roosevelt's "introduction of a number of new systems into the basic American structure" will be "retained forever." F. W. Foote, president of the First National Bank, spoke of the New Deal in glowing terms, upholding it "in all respects" and referring to President Roosevelt as "the savior of the people."[9]

If this mood of optimism was exaggerated, it nonetheless had some factual basis. Although the Commercial National Bank had failed in 1931, along with many other banks across the country, the First National Bank and the Citizens'

Bank survived. Both placed ads several times in 1932 assuring the public that they were on a sound footing and both remained solvent. At the end of August 1933, the state of Mississippi declared that it was out of the red for the first time since October 1930 and by the end of October 1934 state tax revenues were higher than in the previous year, indicating that business activity had improved. Mississippi was not alone. In December of 1934, the paper carried a story on the front page with the headline "Southern Governors Jubilant Over Affairs of States" and reported the governors' claims that their states were now on a sound financial basis.

It was during this period of optimism inspired by Roosevelt, as I learned from the paper, that Jewish businessmen played a significant role in bringing Reliance Manufacturing Company to Hattiesburg. It was a Jewish-owned firm founded by Milton F. Goodman in 1897 in Michigan City, Indiana. It quickly established a place for itself in the garment industry by specializing in work clothes. Factories were opened in the Midwest, Chicago became the home office, and by the 1930s Reliance, with an expanded line of clothing to offer, particularly the Big Yank line of men's shirts and pants, had become one of the largest clothing manufacturers in the country. In the fall of 1932, several officers of Reliance came to Hattiesburg on a tour of inspection, looking into the possibility of locating a plant there. But they chose nearby Columbia for their first plant in Mississippi, the two-story brick building was completed in just a few months, and on June 16, 1933, ten thousand people, it was reported, came to Columbus for the dedication, a parade, and a celebration.[10]

The initiative that brought Reliance to Columbia would soon become a model for bringing industry to Mississippi. Hugh L. White, who for many years had owned several lumber-industry businesses in Columbia (three sawmills, a veneer plant, and a box factory), had been the driving force behind the initiative. During the 1920s, having seen the near exhaustion of the pinewood forests by "timber companies [that had] failed to leave enough trees for re-seeding" and a bleak economic future for Columbia, he retired.[11] Then came the Depression, with results for Columbia that were devastating: "Houses and stores became vacant, homes were lost, families were divided, and the surrounding farms suffered along with the town."[12] White felt a responsibility to do something, not only as the former owner of businesses on which the town's economy had depended but also now as its mayor. When he was elected governor in 1936, he took the Columbia initiative to Jackson and made it the model for a Balance-Agriculture-with-Industry plan, as it came to be known, that he persuaded the legislature to adopt. To qualify for the plan, an industry would have to be free of any need for raw materials such as coal and iron that Mississippi didn't possess. What Mississippi could offer were low labor costs and subsidies for industries that chose to locate there.

After losing out to Columbia, the executive committee of the Hattiesburg Chamber of Commerce continued to pursue Reliance throughout the spring of 1932. To get the plant, however, Hattiesburg would have to come up with $100,000 for a building. The mayor, the Chamber of Commerce, and several special committees, in contrast to the glacial pace of most committees in government and large institutions, acted with remarkable swiftness. At a mass meeting in the late afternoon of the first day, the turning point came when Mayor Tatum—like White, an old lumber baron and one of the richest men in South Mississippi—pledged $15,000. "This was just like touching off dynamite," H. O. Hoffman, president of the Chamber of Commerce, reported, "and in ten minutes another $15,000 was subscribed and a finance committee appointed to give the people of Hattiesburg an opportunity to raise the other $70,000 in the next two days." At the end of the two days they had $78,000 in hand and, confident of raising the next $22,000, they put the "on-to-Chicago" committee on a train with instructions to say to Reliance "We are prepared to sign the contract."[13]

The contract they signed in Chicago on May 1, 1933, was with a Jewish firm in an industry that was itself predominantly Jewish and led to the involvement of a number of Hattiesburg's Jewish businessmen to serve on committees for the "Reliance Garment Plant Enterprise." Most were owners of clothing stores. Their presence on committees helped ensure that they and other Jewish businessmen would make substantial contributions toward the needed $100,000. Simon London was one of seven members on the executive committee of the Chamber of Commerce. He belonged to one of the most prominent Jewish families. His father, Jacob, had come to Hattiesburg in 1915 and founded the London Grocery and Dry Goods Company, which in 1929 was reputed to be "the largest retail grocery in Mississippi."[14] Nathan Fine of Fine Bros.-Matison Company was another. Following the demise of Davidson's, Fine-Bros.-Matison would become the upscale department store in town. He and Matison had first opened a store in Laurel in 1904, then the one in Hattiesburg in 1921, and he had finally moved there with his family in 1930. Other Jewish businessmen on one of the various committees were Harry Botnick of The Emporium and Sam Eisman of Eisman's Ladies' Ready-to-Wear, both having come to Hattiesburg in the early 1920s (and become brothers-in-law, each marrying a sister of the other), and Harry Sapperstein of Famous Department Store. With the help of eight hundred subscribers, the city was able to raise $1,000 more than their goal.

Construction began in July and on October 19 the front-page story of the *Hattiesburg American* reported: "Three months ago the location of the new plant was the site of a rambling row of structures, the city mule barn and several shacks in which negroes dwelt. This location typified the gloom of the depression. . . . Today there stands a two-story brick building on the site, 300 feet long by 150 feet wide."[15] A similar initiative brought another manufacturing plant, Domestic Silks of New York, to Hattiesburg. This time T. F. Dreyfus, Sam Eisman, and Simon London were on the negotiating team. A campaign committee was formed and a telegram similar to the one used in the Reliance initiative was sent to Jewish businessmen. The plant opened in 1935 and, though it closed for a brief time during the war, it was soon acquired by the Julius Kayser Co. and continued operations as The Hattiesburg Hosiery Mill.

The role Jewish businessmen played in these two initiatives represented a greater acceptance of them into Hattiesburg's business and civic life, as well as an example of what sociologist Milton Gordon calls structural assimilation—that is, a form of assimilation that comes about through being accepted into business, civic, and charitable organizations and represents an advance beyond the initial stage of acculturation represented by learning the language and adopting the values and practices of the dominant culture.[16] T. F. Dreyfus became commander of the United Spanish-American War Veterans. Herman Katz served for many years as treasurer of the Odd Fellows Lodge. Nathan Fine was a Kiwanian, Mason, and a Shriner, and was named an "Honorary Colonel" by Governor Paul B. Johnson, Sr.; Marcus London was a Kiwanian, Mason, Odd Fellow, and Shriner; his brother Simon was an Elk, Mason, Rotarian, and Shriner, and was also named an "Honorary Colonel" by Governor Johnson. Sam Eisman and Sam Miller, both members of the Exchange Club, also served on the Library Board. Sam Miller was elected president of the Exchange Club in 1933 and president of the Mississippi Association of Elks in 1937. Other Jewish men, including my father, belonged to one or more of these organizations.

Only a few Jewish women belonged to one of the many organizations and clubs for women. I don't know why, but a possible explanation may be that the women's meetings usually took place in members' homes, in contrast to the men's meetings, most of which took place in a building downtown designated for a specific use—for example, the Masonic Temple, or other buildings where the second floors were rented by the Elks and the Odd Fellows—or a meeting room in the Forrest Hotel. Inviting someone into one's home for a meeting may have seemed to imply more social contact or personal relationship than was wanted. It would have been just here, at the threshold of further social contact in the home, that personal history, religion, education, and language (along with accent) perhaps seemed, consciously or not, and on both sides, to be a barrier. In addition, the interests and activities of many of the women's clubs may have seemed pretty far from the experience of my mother's generation of Jewish immigrant women, many of whom worked with their husbands in a clothing store or other business, some actually running the business.

Jews were not invited to join the country club until the 1960s, something very common throughout the South. But there were exceptions. Levi Rothenberg, president of Marks-Rothenberg Department Store and the Meridian Building and Loan Association, was one of the founders of the Meridian Country Club. Several Jews in Greenville were also members of the country club there. Hodding Carter, the owner and Pulitzer Prize-winning editor of the *Delta Democrat Times* in Greenville, which in 1937 had the largest Jewish population in Mississippi, told an interesting story about his city. On one of his annual visits to Maine, where years before he had been a student at Bowdoin College, he learned from a local resident that the directors of a golf club there "didn't want within putting distance any Jew at all, whether rich or poor, hungry or persecuted, arrogant or humble, smart or dumb, old or young, duffer or champion." Carter relished the opportunity to tell his Maine informant that in Greenville a Jew had served as president of the country club for five years.[17] In Hattiesburg there may have been Jews who longed for an invitation, but I don't think my parents or their friends and fellow Jewish immigrants felt left out or sat around hoping for one. My father belonged to the Elks Club for a number of years, but, having little interest in clubs, he rarely went to its meetings.

I think an even more important step taken toward greater acceptance and assimilation came in 1935 with the hiring of the congregation's first ordained rabbi, Arthur Brodey, and the accompanying turn toward Reform Judaism. Born in Canada, he had earned a BA at the University of Toronto and then an LLB at Osgoode Law School at York University before deciding to give up being a barrister and begin studies for the rabbinate. He graduated from the Jewish Institute of Religion in New York in 1934, where he had studied under its founder, Rabbi Stephen S. Wise, at that time the most prominent rabbi in America. He had founded the Free Synagogue in New York on the principle that a rabbi should be free to address pressing moral and social issues of the day without fear of being restrained by its board of trustees. Prior to its founding and that of the rabbinical institute, he had been offered the pulpit of Tempe Emanu-El in New York, which, as he recalls in his autobiography, was known as "the Cathedral Synagogue of the country." [18] The congregation included members of some of the most distinguished Jewish families in America, including Daniel Guggenheim, Louis Marshall, Adolph Ochs, Jacob Schiff, and Felix Warburg. He turned the offer down in order to remain free to speak out on issues he cared about. He was an ardent Zionist, an early member of the NAACP, and a supporter of the labor movement. Over a period of many years he would win the admiration and friendship of several presidents, including Theodore Roosevelt, Taft, Wilson, and Franklin Roosevelt, and at times served as a consultant about appointments to the Supreme Court. On learning from Brodey that he had accepted the offer in Hattiesburg, Wise wrote, "I knew that if once you and the congregation met and they heard you, they would call you! It had to be. Of course the situation is difficult! What Synagogue situation is not? . . . I think it is a wonderful opportunity to go off into a remote place and build up a congregation, and unite orthodox and reform folk on the basis of uncompromising and undeviating Jewishness!"[19] In his letter Brodey must have mentioned some of his concerns about the potential difficulties of uniting the orthodox and reform contingents of the congregation. It's not clear what's meant by "uncompromising and undeviating Jewishness," but I assume Rabbi Brodey understood what his mentor had in mind.

Over the next eight years in Hattiesburg, in addition to his sermons at the temple on Friday nights and on Jewish holidays, he gave talks at State Teachers College, Woman's College, Walthall School, and Hattiesburg High School. He also gave talks at various local clubs, including Rotary, Kiwanis, Exchange, Review, and the Business and Professional Women's Club, as well as those in other towns and cities, including Laurel, Poplarville, Jackson, Tuscaloosa, and New Orleans. When he spoke at Sinai Temple in New Orleans, Rabbi Julian Feibelman praised him in a bulletin to his congregation for "his pioneering results in building up the Jewish community" in Hattiesburg and for being recognized as one of "the far-sighted young religious spokesmen" in the city and the state of Mississippi.[20]

Although he arrived in the middle of the Depression when economic issues continued to be on everyone's mind, the subjects he chose to speak about with increasing frequency were the moral, social, and political issues posed by the rise of Hitler and Mussolini, who in the late 1930s often dominated the headlines. I was only eight years old when, in March of 1943, he left to become a chaplain in the army. To learn about his seven and a half years in Hattiesburg,

I've had to rely principally on the newspaper's accounts of his activities, though I have memories of seeing him at the old synagogue on Pine Street, one from the day of Fay's confirmation. While reading the paper's coverage of his activities, which usually included substantial excerpts from his talks at schools and clubs, what I wanted to know was not only the subjects he discussed and what he said about them, but especially, to the extent it could be surmised from the paper's reports, the impression he was making and how he, in representing the Jewish community, was shaping the way Jews were being perceived.

What I learned suggested that he was a highly respected voice in Hattiesburg. By his presence and example, this youthful, thirty-five-year-old rabbi from Toronto seems to have done a great deal to advance the city's acceptance of its Jewish community. He knew how to engage the sympathies of an audience for the principles he supported. In one of his first talks, "Character in a Changing World," given at a chapel service at State Teachers College, he began by pointing to a striking contradiction in the middle of the Great Depression. Scientific progress had made it possible for man to live in "unparalleled abundance," yet also find "hunger and impoverishment all about him." To begin to address this problem, he said, one had to recognize that morality and character "are the basis of all religion."[21] In this and other talks he took belief in a divine being for granted, as well as shared ethical principles in Jewish and Christian traditions, but chose not to discuss specific beliefs, perhaps because down that path lay certain irreconcilable differences between the two faiths. Better to focus on areas of agreement—for example, the role of religion in developing individual morality and character or in fighting for "causes which endure, for justice, peace, and love for all mankind."[22] Such causes may have sounded lofty and idealistic to some, but for Brodey they were a way to address real issues, with examples taken from current events and everyday life and adapted for a specific occasion and audience.

The paper's coverage typically wasn't a reporter's summary but instead a series of informative paragraphs taken from a sermon or talk, allowing Brodey to be heard in his own voice (and making me wonder if reporters asked him for copies and he provided them). In reading these excerpts, what impressed me most was how he kept returning to issues affecting everyone, Jew and Christian alike, and how skillful he was in his effort to engage his hearers' (and readers') interests and concerns. But the paper's generous coverage of him also impressed me. It seemed to reflect both the paper's and the wider community's respect for him. As a young, well-educated, and ordained Reform rabbi who also had a law degree, I think the impression he would have made in speech and thought would have been very different from the one made by Hattiesburg's previous rabbis and in that way he contributed to the changing image of Jews held in the wider community.

Every Friday the subject of his sermon for that night was listed in the paper, along with an invitation extended to the public. Among the topics during those years were the following: "Has Science Undermined Religion," "The Marranos—Secret Jews of Spain and Portugal," "The Ethical Power of the Bible," "Capitalism, Character, and Culture," "Palestine—Britain, Arabs, and Jews," "The Right to Be Different," "The Revelation of the Law—Its Meaning and Message for Mankind," "The Jewish Attitude Toward Creation and Evolution," "The Doctrine of Heaven and Hell in Judaism," "A Reply to 'An Epistle to the Jews'—Towards a Jewish-Christian Understanding," "The Sources of Anti-Semitism," "The Jews in the International Scene," "Father Coughlin and the Christian Front," and "Jews and Christians: What We Have in Common."

While Rabbi Brodey was not alone among local and visiting speakers to receive coverage in the paper, the frequency and extent of the attention given to him surprised me. In my reading of the paper from 1920 until his arrival in 1935, I hadn't seen any coverage comparable to it for the congregation's previous rabbis. The attention given to them came mostly in descriptions of upcoming Jewish holidays. In contrast, Rabbi Brodey quickly became the most articulate and public Jewish voice in the city's history. He had arrived in the middle of challenging times—the Depression and the news reports of Hitler's persecution of Germany's Jews—and the times increasingly dictated the subjects he addressed. But his education and the influence of his mentor, Rabbi Wise, had prepared him for the moment. His focus on the moral, social, and political issues of the day made his sermons and talks highly relevant and interesting to a wider audience. What this seemed to me to represent, through his appearances in person and print, was a gradual change that was taking place in the public's image of the city's Jewish community.

Within a month of his arrival, by which time Mussolini had invaded Abyssinia and Hitler had begun to rearm (in violation of the Versailles Treaty) and had marched into the Rhineland, he gave a sermon on the eve of Armistice Day entitled "The Paths of Glory—Shall They Lead to War or Peace?" that was praised in an editorial the next day for his observation that a "nationalism, which, when magnified as sovereign, exalts the state over the church, is mankind's greatest enemy."[23] Over the next few years, his sermons became more explicit about the growing crisis in Europe and the threat of war. On Rosh

Hashanah in September of 1937, the subject was "Two Worlds in Conflict." The paper gave it most of two columns. In one of these worlds, Rabbi Brodey said, the salute "is the clenched fist, and its sovereigns to whom the subjects give their oaths of hate are the Mussolinis and Hitlers of today." In the other, "its trumpet calls its subjects to arms . . . [and] the salute [is] to the sovereign God."[24] Two months later, in a talk he gave to members of the PTA at Walthall School on the subject of "Good Citizenship," he spoke again of the growing crisis in Europe that led to regimentation under dictators and warned of "the necessity to prevent American youths from losing hope and faith in American democracy."[25]

In his sermon at the end of the eight-day celebration of Hanukkah in December, he invoked the spirit of the ancient Maccabees in the modern world's need to confront Hitler and Mussolini. Again, the paper quoted him at length. In developing a parallel between the struggle of the ancient Maccabees, who worshipped the God of the Old Testament, against the Syrians in the Seleucid Empire, who worshipped the gods of the ancient Greeks, he said the war had been fought not to achieve territorial or commercial advantage but "to maintain the integrity of a group's spiritual life, a war for ideas and ideals." The war represented a "clash of civilizations." He then observed that "only as we become Maccabeans of the spirit—only as we stand shoulder to shoulder with the Maccabeans of other faiths shall the miracle of Hanukkah be the miracle of our own survival and the survival of the world itself" in the coming struggle against Hitler and Mussolini.[26] In his use of military metaphors—"a war of ideas and ideals," "stand shoulder to shoulder with other faiths"—he invokes a spirit of patriotism against the dictators in order to support the idea of Christian and Jew fighting together in a common cause. Although he was speaking to his congregation, he knew that what he said might appear in the paper and, perhaps with that in mind, he continued in his frequent talks in schools, universities, and clubs to advance the idea of Jews and Christians being united in sharing common ideals.

As a guest speaker at a meeting of the Review Club in March of 1938, when the territorial demands of Hitler seemed to point to war, he warned that recent advances in civilization had so greatly increased the destructive force of war that it could threaten survival: "We may not be able to wait till history runs its course, because war through science may destroy us in the meantime."[27] Eight months later, with the approach of another Armistice Day, this one after Chamberlain's capitulation to Hitler in Munich, he said in a talk to the Exchange Club that "the peace of Munich" was "a surrender by the democracies to world forces of hate and greed" and that Hitler "now decides the fate of Europe" and predicted that he "intends to take all the territory to the Black Sea and then turn and crush France."[28] Although Hitler would invade them in a different order (Poland first, then France and other countries in the west), Brodey showed remarkable foresight in predicting that Hitler would invade the Soviet Union and other countries surrounding the Black Sea.

At the end of 1938, he spoke at the synagogue to an interfaith audience on the subject "Christian and Jew—a United Front." Those who heard it, the paper reported, labeled it "one of the outstanding holiday sermons." It was based to some extent on a series of articles that had appeared in the *New York Times* about the Nazi perception of Protestant and Catholic churches as "enemies" of National Socialism. "It is not the Jew alone who is in danger now," he warned, "it is the Christian as well . . . it is democracy and humanity which are in peril." In its coverage of the sermon, the *Hattiesburg American* said, "All are aware of the tragic plight of innocent Jews in Europe, but"—now quoting Rabbi Brodey—"'we are not so acutely aware of the danger threatening Christians without Jewish blood.'"[29]

The sermon I most wish I could have found and read in its entirety was entitled "A Spiritual Semite: A Tribute to the Late Pope Pius XI."[30] It was given in February of 1939, a week after the pope died. Rabbi Brodey had good reason to pay tribute to Pius XI. In an encyclical issued in March of 1937 entitled "With Burning Concern," Pius XI criticized the racism, neo-pagan theories, and anti-religious measures of Hitler's new Germany. In September of 1938, in response to Mussolini issuing an anti-Semitic decree entitled "Measures for the defense of race in fascist schools," Pius XI expressed his view that "Abraham is our patriarch, our ancestor . . . [and] anti-Semitism is a hateful movement with which we Christians must have no involvement. . . . Through Christ and in Christ we are the spiritual descendants of Abraham. . . . Spiritually we are all Semites."[31] His last encyclical, which he had prepared just before he died, was entitled "On the Unity of Human Kind." His successor, Pope Piux XII, refused to circulate it.[32]

Brodey, however, was not the first person in the Jewish community to express publicly its concern about the threat that Hitler posed. As early as August of 1933, just seven months after Hitler had come to power, T. F. Dreyfus chaired a local campaign to raise money for Germany's Jews. The paper ran a story about it under the title "German Jews Given Help: Hattiesburgians Respond Liberally to Cause of Distressed People." Dreyfus had received a report on conditions in Nazi Germany from the American Jewish Joint Distribution

Sketch of Rabbi Arthur Brodey, inscribed "To Mr. and Mrs. Paul Waldoff, Loyal friends and co-workers, Arthur."

Committee. Taking its information from the report, the paper stated that "one hundred thousand Jews in Germany have already lost all opportunities to earn a living" and then gave the numbers of Jews dismissed from various professions and left without an income or means of livelihood: 5,000 out of 8,000 Jewish government officials; 1,200 out of 2,500 lawyers; 3,500 out of 7,000 physicians; 3,000 musicians, singers, actors, communal employees, welfare workers; 2,000 dentists; 20,000 merchants, artisans, and so on.[33] In June of 1935, a local committee headed by Dreyfus sought to raise $1,000 to help Jews in Germany, Poland, and Romania, as well as other East European countries. In Germany, Dreyfus pointed out, not only Jews but also Christians in mixed marriages were being made to suffer. "The committee encourages persons of all religions to aid in this campaign, which, it was emphasized, is a humane, not a religious, cause."[34]

The steadily increasing number and forms of Hitler's persecution of Jews up until the war are now well known from newsreels, films, and countless books, especially Saul Friedländer's comprehensive *Nazi Germany and the Jews: The Years of Persecution, 1933 to 1939*. What I wanted to know, however, was what Jews and others in the wider community of Hattiesburg knew at that time from reading the local paper. For example, in June of 1935 the paper reported what had happened to Dreyfus' family and used it to represent the injustices being suffered by Germany's Jews. Nine of his cousins had "fought in the German army during the World War," he said, but "they have since been forced to leave their country."[35] In July the paper ran an Associated Press story detailing some of the ways Jews were being threatened. They were forbidden to have sexual relations with Aryan women or even "to rent apartments to Aryans, engage Aryan domestic help or accept Aryan clients." The warning to Aryan women was made vivid by a postcard showing an Aryan girl standing in a gutter with a Jewish couple and surrounded by storm troopers. Around her neck hangs a placard that reads "A swine am I, the town about / With Jews alone do I go out." [36] After the Nuremburg Laws were adopted in September of 1935, additional restrictions were added and reported in the *Hattiesburg American*. In November came a decree that "the Jew cannot be a Reich citizen, cannot vote or occupy public office," while another, refining the new blood laws, "forbade marriages between Jews and 'quarter Jews,' or between 'quarter Jews' themselves."[37] Over the next four years there would continue to be reports in the paper of Hitler's persecution of Jews. After *Kristallnacht* there was a strong editorial ("Atrocities") condemning Hitler.[38] But the editorial that everyone in Hattiesburg's Jewish community would have been especially pleased to read was the one endorsing a plan proposed by President Roosevelt to accept Jewish refugees. "Some of the world's most talented musicians, most capable scientists, most skilled physicians have lived, and are living, in Vienna. Most of them are of Jewish descent. These people would be welcomed additions to the citizenship of any nation."[39]

An unusual opportunity to hear a firsthand account of what was happening in Germany came when the Hattiesburg-Laurel Zionists, with T. F. Dreyfus serving as president and Rabbi Brodey as honorary president, brought the Christian Zionist and Dutch-Canadian journalist Pierre Van Paassen to town as a guest speaker in 1937. His talk, "A Gentile Views the World Jewish Scene," was given at an open meeting on Wednesday night, April 8, held at the Main Street Methodist Church, where several hundred people from South Mississippi came to hear him and where he was introduced by Rabbi Brodey. He had begun his career as a journalist with the *Toronto Globe*, where Brodey may have first read him, then became a foreign correspondent for the New York *Evening World* and later for the *Toronto Star*. He had traveled widely in Europe. In 1928 he had interviewed Hitler in the Brown House in Munich. "I promise that I will make life impossible for the Jews in Germany," Hitler told him, "and that I will not rest till I have destroyed the influence of the Jews in the whole of Europe—and in the world."[40] In his later travels in Europe, Van Paassen had not only seen how Jews in Germany were being treated but had received similar treatment himself, having been imprisoned for ten days in Dachau, near Munich, Hitler's first concentration camp.

In his talk that Wednesday night, he expressed amazement at the naïve view of Hitler some Americans still had, using as an example their question "Didn't Hitler raise the German people from post-war depths to the heights they have now attained?" He was referring to Hitler's revival of German industry and his building the autobahns. While he said "I do not think a great war stands immediately before the door," he went on to add that the current moment was "a calm before a storm" that Hitler was using to prepare for "a devastating war."[41] As Rabbi Brodey had predicted, Van Paassen brought "a first-hand, graphic report of the position of millions of European Jews."[42] Two years later, those who had come to hear him could read some of what he said that night in his *Days of Our Years*, which became a nonfiction best-seller for 1939.

While reading these news stories in the *Hattiesburg American*, I wondered what my parents and others in our small Jewish community were thinking as they read them in the late 1930s. I have no letters from that time that might have revealed my parents' thoughts. I know only that they read the local paper and subscribed to *Life*, *Newsweek*, and *The Nation* and that Norman subscribed to *The Jewish Daily Forward* and saw the reports of Hitler's rearming Germany, annexing Austria, demanding the *Sudetenland*, and occupying the rest of Czechoslovakia, by which time these and related stories foreshadowing war had long dominated the news, appearing almost daily, and were soon to be followed by headlines of his invasion of Poland in September of 1939.

But I know that the local story of greatest personal interest for my parents and everyone in Hattiesburg would have been the reopening, rebuilding, and expansion of Camp Shelby. Here at the end of the decade, with Old Man Depression not yet dead and food stamps still being distributed, the dazzling speed with which the rebuilding of Camp Shelby was progressing and the increased opportunities for employment would have been developments followed by all with the keenest interest.

September of 1940 became a turning point in the economic history of the city. A contract for $11,000,000 (in today's money, $190,000,000) was signed for construction work at Camp Shelby. When the work was completed, the camp was expected to accommodate 42,000 men. During the war it accommodated between 75,000 and 100,000 soldiers and it became "the second largest army base in the country, second only to Fort Benning in Georgia, making it one of the largest training camps in the country."[43] The population of the city then was only 25,000. As construction began, Congress approved legislation for the first peacetime draft. Approximately 16,500,000 men between the ages of 21 and 35 were required to register. Two days later, President Roosevelt signed the legislation into law.[44] Six-thousand job-hunters now swelled the population and Hattiesburg experienced "the bedlam of a boom town."[45] They came from all across the country. Two young men had driven from Rhode Island in an old jalopy after reading about Camp Shelby in their local paper. Two others had driven a truck from North Carolina. Still others came on a freight train, some hitchhiked, a few walked. A "Negro in tattered clothes" had come on foot from Prentiss, a distance of roughly forty miles. His feet were "bandaged with old cloth," the reporter for the paper, John Frasca, noted, "and were swollen and cut in several places. . . . His last meal, a hamburger at a road-stand nearby, had been purchased the previous night." They all came hoping to find employment. Some Mississippians were concerned about out-of-staters taking jobs away from local people, but others were "philosophical": "'Shucks, they must need work as badly as we do or they wouldn't be here.'"[46]

By the end of September, two weeks after the construction contract was signed, 4,000 men were working at the camp. By the middle of October, the number was 10,153; by October 30, 12,000. The payroll at Camp Shelby for the month of November came to around $1,125,000 (in today's dollars, around $19,000,000), an extraordinary boost to a Depression-era economy, with a little more than half of it going to enlisted men and officers stationed there, the rest to construction workers and other employees at the camp. By January, the total number of troops had reached 40,000. Although the boom that started now would not last as long as the one that had transformed Hattiesburg into a small city in the first twenty years of the century, the speed with which money was pouring in was unprecedented. Despite numerous problems in housing, transportation, and profiteering that accompanied the massive expansion of Camp Shelby and the swift increase in the city's population, 1940 proved to be a miracle year for Hattiesburg. In November *Forbes Magazine* listed the city as one of the best places in the United States for business.[47] Old Man Depression and his Stepson Unemployment moved away, going somewhere else to linger and die.

It also proved to be a miracle year for my parents. My mother had survived the first three years of the five-year period that would determine whether the operations and radium treatments had left her free of cancer. She and my father bought their first house, the one on Mamie Street that Sam and Goldie Percoff had built. My father also bought, together with Norman, the building at 118–20 East Pine Street and remodeled that part of the building, 120 East Pine, that would become their new store (118 continuing to be occupied by Silver the Tailor). The plan going forward was that he would manage the new store and Norman would run the one on Mobile Street.

One day during the remodeling of the building for the opening of the new store, I remember standing next to my father on the sidewalk while he was talking to Sam Eisman. I was five and a half years old. Mr. Eisman said he hadn't known the building was for sale. It was a point of some interest for him, as I've learned from reading the paper of those years. His store, Eisman's Dry Goods, had for a number of years occupied 120 East Pine in the 1920s. Suddenly my confidence in an old memory from that time was revived, specifically that part of it in which I heard Mr. Eisman congratulate my father not only for having bought the building but also for having learned of its availability and moved quickly to buy it before anyone else could. I suppose the emotional content of the memory, a boy's love and admiration for his father, is the reason it has lasted when so many others have slipped away. That fall my father also bought a new 1941 Buick Special. I was in the side yard playing when I saw him behind the steering wheel as he turned into the driveway, with Milton in the front passenger's seat, leaning out over the rolled-down window while yelling excitedly to me and banging his right hand on the outside of the door. Before the year ended my father was elected president of the Hattiesburg Lodge of the B'nai B'rith, as well as treasurer of B'nai Israel Congregation, a position he would be repeatedly asked to hold over the coming years. My parents had arrived, but this time with a sense of belonging and achievement, a sense of feeling at home in Hattiesburg and America, that replaced the mix of excitement and trepidation they must have felt at their first sight of the Statue of Liberty and their first uncertain steps on Ellis Island back in 1922.

A little more than a year later, in the early afternoon of December 7, 1941, when my father was driving back from Camp Shelby, where he had gone to tend to a shoe concession he had there and had taken Milton and me with him, we heard on the car radio that Pearl Harbor had been bombed. That night, or one soon after it, I had a dream in which Japanese soldiers had invaded the West Coast and were now marching east across the country. I knew the shapes of the forty-eight United States from a puzzle I'd been given and repeatedly taken apart and put back together. The image of Japanese soldiers lined up shoulder-to-shoulder from the northern tip of Washington to the southern tip of California and coming towards us—towards *me*—has remained vivid to this day. I don't know what deep, unconscious fears the dream drew upon for its power over me, but its visual details—the faces of the Japanese soldiers, their uniforms, their bodies bent forward, their hands holding rifles pointed forwards with bayonets fixed—could only have come from newsreels or pictures in *Life* or another magazine I'd seen in our house.

In the following years, our teachers in grammar school led us in singing "Let's Remember Pearl Harbor," my mother had ration books for sugar and other food items, and my father had a "B" stamp on the front windshield of the car allowing him to purchase a greater amount of gas for business purposes than an "A" stamp allowed. After I became a Cub Scout, I used to walk with other boys through neighborhoods on Saturdays to collect tin cans, lard, and other materials used in manufacturing weapons. My father served as the air-raid warden for our block on Mamie Street, making sure that lights were either off or not visible during air-raid tests. It's hard to believe that the Germans and the Japanese were even aware of the existence of a small city in south Mississippi, but its proximity to Camp Shelby and Keesler Air Force Base on the Gulf Coast, only sixty miles away, may have been the reason for the tests. German U-boats operated in the Gulf of Mexico in the first years of the war and, since one had surfaced in June of 1942 near Amagansett off Long Island for the purpose of landing saboteurs (who were captured and executed), the precautions must have seemed necessary.

In November of 1942, Norman enlisted in the army, surprising everyone, especially my father. Although he was too old to be drafted, he was caught up in the patriotism everyone felt then. He also had become preoccupied with the fate of the Jews in Europe, following the news closely and spending a good deal of time, some of it at the store, reading *The Jewish Daily Forward*, *The Nation*, and the *Hattiesburg American*. Along with the continuing reports of what was happening to Jews in Germany, he would have read about the speeches and protests of Lindbergh, the America Firsters, and the German-American Nazi Fritz Kuhn and would have seen Kuhn's claim, carried in the local paper, that "all the Jews are enemies of the United States" and that "Jews were the master minds behind the Communist party; that the Rothschilds, through Kuhn, Loeb, & Co., and the Warburgs control the Democratic and Republican parties, that the family of J. P. Morgan 'has Jewish blood' . . . and [that] the Nazi salute 'is the coming salute for the whole United States.'"[48] As preposterous as these claims seem now, the premise of them had become sufficiently fearful as early as 1935 to help make Sinclair Lewis' novel *It Can't Happen Here* a best-seller. In it an American senator from Vermont is elected president, assumes dictatorial powers, and silences opponents by killing them or placing them in a concentration camp, the point of the novel being that *it could happen here*. The specter of a takeover by a fascist dictator was a matter of deep concern for Lewis and his wife, the widely syndicated columnist Dorothy Thompson. During his travels in Italy Lewis had seen Mussolini's black shirts marching and *It Can't Happen Here* was conceived as an attack on the fascist tendencies in American political life.[49] Thompson had lived in Berlin in the early 1930s until she was expelled from Germany in 1934 for her criticisms of Hitler in her columns and in her 1932 book *I Saw Hitler*. In 1939, she had been almost thrown out of a gathering of 20,000 of Kuhn's followers in Madison Square Garden when she shouted "nonsense" during one of the speeches. In the *Hattiesburg American*, Lewis is quoted as saying, "I hope that the third time of her ejection from Swastika-crowned German territory will not be from the capitol at Washington."[50]

At some point during the reactivation of Camp Shelby, perhaps after the bombing of Pearl Harbor, the reception hall on the first floor of the synagogue became an official United Service Organization center, this one for Jewish soldiers. Two additional USO centers were opened in Hattiesburg in 1942, one for whites and one for blacks.[51] Each provided a place where soldiers could read, write letters, play games, and, in the Jewish USO, meet other Jewish soldiers and members of our Jewish community. During World War I, Julian Feibelman, a native of Jackson who, two years before deciding to begin studying for the rabbinate at Hebrew Union College, enlisted in the army in May of 1918 and was stationed at Camp Shelby. Many years later he recalled that "the Hattiesburg Jewish community did their best to help men in the camp and keep us from getting homesick." Although the small, still relatively new congregation had not yet built a synagogue, it managed, he said, to conduct "religious services for us, gave dances, and always provided refreshments."[52] Now, during World War II, the Passover services held in the reception hall in the first week of April of 1942 attracted more than three hundred people, most of them soldiers from Camp Shelby, with Rabbi Brodey presiding (along with a chaplain from the camp, Abba Fineburg).[53] My mother and other members of the Temple

Sisterhood prepared the traditional meal. Throughout the war years, usually on Sunday nights, they used to bring home-cooked meals to the hall for the soldiers. But as I remember those occasions, it was the soldiers' wives who took the initiative to provide entertainment. In front of a large audience sitting close together on folding chairs, they often sang favorites from recent Broadway and film musicals. A memory from that time that keeps coming back to me is of one of the wives, a brunette in a black dress, standing alone in a small space that served as a makeshift stage before her audience of soldiers, their wives, and members of our Jewish community and singing with great feeling George and Ira Gershwin's "Embrace me, my sweet embraceable you."

My mother often invited soldiers to our home for dinner and Norman took a keen interest in them. I remember him sitting next to one of them at the table, engaging him in conversation, sometimes laughing, at other times leaning forward and listening intently. Ever since Hitler's invasion of the Soviet Union in June of 1941, he must have feared what might happen to his family in Kiev. After the bombing of Pearl Harbor, he may have wondered, even though he was too old to be drafted, if people were whispering about him what I remember hearing sometimes being asked about single men around town, "Why isn't he in uniform?" When asked about a Jew, the question echoed the notion, once held by Mark Twain, that Jews didn't fight in any of America's wars. Without identifying it as such, Rabbi Brodey decided to address it in his Thanksgiving sermon of 1942, which the paper summarized and quoted from in a story entitled "Rabbi Discusses Patriotism of Jews." "In this war," he said, "the Jew is found to be in the service of his country in higher proportion than his percentage to the general population." Of Hattiesburg's Jews, he pointed out, "Fourteen of the nineteen single men of military age are in the armed services" and "the other five were rejected because of medical reasons." He went on to provide some history about American Jews in the military. "In the first World War, while the proportion of Jews in the general population amounted to three per cent, the enrollment of Jews in the army and navy was four and five percent. Some 40,000 Jews volunteered, accounting for 18 percent of the Jewish enrollment." Roughly half of those in the army, forty-eight percent, served in the infantry and "Jewish soldiers distinguished themselves by receiving more than 1,100 citations."[54] Now during the World War II and ten years after the appeal in the Wexler case and his lawyers' implying that Jews had not fought for either the establishment or the defense of the country, here was Rabbi Brodey publicly defending the patriotism of Jews. I don't know if Norman heard the sermon, but he would certainly have read the story about it in the paper. He had enlisted just twelve days before. Rabbi Brodey, also too old to be drafted, would enlist the following spring.

My father thought Norman had been foolish to enlist at the age of forty-three. The rigorous physical training might prove to be too much for him. But Norman had made his decision, however unwise it would soon prove to be. I wonder what drove him to enlist. I can't help but think that being single, concerned about his family in Russia, and caught up in the patriotism that everyone felt then were all part of the decision.

For his basic training he was sent to Camp Van Dorn near Centreville (just south of Natchez), one of the many training camps hurriedly constructed across the South in 1942. It became operational in November and Norman would have been among the first group of soldiers to arrive there. After completing basic training and receiving a unit assignment, he continued in the army until September of 1943, when he was given a medical discharge for what must have been early signs of angina. Some months later, I saw him come out of his bedroom one night around nine o'clock gasping for breath and reaching for the telephone in the hallway. After recovering from his heart attack, he decided to move to an apartment. The reason he gave for moving, after having lived with us for seventeen years, was that Milton and I were now older and more active, staying up late and sometimes quarreling, and he thought we needed separate bedrooms and he needed a place of his own where he could rest without noise and interruptions. He rented an apartment from Sam Eisman and the following spring he married Eisman's sister, Ethel. His move out of our house and his marriage changed our relationship with him. As he grew closer to his wife's family, the Botnicks and Eismans, we saw much less of him.

Two years after the war, my father and Norman dissolved the partnership. My father bought Norman's share of the business and the building on Pine Street and Norman took full ownership of the store on Mobile Street. They saw each other only rarely now. There were exceptions, of course, but the only two I remember were Fay's wedding in 1947 and a dinner given by Norman and Ethel in 1960 when Aunt Celia came from Moscow for a three-month visit with my mother after thirty-nine years and Aunt Anne, now a widow, Uncle Abe having died two years before, drove to Hattiesburg to see her. Looking back, it may be that Norman's insistence on a higher price for his share of the building on Pine Street than my father thought was fair became the breaking point. Preceding it, however, were older, deeper sources of tension, including my mother's long-held feeling that he had overstayed his welcome in her home. After Norman moved out, I learned how much she had come to resent his presence.

What I had remembered about him was his washing the dishes on occasion (something my father never did), throwing a baseball bat up into our pecan trees to shake the limbs and make the pecans come raining down, talking with the Jewish soldiers who came to our house, and leaning over a Yiddish newspaper at the store. He bought a flute for Fay when she was in the high school band and took her to New York in 1939 for the World's Fair. He awakened the family on D-Day in 1944 around four in the morning and I have a vivid memory of him in his room sitting on the edge of his bed and leaning over, his ear only inches away from the radio on his bedside table. However, my mother certainly had good reason to feel that seventeen years had been long enough.

I don't know what Norman's thoughts about the break were, but perhaps his enlistment, his heart attack, his move out of our house, his marriage, and his new relationship with his wife's family had brought him to feel a sense of independence he hadn't known before, especially in his relationship with my father, who, as the founder of the business, had always been the senior partner. Whatever the real reasons for the break were, their relationship, dating back to their youth in Russia, had effectively ended. Norman would continue to keep up his relationship with my father's parents and sister in New York and Uncle Ben would continue to work for him at the Mobile Street store, but we saw him only rarely now.

CHAPTER 6

Breaking the Silence about Segregation

Hattiesburg had changed a great deal since the beginning of the war. Its population in 1940 had been 21,000, but by 1949 it had grown to almost 29,000. The economic problems my father and others of his generation had faced during the Depression had been solved largely by the expansion of Camp Shelby that had begun in 1940. The construction had brought the city's population and employment to their highest levels in its history. Following the attack on Pearl Harbor, Camp Shelby, with 75,000 to 100,000 soldiers and only twelve miles away, provided a tremendous stimulus to business activity, making its growth not only one of the most important in the city's history but its impact, as the city's historian, Benjamin Morris, has said, "difficult to overstate."[1] But now, after the war, and as a result of demobilization and the closing of the camp, the primary economic concern in the city became trying to maintain the level of prosperity that had been achieved during the war years.

In the Jewish community, two immediate goals, finding a replacement for Rabbi Brodey and raising $100,000 for the construction of a new temple, were achieved in what now seems to have been record time, a new rabbi arriving in 1946 and the new temple being dedicated in 1947. The congregation had emerged from the Depression and the war much stronger than it had been and over the next five years another generation of young couples and their children would bring a new vitality to the Jewish community, as well as a renewal of confidence in its future. Many of the young couples, in contrast to their immigrant parents, had a college education, among them Fay and "B," and a number of the husbands were veterans, as was "B."

As a result of these developments, the experience of my parents and that of the Jewish community in Hattiesburg had undergone a major change. The problems of economic survival during the Depression had been solved, a successful transition to Reform Judaism (that included accommodations to the congregation's Orthodox members) had been accomplished during the tenure of Rabbi Brodey, and a sense of greater acceptance by the wider community had been achieved. Despite these positive developments, however, the threat of violent anti-Semitism would loom larger than ever over the next two decades and become the issue of greatest concern for Jews in Mississippi.

It was during these first years after the war when challenges to segregation threatened to disrupt the legal and social structure of life in the South and Jews there would eventually find it impossible to remain totally silent about segregation. With the birth of the civil rights movement in the bus boycott in Montgomery in 1955 and its spread throughout the 1960s in the form of freedom rides, sit-ins, demonstrations, and voter registration drives in the 1960s, often involving rabbis and Jewish college students from the North, as well as a few courageous rabbis in the South, one in Hattiesburg and another in Jackson, who began to speak out against segregation, Jews in the South would find themselves exposed to intimidation and violence from the White Citizens' Councils, which were founded in Indianola, and the new White Knights of the Ku Klux Klan, which was based in Laurel, twenty-seven miles north of Hattiesburg.

In July of 1948, President Truman issued an executive order to end segregation in the armed forces. Although he had Confederates among his ancestors on his mother's side of the family, he didn't hesitate to write to several Democrats from the South that "my stomach turned over when I learned that Negro soldiers, just back from overseas, were being dumped out of army trucks in Mississippi and beaten."[2] To avoid such a beating when he returned to Hattiesburg in 1946, Henry Murphy was advised by his father, who had driven to Camp Shelby to pick him up, to change into civilian clothes. "He told me not to wear my uniform home. Because the police was beating up [black] GIs and searching them. If they had a white woman's picture in his pocket, they'd kill him." He took off his uniform and "put on overalls and a jumper, the uniform of a field hand."[3] That same year, another returning black veteran, this one a sergeant who had been wounded in Italy and awarded a Purple Heart, went to the Forrest County Courthouse to register to vote and was told by the registrar, "If you don't get out of here, I'll take my foot, [and] kick you plumb out there in the middle of that street."[4] I first heard of the discrimination against black veterans from Sam Evans, Herbert's son, who began working in the store several years after returning from wartime service in Europe, where, following D-Day, he'd been a driver in a trucking unit. He told me he'd gone to the local VA office to apply for financial aid for education under the GI bill but was told, "You go on home, boy, you don't need no education."

After interviewing nearly fifty black Mississippi veterans, historian Neil McMillen at the University of Southern Mississippi in Hattiesburg concluded that although "the interviews speak directly to the humiliations of separate-and-unequal wartime experience," one could not argue that black soldiers from Mississippi "returned from the war with radical change on their mind." Nevertheless, "the war's impact was decisive." It helped "shape an emerging racial consciousness" of "the moral contradictions of a nation that professed human rights and practiced white supremacy" and that had sent black Mississippians "to fight abroad for what they didn't have at home."[5] This awakening, along with other changes set in motion by the war (economic, political, and social), would evolve into the civil rights movement of the 1950s and 1960s.

In reaction to Truman's executive order, as well as to the National Democratic Party's adoption of a civil rights plank in its platform prior to its convention in Philadelphia that summer of 1948, the southern states rebelled, formed the States Rights Party, and nominated Governor Strom Thurmond of South Carolina for president and Governor Fielding Wright of Mississippi for vice president. In the election, they carried only four states: Louisiana, Mississippi, Alabama, and South Carolina. Then in 1954, with the Supreme Court's decision in *Brown vs The Board of Education of Topeka* that segregation in schools was illegal, segregation would become the dominant issue in the South, often a burning one, and Jews there would soon find their silence about it increasingly difficult to maintain.

It was at the beginning of this crucial period in the history of the Jewish community in Hattiesburg when, in 1951, Rabbi Charles Mantinband arrived. Over the next eleven years he would become active in the civil rights movement, at times speaking to biracial audiences at black colleges or at meetings of national organizations, at other times meeting with individual blacks in his home, Medgar Evers being one, who came to him for help or advice. As a result, his activities attracted both local and national attention, which in turn brought him into serious conflict with some members of the congregation. They wanted him to remain silent on the subject of civil rights. Many of his fellow rabbis in the South, on the other hand, had the highest regard for him precisely because he did speak out despite a number of threats, one from a former mayor of Hattiesburg who told fellow members of the local White Citizens Council that he knew how to get at the rabbi if they wanted to silence him. In 1963, shortly after leaving Hattiesburg for the pulpit in Longview, Texas, Mantinband was one of a number of religious leaders invited by President Kennedy to attend a conference at the White House to discuss the civil rights problem.

I was a junior in high school in 1951 when he arrived and got to know him during my last two years before leaving for Northwestern. Although I continued to see him on occasion when home on vacation, I failed to stay in touch with him and follow the controversy in the congregation stirred by his activities in the civil rights movement. It was the period after college when I was trying to find out what I wanted to do, having tried law school for a semester, served in the army for six months, worked in a commercial real estate firm in Atlanta for three years, and then served an additional ten months in the army at Fort Bliss, Texas (when President Kennedy called up 119,000 reservists following Khrushchev's ordering the construction of the Berlin Wall) before beginning graduate school in 1962 at the University of Michigan and becoming an assistant professor of English at the University of Illinois in 1967.

So it was more than five decades later, and after I had been retired for several years and had begun researching my parents' history and that of the Jewish community in Hattiesburg, when I realized that Rabbi Mantinband's eleven years in Hattiesburg, particularly his involvement in the civil rights movement, were an essential part and natural continuation of the story about Jewish life in Mississippi that I had already begun to write. Indeed, most of what has been written about Hattiesburg's Jewish community since its beginnings has been focused on his time there because it coincided with the rise of the civil rights movement. It was a defining moment. His involvement in the movement and the reaction of the congregation attracted both local and national attention. The more I learned about his experience during those years, the more I realized not only how fortunate I'd been to know him but also how what he'd done had shaped a significant part of the history I was researching and writing about. I could think of no better prism through which to view and try to understand Jewish life in Hattiesburg during those crucial years than his experience.

I was sixteen when he arrived and by that time the four questions I'd been asking at the Passover service each year had morphed into other questions about religion. My relationship with him began when I went to him with my questions. I'd often observed Christianity practiced by teachers and students in high school in the form of prayers and songs, especially during the Christmas season. Local white preachers, as well as others in town for a few days to run revival meetings, were invited to deliver a sermon at one of the weekly meetings of the entire student body in the auditorium. My typing teacher occasionally began class with a mini-sermon five or ten minutes long. Concluding, she would point her index finger at the first student in one of the rows of desks and ask, "Are you saved?" and then go to the next student, and the next, stopping at the third or fourth. The question was rhetorical. She didn't expect us to answer. She wanted us to think about the consequences of not being saved and to instill in us a fear of going to Hell. I was the only Jew in her class (as well as in my graduating class of 135 students) and when she pointed to the row in which I sat in the second or third desk, I kept my head down and waited for her sermon to end. One of my friends in high school told me he'd been ordained and he often led prayer meetings in one of the classrooms during the noon hour. On Saturday afternoons, after eating a sandwich at the Walgreen's soda fountain during my thirty-minute lunch-break from working at my father's store, I used to walk across the street to listen to the volunteer preacher of the day (ordained or not, I didn't know) speak to a small group of people, mostly men, standing in front of the Forrest County Courthouse and near the Confederate monument. While holding a Bible in his left hand, he kept his right hand raised and used it to punctuate the points he was making. What drew me there, aside from my interest in religious questions, was the confident flow of the preacher's words in the rhythms and idioms of Southern speech and mixed with quotations from the English of the King James translation of the Old Testament and the New. On Sundays, I could hear a more refined sermon on the radio given by a preacher from one of the older, well-established churches in Hattiesburg, followed by a hymn such as "Rock of Ages" or "What a Friend We Have in Jesus" sung by the entire congregation.

When I asked my father one day if he thought there was a heaven or hell, he replied "I never got a letter from there." His ironic tone and skepticism appealed to me more than the seemingly perfunctory repetition of prayers I heard in temple. I wish now I'd asked him specifically if he believed in God. Perhaps I hesitated to put the question in so direct a way, or maybe I just assumed from his reply to my first question that the unasked one was unnecessary. In any case, he could hardly object to my adopting his skepticism. But I think he became concerned that my questions about religion might be leading me away from Judaism. Although he'd been eager to adapt to American life and to find acceptance here, he was equally committed to keeping his Jewish identity and he naturally wanted to see his children keep theirs. I doubt he ever thought I was interested in converting, though he would have seen the occasional story in the paper about a converted Jew who had been invited to speak at a local church (such as the one that appeared on April 9, 1929, headlined "Christianized Jew Preaching at Hub Church"). Rabbi Mantinband once took me and two of my friends from the congregation to see a converted Jew speak at a local church. The only thing I remember about his talk, aside from our sitting near the back of the church and people turning to look at us, is that it was rambling and difficult to follow.

I decided to take my questions to Rabbi Mantinband and he took time out from his busy schedule to meet with me on occasion after school. I don't remember exactly how many times we met, but I went to see him intermittently over a period of several months. We used to sit in the two lawn chairs he kept under the oak tree in the front yard of his house, which sat diagonally across the street from the temple and was owned by the congregation. I must have seemed to him to be an argumentative young upstart, rushing into age-old controversies with little knowledge or understanding. Did Jews now really believe in the God of the Old Testament and the prayer books? I also remember asking at one point if Judaism wasn't theologically vague, a little like an Ethical Cultural Society (which I'd recently seen mentioned in a book I was reading, but really knew nothing about), at least when compared to Christianity, which seemed so confident and explicit about its divine trinity, the personal relationship one was urged to have with Jesus, and the certainty of an afterlife. But my interest wasn't as much in the differences between the two religions and conceptions of God as it was in the question of whether there was a God. His reply to that question came in the form of a humorous anecdote. A distinguished Baptist preacher—Harry Emerson Fosdick in the anecdote—once entertained a friend who was a well-known agnostic and when they went into the preacher's library-study the agnostic saw displayed on a table a beautiful replica of the solar system. He was amazed and fascinated and asked who made it. "No one," the preacher said, "it just popped into existence." I doubt that Rabbi Mantinband felt this was all one could or needed to say on the subject, but he offered it in this instance as an amusing and clever response to the question of whether there is a God and I think the anecdote, with its use of irony to mock the notion that something could come from nothing and in that way to affirm the existence of God, serves as a memorable example of the most widely accepted of first-cause explanations of the universe.

For him, however, the most pressing questions weren't philosophical or theological, but moral and social. I didn't know that then, but I've since learned it from reading his published (and a number of unpublished) essays and talks. He believed the moral code embodied in the Ten Commandments and in the words of the Hebrew prophets represented, were revelations of, a divine spirit. The practice of Judaism at its best, in its most thoughtful expression, was an adherence to, a living up to, principles found in those works. After a rabbinical version of the psychoanalyst's fifty-minute hour, he would look at his watch and ask me if I would drop him off at the post office on my way to town. He didn't own a car, he wore extremely thick glasses, and in the last years of his life he was slowly going blind.

Although I've not been able to learn for certain, I believe he was the one who suggested to my father and Jerry Shemper's father that the two of us go to a weekend conference for Jewish youth at the Hebrew Union College in Cincinnati in the spring of 1953. While there I was fortunate to have a brief conversation with a rabbi who listened to my questions and doubts and then replied that he thought there was no difficulty in being both Jewish and agnostic, implying that many Jews were. Obvious now, but liberating then! Despite any concerns my father may have had, however, I never questioned my identity as a Jew or had any interest in another religion. To believe or not believe; that was the question. In some of the poems, novels, and other works I was reading then I found discussions of that question conducted with a directness, knowledge, and understanding entirely new to me, as well as a mastery of language that greatly enhanced both the reading experience and the sense of discovery. I felt drawn to poets, novelists, and other writers who explored that question and other related ones and I still remember the thrill of reading for the first time several of Plato's Socratic dialogues, Edward Fitzgerald's translation of *The Rubaiyat of Omar Khayyam*, Maugham's *Of Human Bondage*, *The Razor's Edge*, and *The Summing Up*, and, a little later, Dostoevsky's *Crime and Punishment* and *The Brothers Karamazov*.

Another important book then was Clarence Darrow's *The Story of My Life*, especially the chapters on why he was an agnostic. It was Rabbi Mantinband who recommended it to me. He never mentioned, however, that he'd once debated Darrow on the question "Is Religion Necessary?" I learned of their debate only recently while reading Mantinband's papers. It took place at the Majestic Theater on November 30, 1932, in Williamsport, Pennsylvania, where Mantinband was the rabbi of Temple Beth Ha-Sholom from 1926 to 1941. In his typed notes for an announcement of the event, he provided a rationale for such a debate and he may well have used these notes in the debate itself. "Religion, like every other phenomenon of man's experience, must be subject from time to time to honest inquiry. It must be tested, likewise, as to its reality and truth." Observing that "the trend of our times and the temper of the age" involved questioning religion, he added that there was a "wave of agnosticism... prevalent on our college campus grounds." But then he pointed out that this wasn't new. "Even back in Matthew Arnold's day," he wrote, "belief in spiritual things was running low," and he quoted the following lines from "Dover Beach," in which Arnold in 1851 said of the "Sea of Faith,"

> But now I only hear
> Its melancholy, long, withdrawing roar,
> Retreating, to the breath
> Of the night wind.[6]

In Darrow's brief reply accepting Mantinband's invitation to debate, he closed with a little humor: "I will try to put some other [speaking engagements] in on the trip, and if I succeed I will endeavor to be as fair as I can about your share of the expenses—at least as fair as a 'Christian' can be expected to be with a Jew." At the debate, Mantinband displayed his own sense of humor when he remarked of Darrow, whose most famous cases—among them, the Leopold-Loeb murder trial, the Scopes evolution trial, and the defense of socialist Eugene V. Debs—were taken on at some self-sacrifice in the pursuit of justice, that he was "an example of a religious man in spite of himself." The next day *The Williamsport Sun* reported that Mantinband's point was "the most amusing of the whole evening" and noted that while the audience was applauding, "Darrow on the stage 'rocked back and forth with high glee.'"[7]

What I remembered from my reading of Darrow's discussion of religion in his memoir was the clarity and directness with which he posed and addressed the questions I was interested in, particularly in three chapters near the end about the existence of a God and the belief in an afterlife. On reading them again recently, I rediscovered the argumentative bent to his discussion of religion that had been so appealing to me then. Eventually I would discover Jewish novelists, literary critics, memoirists, and historians of the Holocaust whose thinking and writing and strong sense of themselves as Jews didn't depend on religious belief or observance. In his attempt to account for the sense of Jewishness that the non-believing Freud felt and expressed in letters and several works, particularly *Moses and Monotheism*, the Judaic scholar Yosef Yerushalmi suggested a "subjective dimension, the feeling, harbored and expressed by committed and alienated modern Jews alike, of the enormous weight, the gravitational pull, of the Jewish past, whether it be felt as an anchor or a burden." He goes on to link this "feeling" to something genetic, "a trilling wire in the blood," in part because of Freud's own speculations in *Moses and Monotheism* about a genetic legacy.[8] What I find persuasive isn't the notion of any genetic legacy but rather "the enormous weight, the gravitational pull" of the long history of a people from biblical times to the present, through slavery and centuries of persecution, who nevertheless made significant contributions to the moral, cultural, and intellectual life in the West. It's with this history and the people who lived it, I think, that many non-observant Jews, not just Freud, have felt a strong connection, a sense of identification, especially after the Holocaust. For me, this sense of identification began with—and is kept alive by memories of—my parents, our home and family, the Passover table, individuals in our Jewish community, and Rabbi Mantinband.

For a number of years now, especially since beginning to write this book and learning about his life and work, I've come to feel a sharp sense of guilt about my failure to stay in touch with him. He showed great patience and understanding in listening to me. Instead of countering with arguments in support of belief, he recommended a book by a famous lawyer and doubter who had set forth a clear rationale for not believing. Like the best teachers I've known, he was helping me toward a better understanding of the issues by encouraging me to read and to think about them and reach whatever conclusion I would. A few years after those meetings, when I had the opportunity to spend my junior year as a student at the University of Munich, he gave me the names of friends in Geneva and London whom I could contact and perhaps stay with (and did) during my travels that year. It was characteristic of him, I would learn, to show this kind of generous concern for many others who came to him for advice.

From our conversations, however, I came away knowing very little about his life prior to his arrival in Hattiesburg, only that he was from Virginia. I don't recall the subject of segregation ever turning up. The *Brown* decision was still a few years down the road. Although I would later hear a little about his activities in the civil rights movement, it was only after beginning to write this book that I became interested in learning what those activities were, how they caused concerns in the congregation, and how he would eventually decide to leave for another pulpit.

In my research, I've not been able to learn if he was asked what his views on segregation were when he was interviewed for the job in Hattiesburg. The issue was one that rabbis interviewed for pulpits in the South could expect to be raised. When Rabbi Ben Goldstein was interviewed in 1929 by leaders of Temple Beth Or in Montgomery, he was "warned from the very start . . . not to speak about 'the Negro question.'"[9] When Rabbi Perry Nussbaum was interviewed for the pulpit of Jackson's Temple Beth Israel, "the very first question the rabbinic search committee posed was 'Doctor, what's your position on school desegregation?'"[10] Two years prior to Rabbi Mantinband's arrival in Hattiesburg, however, the search committee had failed to ask Rabbi Avery Grossfield what his views were and instead simply announced when he arrived, "We don't speak on the 'nigger' problem here." Refusing to be silenced, he immediately told the president that he "would speak on the subject whenever he saw fit" and that he did not intend to remain in Hattiesburg after the expiration of his one-year contract.[11] If, after this experience, the search committee decided not to raise the issue with Rabbi Mantinband, they may have thought, not unreasonably, that since he was a Southerner by birth and had been in Alabama since 1946 as rabbi for the Tri-Cities Congregation of Florence, Sheffield, and Tuscumbia, it was unnecessary.

Though born in New York, he had grown up in Norfolk and attended segregated schools. When he returned to New York to attend CCNY, he unexpectedly encountered the issue and made a decision that would eventually determine how he would be remembered. Finding himself "in a class seated alphabetically next to a black student," as his wife Anna Kest Mantinband recounts in her unpublished memoir, he "promptly walked out of the room in protest." In a meeting with the instructor he was told "you are not in the south now and you had better change your thinking, or withdraw." "That was the beginning," she recalls: "he changed."[12] But the change hadn't been easy, as he recalled many years later. "First, I had to learn—and it was very hard for me, because I am a product of a segregated society—to the degree to which I could exercise control over my attitudes, never to make any distinction between man and man. . . . Second—and this came even a little harder—I schooled myself never to sit in the company of people, whether it be in a service club or a church meeting, in a home or in a chamber of commerce meeting, and listen to a word of bigotry spoken in a context of any importance, and by my silence seem to lend approval to the bigoted utterance." Then, "Quietly, if not always persuasively, I make certain that the opposing point of view is heard in the meeting."[13]

The silence he was disavowing had been a time-honored custom of Jews in the South. Prior to the *Brown* decision and the beginning of the civil rights movement, most Jews weren't opposed to desegregation and some were in favor of it, but they felt they had no choice but to conform to local customs and remain silent. Not to do so was to risk financial ruin or violence, possibly both. In the first part of the century their fear was based on their own observations and experiences of anti-Semitism, their knowledge of it in the old country (kept alive by the memories of the East European Jewish immigrants among them), the lynching of Leo Frank in 1915, the increasing anti-Semitism in this country during the 1920s and 1930s, and the anti-Semitic thunder coming across the Atlantic from Hitler's new Germany.

It was only in looking back, however, that I recognized how the silence about segregation was a feature of everyday life when I was growing up. Segregation wasn't a topic of discussion in our home or in school or among my friends. The exceptions for me were a few occasions when I discussed it with Fay and "B" and, at their suggestion, read a little, probably as much as I could understand then, of their copy of Gunnar Myrdal's *An American Dilemma* and gained a sense of how deep and seemingly intractable a problem it was. It's possible I had discussions with others, but I have no memory of any. Silence on that subject had become second nature. After the bombings of several synagogues and Jewish community centers in the 1950s, as historian Clive Webb has shown, "a pervasive sense of fear seized Jews throughout the South" and the fear reinforced the silence.[14] The fear wasn't new, of course, as incidents from the past, including the Wexler case, make clear, but the danger now was immeasurably greater.

Yet Mantinband was one of a small number of rabbis in the South who had begun to speak out before the *Brown* decision and the beginning of the civil rights movement. In doing so, they exercised caution and discretion and for this reason have been remembered as *The Quiet Voices* in an anthology of essays with that title. They spoke to their congregations and to biracial audiences on certain occasions about the injustices of segregation and they worked quietly behind the scenes, at times alone, at other times in concert with fellow clergymen in the Christian community. For example, in the 1920s Rabbi Morris Newfield in Birmingham joined with a number of Christian clergymen to promote interfaith programs that would combat Klan activities in Alabama. He went against his congregants' wishes in refusing to fire a black janitor of Temple Emanu-El who, though accused of murder, had been acquitted; he developed a friendship with Booker T. Washington and accepted invitations to speak at Tuskegee Institute; and he publicly supported the rights of black coal miners to join the United Mine Workers.[15] In 1917 in Memphis, after a black man accused of raping and decapitating a sixteen-year old white girl was burned alive before 15,000 witnesses in a carnival-like atmosphere of celebration, Rabbi William Fineshriber told his congregation "we ought to be the first to state publicly what we think about the horrible thing of burning a Negro." He met with the editor of the *Commercial Appeal* to persuade him to write an editorial condemning the lynching, then with other clergymen, including six black ministers, to consider a resolution condemning it and mob violence, and then again with the editor to persuade him to publish it. Fineshriber "was the only Memphis clergyman," historian Berkley Kalin points out, "with the courage and conviction to criticize the Ku Klux Klan, even from the pulpit."[16] In 1944 Rabbi Sidney Wolf of Corpus Christi and other clergymen created an interracial commission to deal with racial resentments that were stirred "when black and Hispanic soldiers were refused service at Anglo restaurants and stores"; and in the early 1950s, when "African Americans sought to integrate the city's municipal golf course. . . . Wolf pushed the measure through while sitting on the Park and Recreation Department Board" and later succeeded with a motion to integrate the concessions, locker rooms, and showers.[17]

Without detracting from the courage these rabbis showed, I think it's relevant to note that most of those who spoke up had pulpits in large cities such as Atlanta, Birmingham, Little Rock, Memphis, New Orleans, and San Antonio with Jewish populations in 1950 over 1,000. Atlanta had 12,000, and even a smaller city such as Corpus Christi had 1,100. In contrast, the two cities in Mississippi, Hattiesburg and Jackson, whose rabbis spoke up—Mantinband and Perry Nussbaum, both now widely recognized for their courage in civil rights activities—had congregations in 1950 of 184 and 300, respectively. If there was a sense of security in numbers in large cities, there was one of great vulnerability in small towns and cities. In addition, since Mississippi was the one southern state with no large city, as well as the one most given to violent resistance to integration (despite considerable competition for that distinction from neighboring Deep South states), the roles of Mantinband and Nussbaum seem all the more notable.

Although the bombing of the Temple in Atlanta in 1958 "blew open the wall of silence," in the words of Janice Rothschild Blumberg, and religious leaders and other progressive people there "found the courage to speak," most rabbis and Jews elsewhere in the South, especially in small towns, continued to remain silent.[18] Mantinband was one of those who had the courage to speak. While he knew the fears Jews in small towns felt from his experience in the Tri-Cities area in Alabama and in Hattiesburg, he also knew that a similar fear prevailed in the white, Gentile, middle-class majority. "There is a conspiracy of silence," he wrote in an essay entitled "Rabbi in the Deep South." "The [only] voices heard are those of the blatant, raucous segregationist[s]." Although "everybody here speaks on the subjects I do . . . they do it behind closed doors and in whispers." He understood his congregants' fears of "reprisal, harassment,

Rabbi Mantinband speaking to students at a black college.

[and] violence."[19] "After all," he said, "they are merchants for the most part, and depend for their survival upon the good will of their neighbors. The economic, political, and social pressures on all sides are fearsome. One can understand their misgivings when a rabbi identifies himself publicly with a progressive or liberal cause."[20] Nonetheless, he felt bound to keep his vow. He was following in the tradition of the Hebrew prophets and their message of social justice. He believed that religion should "transcend prayer and ritual . . . to come to grips with pressing matters in the social, educational, and political life of the country."[21] Since he also believed that segregation was "the supreme sin of our day" and "as monstrous an evil as any in our Western civilization," he felt compelled to speak out.[22]

Behind the vow and the tradition of prophetic Judaism lay two experiences from the 1930s that helped me understand what Rabbi Mantinband referred to as "the spirit" that motivated him. In three untitled and undated pages I found among his papers, Mantinband wrote that it was then that he and his wife Anna "sought to rescue the victims of the Nazi holocaust."[23] When he was the rabbi in Williamsport, Pennsylvania, he learned of a Jewish judge in Vienna who found himself in trouble after the *Anschluss* and needed to escape. With the help of friends and with bribes to local officials, the judge had been able to secure a visa to America. But he needed affidavits guaranteeing fulltime employment. Mantinband went to see the president of Dickinson College in Carlisle, who was "sympathetic but reluctant." He next saw the chairman of the board of trustees, who allowed him a ten-minute appearance before the entire board. When one of its members claimed that "this college has never retained a Jew on its faculty, and would be establishing a precedent," Mantinband, having done his homework, was able to reply, "In 1873 there was a Jew on your faculty teaching German and Hebrew . . . Rabbi Michael Wurzel of Congregation Beth Ha-Sholom" in Williamsport, something Mantinband knew from temple records, and the college archives would later verify.[24] The judge was hired. It was also during the 1930s when Rabbi Mantinband and his wife adopted two orphaned brothers from Germany, ages ten and thirteen, who became American citizens and eventually veterans of World War II and the Korean War.[25] Reflecting on his life many years later, on the occasion of becoming the first recipient of the George Brussel Memorial Award at the Stephen Wise Free Synagogue in New York "for exceptional devotion to individual freedom and social justice, in the spirit of the Hebrew prophets," Rabbi Mantinband recalled advice Rabbi Wise had given him: "Charles, the best sermon you can preach, you will manage without opening your mouth. It is by the life you live, the example you set, the influence you exercise."[26]

The period of his life when he set the example for which he is now remembered was his time in Hattiesburg. His commitment to the cause of civil rights, however, preceded his arrival, as well as the civil rights movement itself. In June of 1951 he was asked to deliver the baccalaureate address to the graduating class of Sterling High School in Sheffield. To prepare for it, he wrote to a dozen distinguished Americans—among them, Eleanor Roosevelt, Ralph Bunche, and Walter Francis White—to ask if he should make any reference to "the difficulties facing Negro youth." It may be that the words of Bunche were those best remembered by everyone in the audience that day: "We are Americans, first and last, not Negroes nor Afro-Americans, nor 'colored brethren.' As Americans, we should demand equality for all our citizens. And let not any disadvantage of race serve as a handy alibi. Nothing is easy of attainment, and yet in America nothing is impossible."[27] When I found this talk in Mantinband's papers, I was struck by the initiative he had taken to write distinguished Americans and quote them rather than hold forth entirely on his own. His primary concern was to encourage and inspire the young, reminding me of my own experience with him, and his address, given three years before the *Brown* decision, is an example of the kind of activism practiced by a number of rabbis in the South, who worked behind the scenes years before the beginning of the civil rights movement.

For what he said at another speaking engagement in Alabama, however, this one in Montgomery in February of 1956 (just two months after Rosa Parks was arrested for refusing to give up her seat on a bus and move to the colored section), he received wide newspaper coverage, most notably in the *New York Times*, and brought him unwanted attention in the *Hattiesburg American*, which got him into trouble with some in his congregation. The occasion was the annual meeting of the Alabama Council on Human Relations held at Alabama State College for Negroes. His talk was well received by the integrated audience of three hundred people, especially when he refuted a charge made the previous night by Mississippi's Senator James Eastland at a rally of White Citizens' Councils in the same city. The senator had claimed that the NAACP was a Communist-front organization and on the attorney general's list of subversive organizations. When Mantinband was asked a question about the NAACP, he said that he wasn't a member, didn't want to speak about it, and referred to it as one of "many other militant groups." His decision not to join was deliberate. He knew the NAACP was widely perceived in the South to be a Communist-front organization and, for the sake of his effectiveness in working with local individuals and community organizations, he wanted to be able to say, "I'm not an NAACP member." In fact, he contributed money to its legal defense fund, was a long-time friend of its future president Kivie Kaplan, and became a life-time member after moving to Texas.[28] But now at the meeting in Montgomery he went on to observe that "the NAACP, more than any other group, has made possible the Supreme Court decision," and for this he was greeted with a "loud round of applause." Then, with Senator Eastland's claim of the previous night in mind, he said "I happen to have the attorney-general's list in my coat pocket, and the NAACP's name is not on it." [29]

But it was something else he said at the meeting that sparked the controversy in Hattiesburg. In the paper's front-page coverage of the event the following day, the story was given the headline "Local Rabbi Says Race Problems Stink" and opened with the sentence "A Hattiesburg rabbi says many of his experiences in Mississippi race problems were 'tragic and regretful and smelled to high heaven.'"[30] The headline misquoted Mantinband and when he saw the story he sat down and wrote the following letter to the editor:

> The writer is always embarrassed when he appears on the front page of a news paper. The word "stink" in your headline is not in my vocabulary, nor do I consider it in good journalistic taste. I was quoting *Hamlet*... wherein the King says "O my offence is rank. It smells to heaven. It hath the primal

eldest curse upon it—a brother's murder." It seemed to me that the quotation was both apt and eloquent. But perhaps you do not read Shakespeare.[31]

Several years later in his essay "Rabbi in the Deep South," Mantinband would misquote the headline, substituting "Relations" for "Problems," though the substitution seems more specific and accurate.

To avoid more unwanted publicity for his congregation and himself, he decided not to send the letter. If he had sent it, however, he would have made clear why his use of the quote was so apt, particularly the reference to the "primal eldest curse." King Claudius' crime was not only regicide but also fratricide, as Mississippi's racial killings were in the larger sense that all men are brothers. The brotherhood of all men was often invoked by black preachers, most notably by Martin Luther King, Jr. in his "Letter from a Birmingham Jail," though they naturally had in mind, in addition to whatever moral and religious meanings were attached to that ideal, a more specific reference to legal, political, and social equality in the here and now. But Mantinband had not held back the year before. In his Yom Kippur sermon then, "What Mississippi Has to Atone For," he had condemned the murder of Emmett Till.[32]

Although the event in Montgomery and its aftermath were mentioned briefly by him in his essay "Rabbi in the Deep South" and by his wife Anna in her unpublished memoir, and have since been described by historian Clive Webb, the rabbi's diary record of his meetings with members of his congregation at that time has only recently become available. I learned of its existence quite accidentally from a news item that appeared on the internet on September 15, 2015, reporting that a collection of "eight boxes of personal letters, journals, diaries and scrapbooks" had been donated to the Institute of Southern Jewish Life in Jackson by his daughter Carol Ginsburg and his grandchildren.[33] After contacting Rachel Meyer at the ISJL and making arrangements for a visit, Alice and I drove down to Jackson to spend several days reading the diaries and other materials and found his entries devoted to his meetings with members of the congregation (as well as the entry about the Wexler case that I mentioned in chapter 3). The entries for the next ten days provided me with a detailed and dramatic account of what had actually happened behind the scenes. The fear being acted out in these meetings seemed to me to be a later version of the fear that had been acted out in the Wexler case.

On the Monday he wrote the letter to the editor, he also wrote the following entry: "The Htbg Story Breaks. Temple Board meets in panic—they fear the worst. A few . . . are inclined to support the Rabbi, others censure him.

Committee of 5 . . . wait on me to talk it over. They would like to silence me altogether on the race question, to insure the peace and guarantee security. I try to allay their genuine concerns and promise nothing." Over the next ten days he records how the conflict unfolds, providing brief summaries of the meetings in a pithy style highlighted with a few quotations and revealing the fears behind the silence and low profile that had long been the public face of the congregation on racial issues. In the first meeting, at least, the mood isn't without some humor. "One man says, 'I don't know whether I want to be seen with you tomorrow'—this in jest," Mantinband notes. It was Dave Matison, one of the owners of the Fine Bros.-Matison stores and a strong supporter of the rabbi. He had been invited to accompany him to a Rotary Club meeting where Mantinband would give a talk.[34]

On the next day, Tuesday, he writes "we let the fury rage and hope it will die down," noting that the Rotary meeting was pleasant, that he was welcomed at the Methodist Church in Purvis for the third consecutive year, and that he'd had a brief conversation with a friend, the manager of the Sears store in Hattiesburg, who "kids me about getting free front page publicity, whereas he must pay advertising rate & take the inside pages."[35]

On Wednesday, however, the Congregation held an emergency meeting. He wasn't sure what had taken place, but soon learns from five members. "Again a committee calls on me—this time with new faces—and they demand cancellation of the Tougaloo visit . . . tho I think they are mistaken in their judgment, it is not important and I concur," relenting a little from his earlier "I promise nothing" stand in the meeting with the first committee of five. "They drink tea, eat cake, are friendly—but censure. Again I beg them to cool off—not do so much gossiping about it." During the meeting Professor John F. Nau, chair of the Department of Philosophy and Religion at Mississippi Southern College, comes in and, as Rabbi Mantinband records in his diary, "I ask him point blank in their presence . . . is my status, reputation, acceptability for Religious Emphasis Week o.k. at the College? And get an excellent endorsement. . . . Nau tells my people I 'belong to the College' & can always be relied upon to speak with dignity & propriety, embarrassing no one."[36] Did this committee of five wonder if Nau's appearing that day was purely by chance? Even if they thought it had been arranged, however, they would have had to respect Professor Nau and be pleased to hear his praise of their rabbi.

He spends Thursday in Laurel and there he's told by Milton Fine and Dave Matison that they believe "this is a tempest in a teapot," though they report that "many people who esteem me are surprised at this arch-Southern position" taken by some members of the congregation. They also tell him "that Citizens Councils have been formed in our two counties with respectable membership—but that they [those who have joined] see no need for publicity & so far remain incognito," to which Mantinband then writes, talking to himself, "Draw your own conclusions."[37] Is he thinking that their remaining incognito is an acknowledgment that joining is wrong? Or that some of them are Jews? A small number of Jews in Mississippi did in fact join the White Citizens' Councils, as he knew. During a two-week exchange of pulpits with Mantinband in January of 1958, Rabbi Julius Rosenthal of Vassar Temple in Poughkeepsie, New York, came away from his midwinter sojourn in the deep South believing that there were "only five rabid segregationists" in the congregation, though I don't know if any of these men or others in the congregation joined the local Citizens' Council.[38]

Following the request made by the second committee of five, and in a spirit of accommodation, Mantinband sent a telegram canceling upcoming visits to two black institutions—Tougaloo College, where he was scheduled to be a lecturer for two days, representing the Jewish Chautauqua Society and explaining Judaism, and Copiah-Lincoln Junior College. He also sent follow-up letters. From Chaplain and Professor John D. Mangram at Tougaloo he received a reply expressing disappointment, not simply in the cancellation but also in Jews in the South. "I guess I shouldn't be [disappointed] since I am aware that all religious groups are pretty similar here in the south. Somehow, I had prayed that Judaism here would somehow be an exception to the rule. Somewhere in the back of my mind I had harbored the idea that the Jewish people took the idea of the Fatherhood of God seriously." In spite of his disappointment, however, he reassures Mantinband that he will be welcome "whenever you feel that you are in a position to come." [39]

On Friday, two more members of the congregation come to see him. It's been a long week and now in this "session" he senses something going wrong. One of his visitors, whom Mantinband describes as "now eagerly cooperative," says he "wants to get a large turnout 'as a vote of confidence.' . . . He wants talk of it (both sides) at the Temple." Mantinband is wary of the proposal. A year before, on hearing the Yom Kippur sermon "What Mississippi Has to Atone For" after the lynching of Emmett Till, this man had walked out and "vowed never to return to the synagogue as long as this rabbi was in the pulpit."[40] Now, after hearing the proposal, he rejects it. Later, while recording his thoughts in his diary and recalling this man's past behavior, he explains why. Having seen a Trojan Horse in this man's proposal of a vote of confidence and not trusting him, he remembers the line in Virgil's *Aeneid* (and writes it in his diary in the Latin of the poem) when the priest Laocoön warns the Trojans "I fear the Greeks even when bringing presents."⁴¹ Then he writes of the proposal, "I will not hear of it," presumably having said something to that effect to this man.⁴²

But the attempt at intimidation didn't end here. The man also told him that the president of the congregation had run into the editor of the *Hattiesburg American* on the street and the editor had said "if your Rabbi behaves himself, we'll say no more—Else—we are not responsible for what happens." To this, Mantinband replied: "I don't take kindly to threats, nor scare easily. Tell the Editor he owes me an apology." Then, continuing to describe what he'd just learned about the encounter on the street, he writes, "Andrew [Harmon, the editor] says 'my behavior' reflects on the whole Jewish community—adversely—[and in] his tirade [he] asked 'What has ever happened to your Rabbi [?] Has he lost his mind [?]' Says I live in a fool's paradise if I think I can get away with my radical opinions."⁴³

After the two men left, Mantinband immediately sent the "stink story" to Francis S. Harmon, the brother of the editor and the majority stock owner of the *Hattiesburg American*. He wasn't aware that a letter from Francis was at that moment on its way to him. They were fellow Rotarians and he had once introduced Francis at a Rotary meeting. Francis had read the *New York Times* story about the meeting in Montgomery and probably had also seen the coverage of it in the *Hattiesburg American*. On receiving the letter at the end of this stressful week, Mantinband was pleased and encouraged: "Wonderful letter of admiration and Endorsement from F. Stuart Harmon. . . . If there were any doubt heretofore of my position, I am now doubly reassured." ⁴⁴ Five days later, Francis sent another letter, this one to Herman Katz, a founding member of the congregation and respected figure in the Jewish community, praising Rabbi Mantinband and enclosing a contribution to the United Jewish Appeal. He explains that the contribution "comes as a token of appreciation for the fine leadership which your Rabbi is giving in the difficult field of interracial relations. . . . Also the gift evidences our pleasure that Congregation B'nai Israel is giving your spiritual leader complete freedom to proclaim the truth as he sees it when so many congregations, as for example the Presbyterian Church in Durant, Miss. take an entirely different position. . . . If religious leaders can't speak freely, they can't really lead us." He concludes with "More power to your courageous and talented Rabbi." ⁴⁵

Although he's also received expressions of praise from a number of people in the white Gentile community, he writes, "few Jews discuss the matter." It's as if discussion "would lead to . . . a foul disease."⁴⁶ He's heard that Hodding

Carter "fears that before this business is over, we'll have a siege of anti-Semitism—who knows [?] I hope he is mistaken. But we'll watch carefully & exercise discretion & caution."[47] On Thursday, now ten days after the front-page coverage of the "stink story," he writes, "A quiet day & the incident is completely over. Last night I taught school ... and the respect I get by the teenagers, as they heard of the antics of their Elders[.] 'Aren't they absurd.' Fan mail continues—the students at MSC [Mississippi Southern College]—certain local townspeople whom I do not know." [48] Among the letters he received, one in particular must have brought him a great deal of satisfaction. It was from five students at MSC, one a former high school classmate of mine, Rosa Lynn Hemeter. "To see the condition of the state and the South are in," they wrote, "and to read what the leaders of the state have to say about segregation is very grievous to us.... [We want] to let you know that there are some of us who heartily approve of what you have said and done."[49]

While that incident appeared to be over, there would be others in the next six years that would require him to be not only discreet in speech but also quick on his feet. One occurred two years later, shortly after the bombing of the Temple in Atlanta in October of 1958. As Mantinband emerged from the post office and started to walk home, he encountered a former mayor of Hattiesburg who was now president of the local White Citizens' Council. After a friendly greeting, the president said, "I told my boys at the last Council meeting how foolish it was to bomb a synagogue, which after all was lifeless, and which was a house of God. I hope they would not do anything like that in our city of Hattiesburg. If they want to know who the real mischief-maker was, his name was Rabbi Mantinband. ... I know him; I know him well. I know his personal habits. I know where he lives, and I can tell you how to get at him if you decide that's what you need or want to do." "Well," Mantinband recalled in 1966 when he was interviewed by Rabbi Allen Krause (for a series of interviews with rabbis in the South that could not be published for fifty years and appeared in 2016 in the volume *To Stand Aside or Stand Alone: Southern Rabbis and the Civil Rights Movement*), "I could not believe my ears because this was a threat of violence by a fellow who was in dead earnest, and thought he would impress me. I had to do some quick thinking; I don't scare easily. ... So I took out a pen and a piece of paper and ... I noted the time, I noted the place, and I noted exactly what he had said. 'What are you doing?' said this gentleman." Mantinband replied "I'm going to take it to the FBI, and I'm going to take it to the first five representative white Christians I meet in this town. I'm going to say to them, 'Mr. so-and-so, president of the White Citizens' Council, threatened me in this fashion, and if ever in the next ten years anything ever happens to me, I'm going to ask them to arrest you for creating the climate in which this type of thing would be possible.' 'Oh!' he says, 'don't do that; you know I was only trying to be funny. I was only joking; I didn't really mean it that way.' But I did go to the FBI and I did go to these five people, and that fellow . . . never looked me in the face again because I had called his hand."[50]

In another incident that year the White Citizens' Council took advantage of the Mantinbands' summer travels abroad to write to one of the congregation's prominent members to urge that "this was a good time" for the congregation to get rid of its "mischief-making Rabbi" and to repeat the now familiar threat that "otherwise we cannot be responsible for the consequences." This matter didn't come to full light, however, until six months later when the congregation received a contribution of $2,500 from a national foundation in honor of its rabbi's "sane approach and wisdom in dealing with the race issue." The temple board hesitated to accept the money. They were afraid of reprisals. His response was characteristically direct. "I made it clear that if it were refused, the temple would not only lose the money, but its rabbi as well. I received a five-to-one majority approval, and ultimately life tenure."[51]

Although he now had a strong majority supporting him, he still had to avoid attracting public attention to his activities and put up with thinly veiled threats that came with repeated invasions of his and his wife Anna's privacy in their everyday life. In her memoir, she recalls that "across the street from our home was a bench for the convenience of people awaiting the bus" and "from this bench our front door was under constant surveillance." Once, after she had gotten on the bus, "the watcher on the bench entered and seated himself next to me, although the bus was not half full." "'I see the reverend is taking a trip,' he started right in. 'I seed him get into a car with a New York license yesterday. I got a little book; I knows every move the reverend makes.'" They were also subjected to other forms of intimidation. "When we picked up our mail at the post office, much of it had been opened." Although Mantinband was not a member of the NAACP at this time, Anna Mantinband said they received its magazine *Crisis* in blank brown covers" and, presumably, it, too, was opened. Even their black friends who had been guests at their table "avoided recognition when they met on the steps of the post office or anywhere else in town, lest they create trouble for their friend."[52] In order to avoid publicity he decided not to inform the congregation of all his activities. On one occasion, however, former president of the congregation Maury Gurwitch, after having been told by the rabbi "I'll be gone this weekend," turned on the television and saw him sitting on a stage at an NAACP convention in Miami. More than once Gurwitch said to him, "Rabbi you are scaring us. You know they could burn houses down. They could burn stores down. They could put us out of business and I really wish you would curtail these activities. And he said, 'Maury, I will not be muzzled. I am going to do what I am going to do.' So he really kind of scared us, but we never had any problems" (meaning, I assume, that no houses or stores were burned down).[53]

But there were other occasions when the rabbi knew he couldn't avoid public attention. The most disturbing of these involved a young black veteran, Clyde Kennard. Born in Hattiesburg, he served in the army for seven years in Germany and Korea, earned a Bronze Star and the rank of sergeant, and then completed two years of study at the University of Chicago before deciding to return home to help his widowed mother with her small farm. Wanting to continue his studies, he applied to MSC, in part because it was only a fifteen-minute drive away, but mainly because he wanted to break down the segregation barrier. It was the only way "to attain the goal of first class citizenship," he wrote in December of 1958 in one of several letters to the editor of the *Hattiesburg American* explaining his reasons for applying.[54] Nine months later, following a meeting with MSC President William D. McCain about his application, he was met by two constables waiting for him by his car and was arrested for reckless driving on his way to the meeting and for possession of five bottles of whiskey, though, as Mantinband knew from his friendship with him, he was a teetotaler and someone who made it a point never to exceed the speed limit.[55] Kennard was fined one hundred dollars for speeding and five hundred for possession of five bottles of whiskey.

Mantinband had come to know Kennard through Dave Matison, for whom Kennard had worked over a period of several years, beginning in 1952 when he wanted to earn money to attend the University of Chicago. After returning from Chicago, he again worked for Matison and, through him, for Mantinband, who employed him to do work at the synagogue. Fay and "B" also employed him to do work around their house and lawn. Since Mantinband didn't drive, he asked Kennard to drive him to speaking engagements in other cities. Anna Mantinband recalls that Kennard "sometimes stopped his truck at our front door and felt free to interrupt the rabbi's reading for a brief visit."[56] They used to sit in the same two lawn chairs under the oak tree in the front yard that I remember from my own visits a few years before. Mantinband came to like and respect him for his work, honesty, and intelligence, as did Dave Matison, and both sympathized with his goals of integration and full citizenship. But they tried to dissuade him from applying to MSC, Mantinband advising him to go to some other school to obtain a bachelor's degree and only then return to apply to the graduate program at MSC, to which, they believed, he would then have had a better chance of gaining admission. Following Mantinband's suggestion, Matison offered to finance Kennard's continuing his undergraduate studies at the University of Chicago. Why did they try to dissuade him? One reason would surely have been their fear of the dangers to him. Kennard, a young Negro in a state known for its record of lynchings, would be alone in confronting local and state authorities in an attempt to integrate MSC, and doing so two years before others who also wanted to challenge segregation—for example, the Freedom Riders and sit-in protestors—but on issues less emotionally charged for segregationists than the mixing of the two races in schools. Three years later when James Meredith would attempt to integrate Ole Miss, a riot would break out, President Kennedy would call out the National Guard, and two people would be killed. Mantinband and Matison knew the fierce resistance Kennard would face. They saw him as a young idealist influenced by his seven years in the desegregated army, his years of living in the North, and his readings in political philosophy that stressed human rights. In their separate interviews with an investigator for the Mississippi State Sovereignty Commission, Mantinband said Kennard thought of himself as a "crusader" in the struggle for civil rights and Matison said it was unlikely anyone could change Kennard's mind. But both agreed to try again.[57]

A year after his first arrest he again applied to MSC and was charged with collusion in stealing twenty-five dollars' worth of chicken feed and receiving stolen goods. On Saturday, November 19, 1960, Mantinband wrote in his diary: "Shabos disturbed by the serving of a subpoena to appear as a character witness for Kennard. The same of both Matisons." On the following Monday, after appearing in court, he wrote, "Clyde Kennard on our minds, uppermost. Foregone conclusion the court will throw the book at him entire & violent." In Anna Mantinband's account, "before the trial opened the judge said blithely, 'Go on home, boys. You can't help this bird. We're going to throw the book at him.'"[58] In his diary Mantinband wrote, "We withdraw our character reference & witness, Lena M[atison]. & I—& are spared embarrassment & reprisal. Sentence is swift—10 minute jury guilt verdict, 7 years in penitentiary." He is convinced Kennard will appeal but also fears that "some guard will be rewarded and lionized for popping him off."[59]

It's not clear why he felt "spared embarrassment and reprisal" for not having to serve as a character witness, but perhaps he felt relieved to be able to avoid further unwanted publicity for himself and the Jewish community. He also knew, as Clive Webb has observed, that he was now "powerless to alter the subsequent course of events."[60] Kennard was sentenced to seven years of hard labor, while his supposed accomplice was given a suspended sentence. Though he had to work long, back-breaking hours six days a week on Parchman Prison's cotton plantation, he found time on Sundays to read, write letters for illiterate prisoners, and teach them how to read. On one of Mantinband's visits to the prison, Kennard mentioned that he'd been reading Gibbon's *Rise and Fall of the Roman Empire* and asked the rabbi "Could you get me a copy?"[61] Not long after beginning to serve his sentence in July of 1961, however, Kennard was diagnosed with colon cancer, sent to University Hospital in Jackson for surgery, and returned to prison without the further treatment doctors at the hospital had recommended.

Kennard's case is an example of what Taylor Branch has called the "Kafkaesque reality of Mississippi" at that time: a young black man who had been framed and convicted for theft of a piddling amount of chicken feed and sentenced to seven years at hard labor was now released from prison with "an indefinite suspended sentence," not as an acknowledgment of his innocence, but as a strategy by the governor to protect the state against the national attention his dying in prison would bring.[62] Kennard returned to Chicago to stay with his sister, received further treatment, and died on the Fourth of July.

Events had proved Mantinband's fears fully justified. After Kennard received the sentence, Mantinband wrote, "Our white Citizens Councils have disturbed us with their Gestapo methods of preserving segregation at all costs." Then he added, "those who presume to get in the path of the Councils had better beware."[63] When I read this, I wondered if he had come to regret speaking to the investigator for the Sovereignty Commission, whose reports were seen by Governors Coleman and Barnett, as well as other state and local officials. The character of these reports is suggested by one written by the same investigator who had interviewed Mantinband and who now wrote that "a Negro self-confessed Communist" told him that Mantinband "was an officer and director of the Mississippi Council on Human Relations, which . . . was a transmission belt of Communist infiltration in the South."[64]

Even after what happened to Kennard, however, Mantinband continued to believe that "in the final analysis, the struggle must be carried on by local leadership, white and Negro, Christian and Jew, on the home front—working despite the fear of reprisal."[65] He and Rabbi Perry Nussbaum in Jackson belonged to their respective Rotary clubs, joined the interracial Mississippi Council on Human Relations, spoke at Tougaloo College, and urged Christian clergymen to join them in making a public statement about civil rights. They believed that being active members of local clubs would help to create understanding at the local level for their support of the cause of civil rights. Working behind the scenes in this way, they believed, would, along with the force of Supreme Court rulings, eventually prove to be the most effective approach. From their long experience of living and working in the South they knew the depth of resistance to integration and the very real potential for violence that would result from direct action campaigns such as Freedom Rides, sit-ins, and demonstrations. "We have applauded the objectives of the Freedom Riders," Rabbi Mantinband said on more than one occasion, "but have not been certain of the wisdom of their strategy. Time alone will determine whether the contingents of [Northern] clerics, including some rabbis, have helped or hindered the overall situation."[66]

One of the ironies of Mantinband's and other southern rabbis' approach, I would learn from my reading, was that it could be easily confused with the gradualism favored by most white moderates. "The moderates' call for a gradual dismantling of the racially oppressive caste system," historian John Dittmer has pointed out, evoked the memory of those in the nineteenth century who believed that "slavery could be ended in phases, without outside interference. In both instances blacks were asked to endure their suffering a while longer, as their white counselors went on with their comfortable lives."[67] The white moderates' approach was soon put to the test and dramatized in Birmingham on a public stage with a cast of major actors.

Rabbi Milton Grafman of Birmingham, who had held the pulpit of the city's oldest congregation, Temple Emanu-El, since 1941, was not a segregationist, but in April of 1963 he joined with seven other white clergymen in writing what would prove to be a highly controversial statement that appeared in the *Birmingham News* the day after Martin Luther King, Jr., and fifty other demonstrators were jailed for having taken part in sit-ins and demonstrations. Grafman and his co-signers thought the protests were "unwise and untimely" and called for negotiations.[68] The gradual approach they were advocating had been shaped by their experience of having lived in a state with a militantly segregationist tradition and a strong Ku Klux Klan and in a city with a Commissioner of Public Safety, Eugene "Bull" Connor, who in the last few weeks had overseen the use of police brutality against demonstrators. In January, they had heard the new governor, George Wallace, embolden defenders of segregation in his inaugural address with his defiance of the federal government. It was common knowledge that in the previous six years, from 1957 to 1963, "while Birmingham was still claiming that its Negroes were 'satisfied,'" as Terri Barr has pointed out, "seventeen unsolved bombings of Negro churches and homes of civil rights leaders had occurred."[69]

Given this history of white defiance and violence and the explosive potential of the immediate situation, the gradual approach advocated by Grafman and the other clergymen seemed to be a reasonable alternative. But King, equally familiar with Alabama's racial history, his first pulpit having been in Montgomery, saw that history from the perspective of a Negro citizen. In his now famous reply to the white clergymen, "Letter from a Birmingham Jail," he pointed out that Birmingham's civil rights leaders had already engaged in negotiations in good faith and had received promises, only to see them broken. Then he turned to the gradualists' approach: "We know through painful experience that freedom is never voluntarily given by the oppressor.... I have yet to engage in a direct action campaign that was 'well timed' in the view of those who have not suffered ... from the disease of segregation. For years now I have heard the word 'Wait!' It rings in the ear of every Negro with piercing familiarity. This 'Wait' has almost always meant 'Never.'"

Like King, Mantinband opposed any gradual approach that was in effect a disguise for endless postponement. When Southerners "say they want justice for the Negro, but espouse a policy of gradualism" what they really mean, he wrote, is "building a [new Negro] schoolhouse one brick at a time." [70] I believe he thought that Grafman and other rabbis who espoused such "gradualism" were caving in to those in the Jewish community who feared boycotts, financial ruin, and violence. However justified their fears were, he believed fears shouldn't be allowed to supercede principles of equality and social justice.

Although he continued to have doubts about the freedom rides and sit-ins, he had come to see their value. On my first trip to Jackson to see the materials in the Mantinband Collection at ISJL, I saw a letter he had received from Rabbi Joseph Gumbiner that appears to have been crucial to his thinking. Mantinband had written him to ask for his opinion of the strategy of direct action campaigns, with which Gumbiner had had personal experience during a conference in

Jackson in 1961. He had arrived on Wednesday, July 19, with other rabbis and religious leaders from California, had spent the night at Tougaloo College, and attended bi-racial meetings all of the next day. They heard King speak on the subject of the Montgomery boycott and how the Negro people of that city had set an example that led to the sit-ins, protests, and the current Freedom Riders in Jackson who were testing the right to use public facilities involved in interstate travel. That night at the Jackson airport Gumbiner was arrested along with eight others, two of whom were Negroes, when they attempted to enter the restaurant for a cup of coffee.[71] They spent that Thursday night in jail, went to court the next afternoon, were declared guilty as charged, sentenced to four months in prison and a fine of two hundred dollars, had bond posted for them by CORE, and flew back to California, though they would have to return in August for the arraignment and in October for the trial.

Now in his reply to Mantinband, Gumbiner affirmed his support of the freedom rides and other nonviolent direct actions that King had been advocating. Although he was currently the Director of the B'nai B'rith Hillel Foundation at the Berkeley campus of the University of California, he was no stranger to the South. His first pulpit had been in Selma in the 1930s, giving him eight years of experience in a segregated state. In answering Mantinband's question of whether the conference and "subsequent events accomplished anything," Gumbiner replied with a strong defense of direct-action protests. First, the freedom riders dramatized far more than the injustice of segregation in interstate travel: they helped dramatize "the whole gamut of problems regarding segregation in the United States, including public school integration, the right to freedom of choice with respect to housing, the right to vote, the right to fair employment practices, freedom from police brutality, [and] equal justice in the courts." Second, the protests built up the morale of Negro leaders. "If I were living in a kind of enforced ghetto, as a Jew," he reasoned, "and non-Jewish people came to my ghetto and at inconvenience, cost and risk to themselves engaged in protest against the laws and customs which degraded me, would I not feel much strengthened with respect to the struggle which I would have to carry on?" This may have been his most compelling reason. He was invoking an image of the ghettoes from Jewish history, with its unmistakable allusion to the fate of Jews in Europe under Nazi rule in the 1930s and '40s, which had already become a consideration in Mantinband's mind. Finally, he wrote, "I feel it was good to exemplify the value of direct, nonviolent action over and against the extremist calls to violence which are being sounded in the Negro community. I was happy to enlist under the banner of Martin Luther King because I feel that his approach is best for all of us."[72]

Mantinband came to agree with Gumbiner and King, as well as with a statement issued by the Central Conference of American Rabbis in 1962: "We commend those students who place life and limb in jeopardy for the sake of their convictions. Their objectives and methods—sit-in, kneel-in, read-in, wade-in—are consistent with our [American] heritage, and in keeping with rights granted them by our Federal Constitution. Even when they practice civil disobedience at the risk of community discord, so long as they are non-violent . . . they emulate the leadership of Dr. Martin Luther King."[73] He continued to be concerned about demonstrations that became unruly and disruptive, however, because even peaceful protests in the South could result in violence (as happened in 2017 in Charlottesville, Virginia, when neo-Nazis attacked demonstrators and killed one who wanted to see Confederate statues removed). Two years later, in 1964, after he had moved to Longview, Texas, he again wrote to a fellow rabbi for his views, this time to Jacob Rothschild of Atlanta, who was a friend of King and an admirer of Mantinband. He, too, had at times been critical of certain sit-ins and demonstrations, but was nonetheless convinced that "they were valid because almost nothing had been accomplished without some sort of pressure."[74]

While Mantinband agreed with Rothschild, he expressed concern about a "new trend of militant, insurgent demonstrations, all too often accompanied by threats" and violence. It wasn't only that he thought they were "self-defeating." He also saw them as a sign that "communication between the races" had broken down and that "the Negro no longer trusts the white man," citing as an example James Baldwin, who had once remarked that "the white liberal is our affliction."[75] Despite these concerns, however, he recognized that the demonstrations would continue and that they were "valuable and useful . . . as legitimate means to a worthy end." But he warned "they are never ends in themselves." He was looking down the long road ahead. While "people are on parade," he believed, they should "remember our great needs in voter education, increased opportunities in employment, and on-the-job training, open housing facilities, desegregation of our school system, improved health conditions, slum clearance, and equal penalties under the law."[76] So much of what was yet to be done would require the commitment of local leaders, white and Negro, Christian and Jew, working together despite intimidation, threats, and violence. He knew this would take time but wanted to see it proceed without any of the willful postponement and obstructionist intention associated with gradualism.

His last full year in Hattiesburg, 1962, became his annus mirabilis, bringing national—and even local—recognition for his courage and advocacy in the civil rights struggle. His three best-known publications appeared that year: "Rabbi in the Deep South," "From the Diary of a Mississippi Rabbi," and "In Dixieland I Take My Stand." An essay about him appeared in *New South* (published by the Southern Regional Council), praising him for the moral convictions underlying his commitment and contributions to the civil rights movement. It was also in this year that he became the first recipient of the George Brussell Memorial Award in recognition of his lifetime of commitment to social justice and the spirit of the Hebrew prophets. In Hattiesburg, he was elected president of the local ministerial association and in December at a special meeting of the congregation called by President Abe Pevsner, there was a unanimous vote "that everything be done to keep the Rabbi."[77] In January, shortly after the announcement that he was leaving, he took note in his diary of the story in the *Hattiesburg American* about him: "Front page story in local press of our departure—same space where years ago they said 'Local Rabbi—[Says] R[ace] R[elations] STINK.'" Then, with evident satisfaction, he wrote, "times change."[78] In February, he was highly pleased by a dinner in his honor during National Brotherhood Week. When he got home that night, he wrote: "This is my big day—the 75 men who gather[ed] at the Interfaith Brotherhood Dinner are representative of the best in our Community—the City Government (Mayor)—the two colleges (Presidents, Deans, Faculty), business & professional interests & all Jews." (I think the last three words refer to the Jewish men who were present and part of "the best in our Community," not to all in the congregation. Rabbi Leo Bergman of New Orleans, who spoke at the dinner, would later complain that many Jews had stayed away.) He goes on to say, "I get the key to the city & also a silver platter engraved 'For 11 years of unselfish service.' All very complimentary & [Rabbi] Bergman [of New Orleans] does a superb job of . . . preaching." Then he observes, with his friend Harry Golden in mind, "only in America." On the next day, he wrote in his dairy, "now on to Texas. . . . I need change."[79] Then on June 12, 1963, three months after leaving Hattiesburg for his new pulpit, he received a telegram from President Kennedy inviting him to the White House for a meeting with other religious leaders "to discuss present aspects of the nation's civil rights problem."[80]

But 1962 was also the year when tensions between Mantinband and the congregation increased and he decided to leave. The cumulative effect of the Freedom Rides, sit-ins, and other demonstrations, often including Jewish students and rabbis from other parts of the country, had greatly heightened the fears of Jews in Hattiesburg and strengthened the opposition to his civil rights activities. In early May, after the Jackson papers' coverage of a meeting of the state's biracial Human Relations Council in Jackson, where he had delivered the keynote address, he wrote in his diary "Our congregation is in a dither." Three days later, on May 8, in a meeting with 100 percent attendance, he writes that he was told his "identification with liberal causes does the Jewish people no good." One member asked, "why must the rabbi mix with the niggers? Let us just sell to them and keep them in their place." (Mantinband would include this member's question and comment in his essay "From the Diary of a Mississippi Rabbi," published later that year in *American Judaism*.) The following day, he learns and records in his diary that the tiny Brookhaven congregation has canceled his biweekly visit. On May 10, he writes, "Some of my temple teachers visit the local college president, urging him to restrain 'his friend, the rabbi' in interracial affairs." On May 22, there's another meeting of the congregation, again with 100 percent attendance. "Grudgingly, they concede that my position is morally correct and consistent with the noblest teachings of Judaism. . . . They claim, however, that whenever their rabbi appears in public, people identify him with all Jews and, inevitably, as the spokesman of their congregation." As a result of that meeting and the fact that the *Hattiesburg American* is "hostile and inflammatory," he promises to avoid biracial meetings "for the time being" and the storm appears to be over. But he consulted his lawyer about his legal and moral rights, "making no secret of it to the temple board."[81]

The congregation had reason to be fearful. Marvin Reuben, co-owner of the local television station that ran editorials supporting the *Brown* decision and denouncing extremists, found that crosses were burned in front of the building and the station tower had been shot down.[82] Reuben remained a supporter of Mantinband, but others in the congregation believed the rabbi's activism was putting the Jewish community in grave danger. They wanted him to remain silent. When Clive Webb interviewed Esther Shemper, another supporter of the rabbi and the matriarch of a large family that has been a mainstay of the congregation for many years, she told him "They made it so miserable for him that I think actually in a way they did ask him to leave." Lou Ginsburg also thought he wanted to leave "because the congregation was not happy with him."[83]

The opposition he was facing may have created doubts in his mind but it had also stirred his resolve. In his diary entry for February 14, just five days before the dinner honoring him during Brotherhood Week, he writes that his article "From the Diary of a Mississippi Rabbi" has caused "a dither and stew ... [in] both Hattiesburg and Longview," probably because he had quoted that one member's racist comments. After being reassured by a few phone calls, he writes in defense of the article, "If parts of the story were harsh, they were none the less true. Let the lynch mob see itself as others see [it]."[84] As strong as the last sentence is, I believe his use of the word "mob" refers to only a small number of those who opposed him. After Rabbi Rosenthal returned to Vassar Temple in Poughkeepsie in 1958, he wrote that the majority of Jews in Hattiesburg "lean to a liberal view of the race question" and that he knew of only five "rabid segregationists."[85]

In his interview with Rabbi Allen Krause in 1966, three years after he had moved to Longview, Mantinband cited "circumstances of a personal nature" as the reason for the move: "Most of my colleagues think I left because it was a good time to get out of Mississippi, and that my life was in danger, that he who fights and runs away will live to fight another day. But, actually, that is not the fact—I left under flying colors. I moved because of special circumstances of a personal nature. We were near our grandchildren and we were near our family, it was a new place, there was a brand-new congregation that challenged me, and I still have close contact with Mississippi, even though I no longer live there."[86] Krause wondered, "Is the rabbi being honest with himself? To a good extent, I think so. He has too often shown himself constitutionally unable to run away."[87]

But two historians who have written persuasively about the conflict between Mantinband and the congregation, Clive Webb and Adam Mendelsohn, concluded that he was in effect forced or pushed out, meaning, I assume (since he had life tenure), that he was made to feel unwanted.[88] I had resisted accepting their conclusion, believing that those who opposed him were still the size of the minority in the 1958 vote, which gave him life tenure, and that the large majority continued to support him. I also thought that the unanimous vote in December 1962, even though only twenty members were present, represented strong support, especially in its phrasing "that everything be done to keep the rabbi." But it's clear that the opposition was stronger than I thought. I don't know how strong it had become numerically, but whatever it may have lacked in numbers seems to have been made up for in intensity.

A few of his diary entries suggest how he was reading the situation in his last two years in Hattiesburg. In September of 1960 he wrote, "Still undecided about whether to stay in this job—people need a shock and shaking up and a change for the Rabbi too may be wholesome—we'll investigate and see." In November, after receiving a phone call from a professor at USM to congratulate him on his recent talk on WFOR, telling him "Best yet!" he writes "My own people do not deign to listen—Rabbi is forever taken for granted on the home ground." In January of 1963, a little more than a month before he left for Longview, he writes "Local folk have already forgotten me—they do not telephone to inquire how we are."[89] Of course, everyone has ups and downs, and, as his diary entry on the night after the dinner in his honor during Brotherhood Week reveals, he was highly pleased and deeply moved. Nevertheless, the next day, after receiving a farewell gift from the Levines, being given a dinner by Norman and Ethel, and speaking with Esther Shemper about the dinner honoring him on the previous night, he writes "now on to Texas. . . . I need change."

I think these entries reveal not only how he was reading his standing with the congregation but also how he was responding to it, what his feelings about it were, at that time. In his interview with Allen Krause three years after he had been in Longview, he indicated that there was more than one consideration in his decision to leave and he emphasized the "special circumstances of a personal nature." Among the considerations he did not mention were his age and failing health. He was sixty-seven years old, suffering from arthritis (on occasion having to use a wheelchair), and slowly going blind. They would have made being near his daughter, sons, and grandchildren in the coming years all the more compelling. In late January, anticipating the move to Longview, he wrote in his diary: "Telephone Shreveport & it is pleasant to contemplate the 1 and ½-hour bus ride visit which we can do weekly, if necessary, or they can come to us—How lovely that will be."[90] If his age, health, and being close to his daughter were indeed important in the decision, as I think they must have been, it would not take away from the fact that, as Webb and Mendelsohn have shown, and as his diary entries about a need for change suggest, the opposition to his civil rights activities had intensified, reflecting the heightened fear of the congregation in the years just before

Mississippi would become the bloodiest battleground of the civil rights movement.

No sooner than he was gone and a new rabbi had arrived, the congregation found itself again having to contend with a rabbi who refused to remain silent. Rabbi David Ben-Ami (whom I never met) arrived in December of 1963 and in January went to the Forrest County Courthouse to show his support for northern civil rights activists who had come to Hattiesburg to participate in voter registration demonstrations. Ben-Ami talked with them, invited them to his home, visited them at the jail after they were arrested, and raised funds for the rebuilding of black churches that had been destroyed by white supremacists. Many in the congregation thought he was "far too friendly towards the northern activists and clergymen involved in the Freedom Summer Project.[91] The congregation quickly became unhappy with him. It was said he failed in his rabbinical duties, was unresponsive to the wishes of the president and his board of directors, and lacked the personal and diplomatic skills of Mantinband. In October, after being in the job less than a year, the congregation wanted to terminate his three-year contract and offered him the inducement of three months' salary if he departed early. He agreed to leave in February, but he continued his civil rights activities and in early January of 1965 his upcoming departure was nationally publicized. In *The National Jewish Post and Opinion*, he was said to have "lost his position with the congregation because of his advocacy of civil rights."[92] Three weeks later, he wrote a letter to the editor saying "I was not ousted by the congregation. . . . We mutually agreed to disagree." In the letter, he went on to defend his working "on the front lines of the civil rights struggle" as a personal commitment to "labor in the prophetic tradition."[93]

The last time I saw Rabbi Mantinband was at my father's funeral in March of 1962, and then only briefly. But in my efforts to learn about his last years in Hattiesburg and Ben-Ami's brief time there, I've been struck by how the fate of Jews under the Nazis figured in their memories as a major reason for Jews, particularly rabbis, to speak out against segregation. Ben-Ami had been born in Germany in 1924 and had lived there until 1937. "When I walked in the street or when someone knocked at my door," he said of his experience in Hattiesburg, it "reminded me of Germany."[94]

Another rabbi, Andre Ungar, who came to Hattiesburg in January of 1964 to participate in the demonstrations at the courthouse, had lost many family members in the Holocaust, but had managed to survive in Budapest by means of false papers. In London after the war, where he went for his rabbinical training, he was influenced by the teachings of Rabbi Leo Baeck, who had decided to remain in Berlin to serve its remaining Jews ("I shall be the last to leave. . . . As long as a minyan exists in Berlin, here is my place"), had eventually been sent to Theresienstadt, had survived, moved to London where his daughter and son-in-law lived, and become both a British citizen and an internationally recognized figure for the stand he had taken against Nazi oppression.[95] For Ungar and other progressive rabbis, he became, as Adam Mendelsohn has observed, "a distinguished role model for an activist rabbi."[96]

When Ungar went to South Africa in the 1950s to be the rabbi of the Reform congregation in Port Elizabeth, he saw blacks being forced out of white areas and he was appalled. "There was a sense of deja-vu in many ways," he told Roger Cohen in an interview decades later. "I remember being ordered into a ghetto in Budapest in 1944, and the attitudes of racial superiority in South Africa seemed to me to be cut from the same cloth." From his pulpit he spoke out against the injustices of apartheid. "I knew I had a clear mandate to say what I was saying from the Jewish experience itself."[97] But most in his congregation didn't agree and when in late 1956 the Interior Ministry ordered him to leave South Africa, they did not oppose the expulsion order.

Of course, one didn't have to be a survivor of Nazi persecution to see its relevance for the civil rights struggle in America. In Rabbi Gumbiner's letter to Mantinband, he justified his support for Martin Luther King and the strategy of demonstrations by comparing the evils of segregation to the ghetto life that Jews had experienced under the Nazis. Mantinband himself was very clear on the subject. "How can one answer the question, 'Is the Negro race situation and the desegregation issue of special Jewish concern?' All too often many of our people feel themselves relatively safe, as long as it is another underdog who is the scapegoat. But those of us who have studied Jewish history—and the experience of Nazi Germany is still vivid in our memory—recognize that there can be no measure of freedom as long as any one segment of our population is enslaved."[98] For Mantinband, as well as for Ben-Ami, Ungar, and other rabbis, Jewish silence about segregation was haunted by the experience of Jews under the Nazis.

I believe Mantinband did everything he or anyone could to bridge the divide between his commitment to prophetic Judaism and social justice for all, on one hand, and the concerns for personal safety and economic survival in the minds of his congregants on the other. But there was no way to be equally true to both without putting one of them in jeopardy. That was the dilemma he and Jews in the South faced. What he's now best remembered for is taking the stand he did and breaking the silence. The example he set by the life he led, which his mentor Stephen Wise had told him would be his best sermon, held up a high moral standard for Jewish life that many Jews in Hattiesburg, living under the threat of boycotts and violence, felt they could not publicly support. In the next few years, the violence in Mississippi would increase dramatically and the synagogues in Jackson and Meridian would be bombed.

CHAPTER 7

Fear in High Profile: Terrorism in the 1960s

On a Sunday morning in early September of 1946, Fay, now in her junior year at LSU, went to the recently formed Liberal Synagogue for the first meeting of its Sunday-school teachers with their new rabbi, Arthur Brodey. After leaving the pulpit in Hattiesburg in March of 1943 to become a chaplain in the army and serving in the States for a year, he landed on Omaha Beach three weeks after D-Day and went with American troops into France, Belgium, Holland, and eventually Germany, where he was among the first to enter Buchenwald following its liberation, and would remain with the occupying forces in Europe until early 1946. In the meantime, two months after the end of the war, his former congregation, knowing how well he had succeeded in the task Rabbi Wise had expressed concern about—creating a harmonious relationship between its Orthodox and Reform members—passed a unanimous resolution requesting the Chief of Chaplains, United States Army, to "do any and all things possible to effect the prompt return of Chaplain Arthur Brodey to his Congregation in Hattiesburg, Mississippi."[1] But the decision was Rabbi Brodey's to make and he chose the pulpit in Baton Rouge.

Following the meeting that Sunday, Fay told me, Rabbi Brodey invited her to have lunch with him and Mrs. Brodey at their home. He also invited "B," who was another new teacher and, like Rabbi Brodey, had recently returned from Europe, where he had served in the infantry and later in the office of the Judge Advocate General in Paris, and now, after being discharged from the army, was a freshman at LSU. The younger son of Louis Botnick (and the nephew of Harry Botnick and Lotte Eisman), he had been born in New Orleans, grown up in Baton Rouge, attended Gulf Coast Military Academy in Gulfport, and enlisted in the army immediately after graduation in 1943. Fay remembered seeing him in the synagogue in Hattiesburg in the years when he was at GCMA and came to stay with his uncle Harry to attend services on the High Holy Days. At the end of their long conversation that Sunday afternoon in Baton Rouge, he asked her to go out with him. She said she couldn't because, as she knew from a mutual friend, he was engaged to a young woman in Jacksonville. But he was persistent. A few days later he called to say he was no longer engaged and he and Fay were married the following year. He completed the coursework for a BA in three years, they moved to Hattiesburg in January of 1949, and he went to work for my father in the store.

After ten years in the clothing business, however, and now in his mid-thirties, his interest in it had waned. This wasn't something "B" told me but rather something I inferred from our conversations, many of them at the store when we weren't waiting on customers or when we took a coffee break at the Yellow Pine Drug Store across the street, though I had no idea then that he would one day decide to look for work in another field. When he was at LSU, in addition to meeting the requirements for his major, which was history, he had also taken courses in philosophy, the social sciences, and government, including one on race and race relations. I noticed that his interests in these subjects came up more often in our conversations than business did. He began to give some thought to other vocations and took a course in sociology at Mississippi Southern, indicating an interest in social issues and the possibility of pursuing some kind of social work. Eventually, and with strong encouragement from Fay, he turned to Rabbi Mantinband for advice.

One role for which Mantinband has received little recognition was that of counselor. His principal role as a rabbi, he once wrote, was "teaching Judaism to Jews and interpreting it to the outside world." On another occasion, he made a more inclusive list of rabbinical responsibilities, beginning in a somewhat light-hearted, self-disparaging vein with "general factotum" and continuing with "teacher, preacher, counselor, social worker, public relations specialist, fund raiser, and ambassador to the goyim."[2] Individuals in his congregation, other rabbis, and many other people (including a few who, like him, were involved in the civil rights movement) sought his advice. "B" met with him a number of times, beginning in 1960 and continuing into 1961, and eventually, following his suggestion, applied for a position with the Anti-Defamation League. In June of 1961, while Rabbi Mantinband was in New York for the annual meeting of the Central Conference of American Rabbis (CCAR), he went to the ADL headquarters in New York and personally recommended "B" for the position. At some point in the spring or summer "B" went to New York for an interview and in September he was offered the position of assistant director in the ADL's regional office in Atlanta. I was still in Atlanta then (though in September I received notice that my army reserve unit had been recalled and that I had to report for duty at Fort Bliss, Texas, in early October) and was able to help him find an apartment. After three years in Atlanta, he was promoted to director of the ADL's south central regional office (for Arkansas, Louisiana, and Mississippi) in New Orleans and he and Fay moved there with their three children in the spring of 1964.

His new appointment came at a fateful period in the history of the civil rights movement in Mississippi. The previous year had been marked by increased Klan violence, most notably the assassination of Medgar Evers by Byron De La Beckwith (who ten years later would drive to New Orleans with a bomb and a map marked to show directions to the neighborhood where Fay and "B" lived). It was also the year Samuel Bowers of Laurel—who believed that the Kremlin "was a front for Jews trying to topple Christianity"—had founded the White Knights of the Ku Klux Klan.[3] Then, beginning in 1964 and continuing for the next four years, the Klan would convulse the state in murders of civil rights workers, burnings of churches, and bombings of the synagogues in Jackson and Meridian and the home of Rabbi Perry Nussbaum in Jackson. The summer of 1964 would prove to be like no other in Mississippi's history.

As momentous as the events of that summer were not only for Mississippi but also for the nation, and as often as they appeared in the headlines and on the television screen, I wasn't paying much attention to the news then. Having just completed my second year of graduate school, I was preparing to take the preliminary exams for the PhD that would be given in early January. I had been late going to graduate school at the age of twenty-seven and for that reason was all the more intensely focused on my studies that summer and fall. In addition, while Alice was working at the English Language Institute, having completed the coursework for her BA the previous year, we were also making preparations for the arrival of our daughter Jessica in October. Three years later, after I was offered an assistant professorship at the University of Illinois and had completed the requirements for the PhD, we moved to Champaign-Urbana and I turned my attention to teaching English literature and writing articles about the English Romantic poets with the hope of getting tenure.

What seems so strange to me now, after all the times I saw "B" over the next thirty years, usually for a family occasion in Hattiesburg or New Orleans but at other times for just a visit, is that I have only a few memories of talking with him about his work. I knew a little about it from two books and several pamphlets published by the ADL that he gave me and that described its purpose and work and I knew he felt he was now doing something that engaged his interests. It was work he found personally rewarding and knew was important. On one occasion when Alice and I were visiting Fay and "B" in New Orleans, I remember meeting one of "B"'s close friends, Barney Mintz, who was a long-time member of the ADL board in New Orleans, and hearing the two of them discuss some recent issues that were to come before the board. On another occasion, I remember "B" telling me about a meeting he'd attended in Atlanta at which a member of Martin Luther King's Southern Christian Leadership Council had said to him that Jews hadn't shown much interest in or commitment to the civil rights movement. "B" was surprised and disappointed by what this man had said. But for the most part, when he and I were alone together in New Orleans or the four of us were out at a restaurant in the French Quarter, we talked about other things. He was a lively conversationalist and storyteller, he had a wonderful sense of humor, and together we enjoyed reminiscing about the past or talking about recent goings-on in the lives of our families in Hattiesburg, Baton Rouge, and Mobile and of other people we knew. At these times, I think he was happy to leave his work-life at the office and give himself over to the pleasures of the moment. My regret now is that I failed to ask him more than I did about his work, especially about his experiences during Freedom Summer and the next few years when Jews in Mississippi—and he himself—became targets of the Klan.

When, a few years ago, nearly a decade after I'd retired and "B" was no longer there to answer my questions, having died in 1995, I turned to Fay and she answered those she could and then suggested that I read the memoirs "B" had left as part of the ADL's Oral Memoirs Project. My niece Lori Botnick Fireman had a copy and made one for me. Since then I've been able to get additional information from my nephew Michael Botnick, who is a Past Chair and Honorary Board Member of ADL's South Central Region, as well as Honorary Life Member of the National Commission. For the rest of the story of the experience of "B" and that of the Jews in Mississippi during those years, I've had to rely on the various primary and secondary sources I was able to find.

More than a thousand young people came to Mississippi that summer of 1964, most of them college students, the majority white, many Jewish. They came from the Northeast, the Midwest, and the West Coast to open Freedom Schools, live with local blacks in their communities, some in their homes, and work with them in the schools and in voter registration drives. Martin Luther King said of the Freedom Summer project that it was "the most creative thing happening today in civil rights."⁴ But it was also the summer when the three civil rights workers, Cheney, Goodman, and Schwerner, disappeared, beginning a national ordeal of uncertainty about what had happened to them that lasted six weeks, with continuous newspaper and television coverage of the search for them until their bodies were discovered on August 4. As a result of their disappearance, President Lyndon Johnson urged J. Edgar Hoover to open an FBI office in Jackson and staff it with fifty to a hundred agents. It would eventually have over two hundred.

On the same morning that Hoover arrived to speak at the opening of the new office, July 10, Rabbi Arthur J. Lelyveld of Cleveland, Ohio, was walking in Hattiesburg with four civil rights volunteers—two young white men and two young black women—when he and the other two whites were attacked and beaten by a man and his nephew who had been riding around in a truck looking for some "white niggers" to beat up. Rabbi Lelyveld was bludgeoned with a tire iron. A now-famous picture of him sitting on a bench with a bandage on the right side of his temple and the front of his shirt soaked in blood would soon be circulated in newspapers and magazines across the country. Members of the congregation went to see him in the hospital and urged him to leave. Fifty years later, Maury Gurwitch, who was president of the congregation then, recalled their visit in an interview with journalist Marc Fisher: "We said, Rabbi, we have enough *tsuris* [trouble] being Jews here. You're going to get us burned out or killed."⁵

The fear that he and others in the congregation were experiencing was real. Former Congressman Barney Frank was one of the Jewish students from the North who came to Mississippi that summer and he recalled the fear he had observed. Having been invited to dinner at a Jackson restaurant by the family of a student at Wellesley College whom he knew, he learned from the family that they "had received 90 phone calls from friends and neighbors asking why they were hanging around with those outside agitators." "Just their having dinner with me was an act of bravery," he told Fisher. "I knew they faced ruin and maybe violence if they were seen with people like me."⁶ Southern rabbis knew and understood their fear. Although Mantinband wrote a letter to Lelyveld following the incident to "apologize for my former community," two years earlier he had expressed some of the same fear many in his congregation now felt. He had written to Rabbi Perry Nussbaum in Jackson to say, "If only we can keep the northern rabbis from invading our precincts."⁷ Freedom Summer captured the attention of the nation and revealed the dangers to be faced by anyone who went to Mississippi and was known to belong to, or believed to be in sympathy with, any organization that supported the goals of the civil rights movement.

As the regional director of the ADL, "B" became an easily identifiable target, though not immediately an actual one. A number of years prior to his appointment as director of the regional office, there had been a bombing of the Lafayette Furniture Company in New Orleans, owned by Barney Mintz, who at the time was at an ADL meeting in New York. "Somebody put a hand grenade in the lobby of our store," he recalled in his oral memoir, "filled with black powder, and attached to it was a rag, apparently soaked in gasoline." Although the bomb blew out several windows, it otherwise did not do great damage. But his wife warned him, "It's all right as long as they bomb the store but the moment they bomb my house you have to get out of the ADL."[8] "B" would become a potential target only after Beth Israel Synagogue in Jackson was bombed in September of 1967, which marked the beginning of what journalist Jack Nelson would call *The Klan's Campaign Against the Jews* (in the subtitle of his 1993 book *Terror in the Night*), as well as the beginning of "B"'s cooperation with the FBI and local police in their efforts to apprehend the perpetrators. Until then, his job had been primarily one of monitoring anti-Semitic organizations, activities, and publications, investigating reports of anti-Semitism by individuals who had experienced it in school or the workplace, organizing seminars at local seminaries, colleges, and other venues on various subjects regarding human relations, and making regular visits to the Jewish communities in the three states in his region.

But within a month of his arrival in New Orleans the state of Mississippi would claim most of his attention. In June he and two other ADL regional directors, Ted Freedman of Houston and Sherman Harris of D.C., went to Jackson to meet with the leaders of the Jewish community about the upcoming Freedom Summer project. They gave a brief summary of the expected activities of those involved in the project and later provided a three-page report listing its sponsoring organizations, the number of volunteers coming to Mississippi, what they would be doing, and a list of the twenty-three cities where they would be active. As valuable as this information was, however, it did not address the most pressing concern of Jackson's Jewish community. What it wanted from the ADL was help in preventing "Jewish leaders from coming into Mississippi to participate in the desegregation process."[9] It feared a repetition of the summer of 1961, when rabbis from the North and West had come to Jackson in support of the Freedom Riders. The presence of out-of-state Jews—"outside Jewish busybodies," in the words of one Delta rabbi—would threaten the security and welfare of local Jews.[10] "B" and the two other directors explained that they couldn't control the behavior of Jews who chose to travel to the state.

As an alternative they proposed a special program in which the ADL would come to Mississippi and "circuit ride the state" in an effort "to strengthen law and order" and prevent outbreaks of violence, as well as visit its Jewish communities and allay fears. The ADL had initiated a similar though much larger and crisis-driven "Crash Program" following the 1958 bombings of Jewish community buildings in Jacksonville, Miami, and Nashville. Additional staff had been added from other offices and two ADL directors from other regions had joined Irwin Schulman, "B"'s predecessor in New Orleans, enabling them to travel widely in the three-state area. Within a week they had visited virtually all the Jewish communities in Arkansas, Louisiana, and Mississippi and held meetings with rabbis, congregation presidents, and Jewish community leaders. The program being proposed now would be similar, but its focus would be on one state, Mississippi.[11]

Following its approval, "B" drove to more than twenty towns and cities in a three-week period of the summer of 1964. "I would leave New Orleans on Monday morning and go from community to community in Mississippi meeting with our constituents, church leaders, educators, and friendly law enforcement officials (some of them not so friendly—some were even Klansmen). Our message was simple. There was going to be more bloodshed if they did not speak out against the lawlessness which pervaded the state." In meetings with each Jewish community or in private conversations with individual members he often had to respond to difficult questions. "One important question that arose repeatedly was whether or not they should join the White Citizens' Councils."[12] The first council had been organized soon after the *Brown* decision in the small town of Indianola, but others quickly sprang up in towns and cities across the state. The Councils' leaders "sought to identify their movement with 'the finest and the best intelligence, the best law-abiding group, most courageous, the most honest' elements in the region" and they "quickly condemned the hooded night riders of the Klan."[13] The investigative unit of the state's Sovereignty Commission was constantly interviewing individuals, as it had Rabbi Mantinband and Dave Matison about Clyde Kennard. In addition, the White Citizens' Council in Jackson, which Mantinband believed used "Gestapo methods," had "built up a card file containing the racial views of nearly every white person in the city." Because of the pressure the Jewish community in Jackson felt it was under, its B'nai B'rith Lodge invited a member of the Jackson Citizens' Council to address its members during one of its meetings and as a result Jackson's Rabbi Perry Nussbaum "castigated the lodge from his pulpit and in public."[14]

As strong as the pressure was in Jackson, it was even greater for Jews living in small towns, especially in the Delta. Although very few actually joined the councils, one wrote an essay entitled "A Jewish View on Segregation," which was published in Greenwood by the Association of Citizens' Councils in Mississippi. The author of this thirteen-page pamphlet preferred to remain anonymous, but Rabbi Mantinband wrote "we know who it is" in one of his unpublished papers, though he doesn't reveal the man's name.[15] The fact that it was published in Greenwood suggests he may have lived there or in a nearby rural community in the Delta. He praised the White Citizens' Councils and criticized national Jewish organizations, singling out the B'nai B'rith and the ADL. "As a Jewish Southerner, I objected, and still do object, to the stand taken by national (?) Jewish organizations, and most particularly B'nai B'rith and the Anti-Defamation League," especially the latter for taking "the position it did in filing a brief as a friend of the court [in the *Brown* decision]" and having done so "in the name of American Jewry."[16] With the question mark after the word "national," he tries to raise doubts about how national these organizations can really be if, as he believes, they do not represent the position of southern Jews. The "Publisher's Note" on the title page states that "this article is entirely voluntary by a Jewish Southerner who prefers to remain anonymous" because "the cranks and crackpots who will wish to revile him for his right to form his own beliefs and act upon them will not remain silent" and "The author is unwilling to subject his family to abuse from such quarters." Rather than the independence of mind that the words "entirely voluntary" are intended to suggest, however, the impression they leave may be the opposite. In the view of one historian, the pamphlet was an example of the "pressure [that] was occasionally applied to force Jews to join the movement."[17]

Once, after "B" returned to New Orleans from a trip into Mississippi, he received a telephone call from a man who had joined his local council and reported that local stores in his small town were being boycotted and picketed by blacks. He was on the Executive Committee of the White Citizens' Council in that community and they had a meeting one night and at this meeting they were passing photographs around of the blacks who were picketing and asking if anyone in the room knew them. One of the council members said, "You know all niggers look alike, they are like Jews, every one of them, they all look alike." I said to him, "And how do you feel about that?" "Oh," he said, "they are not talking about me, you know, they're talking about other kinds of Jews, not me." This man believed he wasn't included in the stereotype because the one they had in mind, as "B" went on to explain, was that "of an old Jewish man with payess [side earlocks or curls], a beard, a beaver hat and a long frock coat."[18]

While the councils weren't openly anti-Semitic, there was an undercurrent of anti-Semitism running through them. Most of the literature on their list of recommended reading about desegregation was anti-Negro, but the list also included works that made no effort to disguise their anti-Semitism—for example, by Gerald L. K. Smith, at the time the best-known anti-Semite in the three states "B" monitored. Smith had begun his career as a preacher in Indiana in 1916 and had enjoyed some success there, but in 1928, because of his wife's poor health, they had moved south to Shreveport, Louisiana, where much of his attention and energy shifted from his pulpit to politics, becoming a devoted follower of Huey Long and a valued organizer. After Long's assassination in 1935, Smith's political activities continued and in the 1940s he ran once for the U. S. Senate in Michigan and twice for president. He had all along been drawn to the anti-Semitism of Henry Ford and Father Coughlin, becoming friends with both, and eventually he settled in Eureka Springs, Arkansas, where, out of a mix of his Christian faith, white supremacist ideology, and anti-Semitism, he founded a religious theme-park on his own property and built a sixty-five-foot-high statue of Jesus known as the Christ of the Ozarks. I remember seeing it once when Alice and I were visiting friends in Fayetteville who drove us to Eureka. It could be seen for miles around and had become a popular tourist attraction.

In an article that "B" wrote about Smith entitled "The Business of Bigotry," he provided a detailed description of the range of Smith's political activism in the 1960s, one of the highlights of which was the publication of the racist magazine *The Cross and the Flag*. Another was the repeated staging in a large amphitheater—"five nights a week, five months of the year"—of the original version of the Oberammergau Passion Play, a work which charges Jews with deicide.[19] Moreover, in his theme-park he sold anti-Semitic tracts such as a four-page outline of *The Protocols of the Learned Elders of Zion* and a copy of Henry Ford's *The International Jew*. While Smith's Christian National Crusade never attracted a large enough following to become a significant political presence on the national stage, it nonetheless received contributions of more than $300,000 (more than $2,000,000 today) in each of the three years from 1965 to 1967.[20] These were the very years when Bowers' White Knights were moving toward their campaign of violence against Jews in Mississippi. Taken together, Smith's Christian National Crusade, the Ku Klux Klan, and the White Citizens' Councils represented a strain of anti-Semitism running through the white population, from the lowest economic and social levels to the highest and most politically influential in the three-state

"B" in Jerusalem in 1973.

region where "B" traveled, met with the Jews in one community after another, and conferred and cooperated with local officials.

Looking back, he wondered what changes he and the ADL had succeeded in making in Mississippi: "It's hard to be able to say in X or Y communities the following changes took place. We do know that we were instrumental in being a catalyst to convene ministers, newspaper people, churchmen and, in certain instances, politicians to come together and say to them, 'You must exercise every effort to stop violence, to stop the church bombings and to stop the false arrests of civil rights workers who come to Mississippi.'" His description of what he sought to do and how he went about it was in this instance not unlike what Mantinband and a number of other rabbis in the South thought was the best way to proceed: meeting with members and leaders of prominent civic organizations and religious groups in an effort to persuade them to speak out. "Up until this point," "B" believed, "the good people" still didn't "really know each other." So, in effect, "we were acting as a catalyst to find out who they were and bring them together for some sort of effort to bring about a sense of law and order and a diminution of the violence which was pervading the state."[21] Who were these "good people"? Those who were sympathetic to the Negro demand for equal treatment under the law but who, out of fear, remained silent. In a letter to Mantinband in 1964 (now in his second year in Longview, Texas), Rabbi Nussbaum said of "the good people" that at times they were afraid to attend a meeting of the Human Relations Council on the campus of Tougaloo College and that the protests and demonstrations had "led most of the 'good people' to renewed rationalizations about 'keeping the peace.'"[22]

It was the bombing of the synagogue in Jackson on the night of September 18, 1967, that would prove to be the most effective catalyst and begin to make clear who would speak up and who would continue to remain silent. The *New York Times* reported that the bomb "heavily damaged offices and a conference room in the temple's administrative wing" and that "walls were buckled and 14 windows were blown out."[23] The explosion could be heard a half-mile away. Although no one was in the building and the damage to it was limited, the Jewish community suffered a severe shock. The president of the congregation, Emanuel Crystal, called a meeting of Jewish leaders for the following day to discuss what had happened and what to do. The meeting was held in the conference room of a motel near the state capitol in downtown Jackson and was attended by forty men. "B" was invited to attend and immediately drove to Jackson. The meeting was already in progress when he arrived. "The rabbi was talking about the damage to the temple. When he noticed me . . . [he] indicated that it was not necessary to bring in any 'outside experts.'"[24] Such a remark directed at someone who had been invited to attend the meeting was, to say the least, undiplomatic, as well as characteristic of a man who, despite his well-deserved reputation for commitment and courage in the cause of civil rights, was also known for his "difficult" and "abrasive personality."[25] Nonetheless, the remark reflected the very real tensions that not only Nussbaum but also other southern rabbis and their congregations had been experiencing during these years in their relationship with the ADL. They naturally felt that they knew best how to deal with a crisis on their own turf and they didn't need advice from the ADL or other national Jewish organizations.

While the ADL's investigative work appears to have been appreciated in the South by rabbis and Jewish communities for keeping them informed about the activities of the Klan and about the campaigns and programs of various civil rights groups that might affect Jews (sit-ins, boycotts, protests, Freedom Rides, voter registration drives), opinions about its policies were divided. Rabbi Alfred L. Goodman of Columbus, Georgia, for example, believed that, despite "many unfavorable comments" elicited by the ADL's "entrance into the school situation," it had been helpful in giving "local rabbis and the local community leaders advice as to how to proceed when faced with particular situations. The regional director . . . came into Columbus and met with our human relations council and advised us as to the best policies to follow, both in regards to the school desegregation and the parks and the library problem."[26] Rabbi Julian B. Feibelman of New Orleans acknowledged that representatives of national Jewish organizations had at times "caused some resentment and some embarrassment," but then went on to say that in the local regional office of the ADL "we've been fortunate to have a series of very fine young men who are outstanding in their liberalism [and] in their activity, and they have won the respect of Catholics and Protestants all over."[27] "B" was one of the men he refers to. Many other rabbis, however, had reservations about the effectiveness of certain ADL policies and practices because, as Mark Bauman has pointed out, they understood "local community dynamics from a different perspective."[28]

The ADL's perspective too often appeared to be from the top down. Its statements of general principles, while morally indisputable, seemed to some to show a lack of understanding for the complexities of local issues and a failure to appreciate the vulnerability of Jews in the South. The ADL's headquarters were in New York and the views and policies on civil rights issues it advocated were being shaped by Jews in the North, where by far the largest percentage of Jews in the country lived. From the late 1940s on, northern Jews had become more active in supporting civil rights causes and expressing opposition to segregation. After the *Brown* decision, as Gary P. Zola has pointed out, "National Jewish organizations such as the Anti-Defamation League, the American Jewish Committee, and the American Jewish Congress aggressively proclaimed the need to dismantle segregation in the South. These efforts unnerved southern Jews."[29] One southern woman told a representative of the ADL from the North "Every time one of you makes a speech, I'm afraid my husband's store will be burned up."[30] In addition, the ADL was known to have joined with the NAACP in taking the *Brown* case to the Supreme Court and afterwards to have cooperated with the NAACP in its challenges of individual racial injustice, a partnership that posed distinct risks for Jews in the South, where the NAACP was widely believed to be a Communist-front organization, a charge repeated by Senator Eastland and by the Sovereignty Commission investigator who interviewed Mantinband.

An example of the ADL's top-down perspective, as well as the way southern Jewish leaders reacted to it, may be seen in the sample editorials the ADL sent to rabbis with the suggestion that they take them to editors of their local papers. Rabbi Nussbaum had received a letter from "B" with such a suggestion three years before the Temple was bombed: "Please find enclosed sample editorials on the question of lawlessness and violence about which we spoke at the meeting in Jackson on October 18, 1964. These are very carefully designed to stimulate and generate a tone and a climate in your community to discourage overt actions of extremists."[31] I don't know what Rabbi Nussbaum's response to the letter was, but Mantinband's comment on these sample editorials represents the opinion of many rabbis in the South at that time about the ADL. "I don't belittle their efforts; I don't even question their methods. It may be all right for the ADL, but it's not the way a rabbi usually works. A rabbi works quietly, behind the scenes." He gave an example from his time in Alabama when the Klan was expected to come to town with the aim of organizing and gaining support and an ADL representative came to him with sample editorials and instructions for their distribution to local editors. "Is that all you're going to do?" he asked. "What else is there to do?" asked the ADL representative. Mantinband explained he would go to the leading white Christians in the community, both lay and church people, and urge them to speak up when they are at their country clubs or Rotary meetings or "somewhere else where there's power structure and public influence."[32] Mantinband's response illustrates the crucial difference in perspective that often accounted for the tension between rabbis and Jewish communities on one hand and the ADL's representatives on the other.

"B" was eventually offered the opportunity to speak at the meeting in Jackson. "I told them what we knew about Klan activity and the Klansmen in the area," he recalled, "[and] I indicated to them that earlier in the day I had talked to law enforcement people who were totally on their side and would be supportive of every effort to apprehend and prosecute those responsible for the bombing."[33] I don't know if those at the meeting, particularly Rabbi Nussbaum, would have been pleased that he had gone to speak with law enforcement officials prior to the emergency meeting. They may have felt he should have consulted with them first. Who was speaking for Jackson's Jewish community?—its rabbi and the leaders of the congregation or a representative of a national Jewish organization? Rabbi Jacob Rothschild said that the only conflict he ever had with the ADL within the area of civil rights came after the Temple was bombed in 1958 and "the ADL wanted to take over" and "run the public relations aspect." As he went on to explain, "Anything that happens that they can get involved in, and show their value, helps them in their fundraising."[34] But he thought that public exposure—making statements for newspapers and appearing on national television—would jeopardize the support the Jewish community had in the political and religious structures of Atlanta. Rabbi Nussbaum's suspicions of the motives of the ADL were more direct and explicit. Noting that "in recent years the specter of Antisemitism has become very much a problem in Jackson and Mississippi," he said "the ADL is taking every advantage of that and has consolidated its stance as the defender and preserver of Jews and Judaism."

But there also appears to have been, notwithstanding these criticisms, a general recognition that the ADL and other national Jewish organizations often did important work in the South in support of both the civil rights movement and Jewish interests there. In this instance, it was important for "B" to have contacted local officials, in effect letting them know that a representative of a national Jewish organization was in Jackson to observe and report what actions would be taken to defend the city's Jewish community. Given the fact that law enforcement officials in Mississippi at that time did not have a good record of upholding the law and indeed, as in the burning of scores of black churches, where police and prosecutors had shown little interest in pursuing and prosecuting those responsible, and particularly in the murder of the three civil rights workers in Philadelphia, where police had joined with the Klan in subverting the law, it was also important that "B" was able to report that the officials had told him they were on the congregation's side and "would be supportive of every effort to apprehend and prosecute those responsible for the bombing." Addressing those at the meeting, he said they should work not only with law enforcement people but also, as he had been urging Jews to do in his travels throughout the state, with others in the community—"the good people," he called them—who would be supportive in creating "a climate that would be prohibitive of... continued violence."[35]

Whoever they were, they had so far been hard to find. Martin Luther King remarked that Chaney, Goodman, and Schwerner had been "murdered by the silence and apathy of good people."[36] Jews themselves—most, anyway—had been unwilling to speak out. But the bombing had changed things and the mood of the meeting was "tumultuous," as Nelson learned from interviewing a number of those who had been there. "Many of the younger men... wanted immediate action. After years of distancing themselves from confrontation, they suddenly came to see things differently." Given what had happened, the change is not surprising. As one of the men put it, "The blacks had problems with these people, but that was solely their problem until the Temple was bombed and it became our problem, too."[37] Of course, in a larger sense, one that Nussbaum, Mantinband, and other rabbis in the South understood, what was thought to be the blacks' problem had all along been everyone's problem. Now several of the men suggested forming "a vigilante group to protect the Jewish community," but the meeting ended inconclusively.[38] The next day, Alvin Binder, a distinguished lawyer and a former segregationist whose recent meetings with Martin Luther King and William Kunstler had, along with other experiences, changed his attitude toward blacks and the civil rights movement, went to the FBI office in Jackson to meet with Roy Moore, the head of the FBI in Mississippi. Moore persuaded Binder that "the best way to catch terrorists... would be to pay informants."[39] This approach was adopted by the FBI and local police, as well as supported by Binder, others in the Jewish community, and the ADL.

Just two months later, however, and before much headway in the investigation could be made, the rabbi's home was also bombed. "The front of Rabbi Nussbaum's home was shattered by an explosion at 11:10 p.m. Tuesday," reported the *Jackson Daily News* on its front page with a large photograph of the rabbi and his wife walking "amidst the shambles" of damage to their home.[40] The bomb had been placed under an air conditioning unit outside the dining room in the front of the house and, although the Nussbaums had not been seriously injured because their bedroom was in the rear of the house, the blast had "caved in the front wall and hurled debris as far as 100 feet from the house," shattering windows of neighboring houses, causing glass and debris to fall on the Nussbaums in their bed, and leaving tiny bits of glass in their skin, hair, and clothes. It was the fourth bombing in Jackson in two months, the other two having also been at night, one on October 6 that demolished the home of a dean at Tougaloo College and the other on November 18 that damaged the home of a religious worker and civil rights sympathizer. "I don't know who is responsible for these acts of violence," the rabbi said, "but I think I can make a pretty educated guess," referring to a meeting of the Americans for the Preservation of the White Race in Jackson "less than two weeks ago" that had been held in Jackson for the purpose of raising money for four of the seven men involved in the murder of Chaney, Goodman, and Schwerner and convicted on a charge of conspiracy in a civil rights trial in Meridian. "I understand the meeting was attended by a former candidate for governor and one of Jackson's city commissioners," he added, "and when men of this importance share sympathy with these groups—nothing can result but terror."[41] He was not the only one to use the word "terror" in referring to the bombing. The reporter used it in his story, the paper in its headline "Rabbi Says Terrorists Thumbing Their Noses," and Nelson in his reports for the *Los Angeles Times*, as well as in the title of his 1993 book, *Terror in the Night*. For decades, the Klan in Mississippi had used terrorism against Negroes; now it was being used against Jews.

Since coming to Jackson in 1954 Rabbi Nussbaum had been following his conscience on the cause of civil rights, though always with due concern for the safety of his congregation. In his first years there he had tried to establish ties with moderate clergy and politicians who might share his views on racial issues and he had helped to establish an interfaith fellowship that would eventually become the Greater Jackson Clergy Alliance and "the first racially integrated association of Protestants, Catholics, and Jews in Mississippi." He had also addressed his congregation on civil rights issues, attempting to create a more sympathetic understanding of the plight of the Negro by "stressing the common bonds of understanding that linked Jews and blacks."[42] He is best known, however, for the commitment he made to the civil rights cause when he decided to go to the Jackson jail and later to Parchman Penitentiary to provide chaplaincy services to the Jews among the Freedom Riders imprisoned there. Once a week that summer he drove one hundred and thirty miles to the penitentiary to hold services and provide counseling, something other rabbis in Delta towns that were closer to the prison had refused to do. After he returned home he spent many hours writing letters to the worried parents of the young Jews held there. On several occasions, he conducted services that were attended by Jews, non-Jews, whites, and blacks and years later, as Gary P. Zola recounts, he "asserted with pride that the prayer services he led at Parchman may have been the first racially integrated worship to take place in the history of Mississippi."[43]

But throughout this time, he tried to conceal the extent of his civil rights activities. While driven by his conscience and his commitment to the ideals of social justice in prophetic Judaism, he wanted to protect his family and the Jewish community from any possible repercussions on account of his activism. The vulnerability of Jews in the South was never far from his mind. After the Temple in Atlanta was bombed in 1958, he wrote a short piece in his temple bulletin entitled "It Can Happen Here," alluding to the bombing, of course, but also to Sinclair Lewis' best-selling novel and its depiction of a fascist takeover in this country and the possibility that it could happen here, though in Rabbi Nussbaum's memory and fears it may have been the fanatical anti-Semitism of Hitler's Nazism that loomed larger than the comparatively tepid version of Mussolini's fascism.

Three years later, on learning that a number of rabbis would be among the next group of Freedom Riders, he went to see William Kunstler late one night at the motel where he and other civil rights lawyers were staying. They had come from New York and other parts of the country to defend the Freedom Riders and had been delayed at the courthouse until eleven o'clock.

The delay had been caused by witnesses for the prosecution (highway patrolmen, city policemen, newspapermen, and Jackson businessmen), "each trying to outdo his predecessor in depicting the fear generated by the approach of the Riders," Kunstler recalled, "as if they were describing a Martian invasion rather than a few busloads of peaceful American citizens."[44] When he and the other lawyers got back to their motel, "we were surprised to find Rabbi Perry Nussbaum . . . waiting for us. He had come . . . to beg us to keep Jewish clergymen out of the Freedom Rides. He was afraid that their continued participation would cause a wave of anti-Semitism in Mississippi." Nussbaum spent the next two hours voicing his concern, one shared by most Jews in Mississippi. "B" had also been asked to help prevent Jews from other parts of the country coming into the state to support civil rights activities.[45] Knowing that Kunstler was Jewish, Nussbaum pleaded with him, "You have an obligation to your fellow religionists." But Kunstler sided with those who were among the Freedom Riders. "As a Jew, I had been very proud of the many rabbis like Joseph K. Gumbiner and Allen Levine who had joined the Rides. It seemed to me . . . that religious leaders, of all people, have an obligation to put into practice the principles that fill their sermons."[46] What he didn't know was that Nussbaum had for years been doing that very thing, most recently by going against his congregation in visiting the Freedom Riders held in Jackson's jail. Nelson, who had grown up in Biloxi, thought Kunstler did not have "the slightest idea of the conflicting pressures and fears of reprisal and violence that weighed on Nussbaum . . . [including] the keen awareness of his congregation's vulnerabilities, [and] the hard-earned knowledge that in Mississippi it was often necessary to put realism before idealism."[47]

Now, on the morning after the bombing, and after his long sleepless hours following the explosion, with the continuing presence of police officers, FBI agents, newspaper and television reporters, and cameramen coming and going in and out of the house, Rabbi Nussbaum, still in a state of shock, found himself having to stand and talk with a number of prominent men in Jackson's religious and political life who had come to express their sympathy. One was Rev. Douglas Hudgins of the First Baptist Church, founded in 1838 and now the largest church in the state. Former Governor Ross Barnett and the Hederman family, owners of *The Clarion Ledger* and the *Jackson Daily News*, were among its members. In his brief conversation with Rev. Hudgins that morning, Rabbi Nussbaum let loose of whatever self-restraint he had so far managed to hold onto and, in the presence of others, including Governor Paul B. Johnson, Jr., FBI agent Jim Ingram, Kenneth Dean of the Human

Rights Council, and an NBC cameraman, he turned to address his fellow clergyman and, "wagging his finger under Hudgins' nose", said to him, "If you had spoken out from your pulpit after the synagogue was bombed and told your people it was wrong to have done that, this wouldn't have happened! Don't tell me now how sorry you are. Those sons-of-a-guns attacked me and my family! They've attacked my house! I don't want to hear how sorry you are!" Then, in a calmer tone, he said, "Doug, if you're really sorry about this, get on the pulpit Sunday and tell your people this is wrong. Talk to all those segregationists that fill up your church."[48] Ingram, who was standing next to Nussbaum at the time, provides a similar account.[49]

On the following Sunday, Nussbaum listened to the regular Sunday morning radio broadcast from the First Baptist Church to hear what, if anything, Rev. Hudgins would say about the bombing. He said it was wrong to bomb someone's house, but did not mention that "it was a rabbi's house that got bombed" and concluded with the evasive comment that "the Lord works in mysterious ways."[50] Another clergyman who came to the house to express his sympathy first denounced both the bombing and the bomber, then added, "But isn't it a shame that the rabbi doesn't know Jesus."[51] Some time later, however, according to Ingram, a number of clergymen "held a small demonstration led by an inter-faith group, composed of whites and blacks, and marched to the synagogue. Some, but not many, of the white clergy did step forward."[52]

I don't know what degree of support Rabbi Nussbaum had prior to the bombing, but according to Nelson, the "great majority of the congregation" now rallied behind him. A day after the bombing a group of "about fifty business and professional leaders of the Jewish community" met at a motel in Jackson to discuss what was to be done. It was decided that Nussbaum and the president of the congregation, Emanuel Crystal, should go to see Mayor Allen Thompson to ask him "to rally the Jackson community behind greater cooperation with the FBI in its efforts to catch the terrorists." Thompson, an uncompromising segregationist, responded to their request by telling them "he didn't think the rabbi's house would have been bombed in the first place if the rabbi hadn't been involved in civil rights activity." When Crystal and Nussbaum presented an account of the meeting to members of the congregation, they became convinced they would have to rely on themselves and the FBI, not on Jackson's police and city officials.[53]

Along with this new resolve, however, came an increase in dissatisfaction with Nussbaum over his civil rights activities. It must have been building over a period of years. "Officially, the congregation continued to express support for Nussbaum," as Gary P. Zola has explained, "but some members . . . were fed up with the controversial rabbi. 'If only the rabbi had kept quiet. . . . If only he hadn't gone to all those meetings,' they would say." They urged him to find another pulpit and "the board of trustees voted not to allow non-Jewish groups (by this, they meant the rabbi's interracial gatherings) to use the temple" without prior approval by the board.[54] Nussbaum had been angered by the failure of Hudgins and others in Jackson's white clergy to take a stand after his house was bombed and now he was bitterly disappointed by the board's new policy. He saw it as a vote of no-confidence and decided to leave Jackson, but was unable to find another pulpit and so remained in Jackson until his retirement in 1973, when he and his wife moved to San Diego.[55]

But now, in January 1968, two months after his house was bombed, the FBI learned from an informant that the Klan was turning its attention away from Jackson and toward Meridian. FBI agent Frank Watts, a native of Hattiesburg, had met with the informant and was shown a hit list. First on it was Meridian's chief of police Roy Gunn. Watts himself was also on the list. Others were prominent Jewish businessmen in Meridian, including Meyer Davidson, president of the Southern Pipe Company, a major distributor of plumbing supplies across the South, and I. A. Rosenbaum, who had been a Marine during World War II, the founder of an insurance agency in Meridian after the war, president of the congregation, and eventually the city's mayor from 1977 to 1985. Police Chief Gunn had recently learned that more than half of Meridian's policemen were members of the Klan and he had recently required all officers to sign a loyalty oath denying membership in the Communist Party or the Klan.[56] The extent to which the Klan had infiltrated the law enforcement establishment was not widely known, but Governor Johnson had learned of it from an FBI letter that had been hand-delivered to him two years before. It reported that the problem was statewide and it provided a list of names that included sheriff's deputies, constables, state highway patrol officers, and judges.[57]

Meridian's Jewish community had long played a prominent role in its city's history. Its first Jews had come from Germany before the Civil War and the congregation began as Reform, in striking contrast to Hattiesburg's congregation, which began to make that transition only in 1935 with the arrival of Rabbi Brodey (suggesting how different two Jewish communities in Mississippi, only eighty-five miles apart, could be, depending on whether they stemmed from the more liberal Reform tradition in Germany or the more orthodox one in Russia and Poland). After becoming an important railroad center in the 1880s, Meridian became the second largest city in the state. It had a long period of prosperity from the late 1800s on, despite intermittent economic downturns, and several Jews became significant figures in the city's business and civic life. They owned highly successful businesses and, with others in the Jewish community, supported major philanthropic endeavors. The four partners of the Marks, Rothenberg and Company built the Grand Opera House in 1890 next to their own grand five-story department store. They also gave land to the city for Highland Park and Israel Marks was honored with a statue of himself in the park for his work as president of the commissioners of Highland Park. Arthur Lyons, a partner in a company dealing in cotton, grain, and hay, donated a building to the Tuberculosis Sanatorium. Rabbi Judah Wechsler had a school named for him "on request of the Negroes of Meridian," the plaque in the school states, "because he led the movement to provide public school facilities for their children."[58] In its fanatical anti-Semitism, the Klan had no need to search for reasons to attack any particular Jewish community, but Meridian's long history of prominent Jews in its business and civic life made it an attractive target.

Beth Israel Temple was bombed on May 29, 1968, eight months after the bombing of Jackson's Beth Israel, six months after the bombing of Rabbi Nussbaum's home, and one month after the assassination of Martin Luther King, Jr. On learning of the bombing, "B" drove to Meridian to assure the Jewish community of the ADL's support, including the possibility of helping to raise money to pay informants in the effort to solve the case. He also told Chief Gunn and Meridian Mayor Al Key "to call on him and the ADL for any assistance they might need in the investigation." Three of Jackson's Jewish businessmen who were involved in raising the money to pay informants, however, "scoffed at Botnick's assurances." In Nelson's account, the ADL contributed only a small amount, $2,500, of the eventual total that was raised—somewhere between $45,000 to $100,000—most of it coming from Jackson's and Meridian's Jewish communities. But, as Nelson points out, the three "were selling Botnick short." Jewish leaders in Meridian thought "B"'s "close relationship with the FBI was helpful." And, in Washington, Nelson went on to say, "the ADL kept the political pressure on the FBI to make sure agents in the field had whatever mandates and resources they needed for the investigation."[59]

In the course of the investigation both the FBI and Meridian's Chief Gunn had come to focus on two brothers in the Klan, Raymond and Alton Wayne Roberts, who, they believed, could be persuaded to become informants. They had both been involved in the murder of the three civil rights workers in Philadelphia and were interested in the reward money, but Alton Wayne, having been recently convicted in a federal court of the killing of Goodman and Schwerner, and now out on bail while appealing the conviction, hoped for some leniency in the event the appeal was denied. Eventually, after extended and often frustrating late-night negotiations, usually in a trailer hidden from sight in a remote wooded area near Meridian, but sometimes in the home of Watts, the brothers agreed to become informants.

One of the first things learned from them was that the Klan was planning to bomb Meyer Davidson's house. Not only was he a prominent member of the Jewish community; he was also a member of Meridian's biracial Committee of Conscience, which raised funds for the rebuilding of the black churches—as many as two hundred—that had been bombed or burned in Mississippi and he was therefore, in the eyes of the Klan, one of those "Jews [who] are the biggest nigger-loving people in the world." [60] The Roberts brothers revealed the date of the scheduled bombing, the night of June 27, and the names of the two Klansmen who would place the bomb at the Davidson house, Tommy Tarrants and Danny Joe Hawkins, the same two who had bombed the Temple the previous September. In the counterplan developed by FBI agents Watts and Tom Tucker together with Meridian police Chief Gunn and Detective Scarbrough, FBI agents and Meridian police would be waiting at the Davidson house that night, as well as in the neighborhood. Their plan was to apprehend Tarrants and Hawkins in the act of placing the bomb.

But things didn't go exactly according to either plan. Based on what the FBI knew from informants, it decided to surround the Davidson home with agents and police officers on the night of the 27th. But after everyone was in place the FBI learned from the informants that the date for the bombing had been changed by the Klan for the 29th. Then, in the actual event on the night of the 29th, Tarrants was accompanied not by Hawkins but by a young woman, Kathy Ainsworth, who, it would be learned later, had been Tarrants' accomplice in several other attacks. As Tarrants began to walk up Davidson's driveway toward the house with the bomb and an automatic pistol in his hands, he heard a voice cry out "Halt! Police!"

What happened next remains in dispute. In both Nelson's and Ingram's accounts, it was Tarrants who fired the first shot. In his account, it was the police.[61] The most striking feature of his account, however, is not in how it differs but in how it emphasizes understanding what happened that night: "Whether or not the Meridian police gave me proper warning before opening fire is a matter about which we have always differed. But this difference of opinion is no longer relvant to me. Policemen are human—just like the rest of us. These particular men were under great pressure to stop a dangerous, terrorist organization that would certainly have claimed innocent lives had it been allowed to continue unopposed.... So I could understand how the Meridian police could not afford to take any chances."[62]

After dropping the bomb and the pistol on the driveway, Tarrants, though hit in his right leg with buckshot from Scarbrough's shotgun, managed to get to the car. Kathy Ainsworth had been hit by a rifle bullet in her spine at the base of her neck and died soon afterwards. Tarrants managed to drive past a roadblock that had been set up, but wrecked the car, got out and tried to escape, and was eventually captured. He was tried, convicted, and sentenced to thirty years in Parchman Penitentiary. But his story doesn't end there. He escaped from Parchman, was caught, brought back, sentenced to an additional five years, had a religious conversion over the next few years, received an early release (in part as a result of a recommendation from Watts), attended the University of Mississippi, and went on to earn a Master of Divinity degree, become a minister, and write *The Conversion of a Klansman*.

The disputed course of events on the night of the stakeout at the Davidson house, particularly regarding the question of who shot first, involved a potential legal issue and became a matter of special concern for "B" and the ADL. Nelson argued that the FBI's counterplan was one of illegal entrapment that "raised serious questions about law enforcement methods used in this case."[63] He quotes FBI agents and local police who used words and phrases such as "set up," "lay a trap," "lure," "ambush," and "lured into an ambush" in their discussions of the plan enacted on that night at the Davidson house and he at times uses the same or similar language himself in telling the story of what happened. His interpretation of the events that night was also based on a memorandum entitled "Memo on Reported Activities of the ADL, FBI, and the Meridian Police Department Concerning the White Knights of the Ku Klux Klan and Anti-Semitism in Meridian" that had been written and given to him by Ken Dean, who was head of the Human Rights Council in Mississippi then and had met with "B" a number of times to discuss what was going on in Meridian. At the heart of the memorandum was the charge that "the FBI and the Meridian police had used money supplied by the Anti-Defamation League and Mississippi Jewish community to pay the Roberts brothers to arrange for two Klan hitmen to attempt a bombing so that the police could execute them in the commission of a crime."[64] "B" was said to be one source for the information in Dean's memorandum and he and the ADL, along with the police and the FBI, were said to be involved in an illegal entrapment.

From the FBI's point of view, however, as Roy Moore wrote in a memorandum, what happened was "not an entrapment in that no one was caused to do anything that had not been already planned by the Klan[;] rather, officers were successful in convincing one of the participants that he should cooperate and furnish them with the time and place of the next planned act of violence." [65] Tarrants himself confirmed what Moore said: "the truth is that Meyer Davidson had become a high-priority target in my mind before the Roberts brothers became FBI informants. So the FBI did not lure us into doing something we had no intention of doing."[66] Although "B" remained focused on defending his and the ADL's role, his references to "marked targets" and to "a Jewish businessman" in Meridian (Davidson) in the following passage from his oral memoir assume Moore's point that the bombing had already been planned before the FBI and Meridian police became involved: "Notwithstanding the charges and allegations of the national press that [the] ADL was in complicity with the FBI to entrap certain individuals who had marked targets, in this case a Jewish businessman in Meridian, we felt we should participate in offering reward money for the apprehension and capture of those responsible for these bombings." [67] In other words, what happened that night was an effort in apprehension and capture, not entrapment, and the role of "B" and the ADL was limited to helping to provide information and raise funds.

The ADL was even more explicit in a statement issued in December of 1992 just prior to the publication of *Terror in the Night* and intended as a response to the entrapment claim in it. The ADL's purpose was to explain its role and to help ADL representatives in "responding to press inquiries" following the book's appearance. I learned of the statement's existence from Fay and she gave me a copy of it. Entitled "Statement Concerning Jack Nelson's Terror in the Night, December 1992, for responding to press inquiries," it begins by noting the recent "tide of actual bombings of Jewish houses of worship and other communal establishments by the Ku Klux Klan." It then acknowledges that "the Jewish community of Mississippi raised funds to enable the FBI to obtain information leading to the apprehension of these terrorists" and that "B," as the ADL's representative in the region, "recommended to Jewish leaders that they assist in this fund-raising effort as a matter of civic responsibility." The statement denies the charge of an entrapment: "So far as we know, there is no basis for criticism of the law enforcement authorities. Even Thomas Tarrants, the convicted KKK terrorist who was wounded in the attempted bombing of a Jewish family's home in Meridian . . . specifically denies Mr. Nelson's claim that he was lured . . . into a trap" and notes that "the intended Jewish victim had already been a high-priority target for the Ku Klux Klan's assassination squad."[68]

Everything seems to depend, as Maryanne Vollers observed, on "who's telling the story" at the point when Tarrants reached the driveway: "either the cops shouted 'Halt! Police!,' Tarrants fired twice with his handgun, and the cops opened up" or "the cops simply opened up."[69] Nelson's and Ingram's different accounts of the events that night reveal an uncertainty that persists to this day about that crucial moment and who shot first. Nelson reports that Ingram told him "It was an ambush, that's what they meant to do. . . . No question about that. They meant to kill them out there that night."[70] Nelson, who died in 2009, remained convinced that there had been an entrapment and an abuse of power by the FBI and Meridian police and he restated that view in his posthumously published memoir, *Scoop: The Evolution of a Southern Reporter*.[71] But in Ingram's memoir, published four years after Nelson's death, he doesn't mention an ambush and instead provides a very different account of what took place. As Tarrants "began walking slowly toward the Davidson home," Ingram wrote, "the stillness of the night air was broken by the sound of a human voice—'Halt! Police!' Hearing that, Tarrants turned and fired his weapon, drawing the fire of the police officers."[72]

Probably only through a detailed reexamination of all the relevant documents and a study of the various issues by legal scholars, or at least with their aid, could one hope to resolve the differing points of view into a definitive account of exactly what actions were taken, by whom, and with what intentions, but perhaps not even then.

For a number of years afterwards, what took place that night in Meridian appeared to mark the end of the Klan's campaign against the Jews in Mississippi. The Klan had been so well infiltrated by FBI informants that membership declined and those who remained ceased to be able or willing to mount the kinds of attacks they had in the past. The exception was Beckwith. He had managed to remain free after assassinating Evers in 1963 because the first two trials had ended with hung juries that were all white and all male. "B" thought that "a hung jury . . . in Mississippi in those days . . . was progress because a white man had always gone scot-free . . . in the murder of a black man."[73] But Bowers remained confident that Mississippi hadn't changed and boasted "no jury in the state of Mississippi is going to convict a white man for killing someone black."[74] Although Bowers was convicted in 1970, along with other Klan members, of conspiracy to deprive Chaney, Goodman, and Schwerner of their civil rights, and served six years in federal prison from 1970 to 1976, for more than twenty years he successfully evaded conviction for the 1966 murder of Vernon Dahmer, president of the NAACP chapter in Hattiesburg, by means of hung juries, though he was eventually convicted in 1998.

The long histories of the Bowers and Beckwith trials and hung juries reveal how deeply embedded in Mississippi's social and political culture was the determination to defy the Supreme Court and the federal government in the decades following the *Brown* decision. The Klan operated with a good deal of confidence that its defiance, though not necessarily its resort to violence, was secretly approved of by most white Mississippians, and at times not so secretly, and even blatantly, as when former Governor Ross Barnett, who was a partner in the law firm whose attorneys were defending Beckwith, "made frequent appearances at the defense table" during Beckwith's second trial and "more than once ... shook Beckwith's hand and clapped him on the back in full view of the jurors."[75] Barnett was also, according to Beckwith biographer Reed Massengill, "personally delivering contributions to Beckwith's defense fund, even as the state was mounting a murder case against him."[76]

During the nine years between the end of the second trial in 1964 and his drive to New Orleans to assassinate "B" in 1973, Beckwith remained active in the Klan, though he denied being a member with his characteristic reply "I have been accused of it," which he also employed from time to time in reference to his assassination of Evers, relishing the ambiguity in his reply that enabled him to seem to be denying he had killed Evers while enjoying whatever fame and celebrity-status went with the accusation. In August of 1965 he felt free to brag about it when he went to a Klan gathering at a fishing camp south of Jackson and proudly stated that "killing that nigger gave me no more inner discomfort than our wives endure when they give birth to our children." Later that year when he appeared before the House Un-American Activities Committee, having been subpoenaed along with other Klan members, he, like Bowers, invoked the Fifth Amendment for the right not to testify, though he, in contrast to Bowers, clearly enjoyed the attention he got from appearing before the committee. At other times, he was eager to let someone know that he was the one who had killed Evers. In 1967, he helped raise legal defense funds for Alton Wayne Roberts, Bowers, and other Klansmen who had been convicted on federal conspiracy charges in the deaths of Chaney, Goodman, and Schwerner but were free on bonds pending appeals.[77] Bowers began serving his six-year sentence in 1970, as other convicted Klan members began serving theirs. Then, after a couple of years, the paid informants who were still in contact with the few remaining White Knights learned that "another job was being planned." The target was

"B" and the person chosen for the job was Beckwith. His assassination of Evers made him seem, in the eyes of those few White Knights, the obvious choice for the job. Now, five years after Meridian and the seeming end of the Klan's campaign against the Jews in Mississippi, there was still one job left to do: avenging what had happened at Meyer Davidson's house, the death of Ainsworth, and the imprisonment of Tarrants.[78]

Beckwith initially planned to use a bomb to blow up the ADL headquarters in downtown New Orleans. His experience as a marine in World War II, as a life-long deer hunter, and as a Klansman had been with guns. But his accomplice in this job, the bomb-maker Klansman L. E. Matthews, had criticized him for having left his rifle at the scene of the shooting of Evers. Beckwith went to the ADL office in a building on Gravier Street to see "B," though for what reason isn't known. Perhaps he needed to see what the office looked like if he was thinking of placing a bomb there, or perhaps he was still considering the possibility of using a rifle and had never seen "B" or a picture of him. After being told by the secretary that Mr. Botnick wasn't in, and perhaps concluding that placing a bomb in downtown New Orleans was too difficult or risky, he decided to target him at his home. Although there were difficulties there, too, they apparently weren't important considerations for him. Fay and "B" lived in a large apartment on the second floor of a two-story house on South Galvez Street in a quiet neighborhood lined with crepe myrtle trees. Of their three children, Michael was in law school at Tulane and the older of their two daughters, Wendy, was a senior at Sophie Newcomb. Their younger daughter, Lori, fourteen, was still living at home. Another family lived in the apartment on the first floor. Exploding a bomb at the house would have killed or severely injured Fay, "B," and Lori, as well as the family in the apartment on the first floor.

In the meantime, the FBI had learned of the plan from an informant and had notified the New Orleans police department. They knew the model car Beckwith would be driving, the number on the license plate (which he had stolen), and the route he would be taking into the city. In the late afternoon of September 26, 1973, Beckwith picked up the assembled bomb from the home of his accomplice south of Jackson and began the drive on Highway 49 that would lead to Interstate 10 and to New Orleans. The informant called the FBI immediately and the FBI notified the New Orleans police. As Beckwith began to cross the southbound of the twin bridges over Lake Pontchartrain, the police were waiting for him on the other side in patrol cars parked off the highway and stopped him about a mile after he exited the bridge. When asked if he had been ever arrested before, he replied, "Yes. They said I killed a nigger in Mississippi."[79]

One of the arresting officers, I've recently learned, had many years before been a school friend of Lee Harvey Oswald in New Orleans. His name was Fred O'Sullivan and they had sat next to each other in junior high school because the order of seating in homeroom was alphabetical. O'Sullivan would later tell the Warren Commission investigating President Kennedy's assassination that in high school he had tried to recruit Lee (as he had known him then) to the Civil Air Patrol. Oswald's erect bearing, with his "eyes straight ahead, head straight, [and] shoulders back," seemed to O'Sullivan to indicate that Oswald "would really fit well on the drill team."[80] Oswald would go into the Marines, live in Russia for a time, return, and move to Dallas. O'Sullivan, following in his father's footsteps, would become a policeman and then an intelligence officer in the New Orleans Police Department. It was there, Fay told me, when "B" came to give seminars on anti-Semitism, that the two met and became friends. O'Sullivan had once taken a course at Loyola University in comparative religion and in 1967, though raised as a Catholic, had decided to convert to Judaism. Six years later, having caught "the Zionist bug," in the words of Dina Kraft in an article in *Haaretz* about him, he would move to Israel with his family just before the Yom Kippur War, become a policeman in Jerusalem, and change his first name from Fred to Ephraim.[81] But it was in the week just before his departure, on Rosh Hashanah Eve, September 1973, that the police department received a tip from the FBI that Beckwith was headed to New Orleans to bomb the Botnick home and it was then that O'Sullivan and other police officers made the arrest.[82]

Beckwith was searched and found to be carrying a .45 automatic pistol. On the front passenger's seat of the car lay a photocopy of a city map marked with directions to within a block of the house where Fay and "B" lived and near it on the floor board lay a black box in which there was an alarm clock set for 4:30 a.m. attached to a bomb requiring only a few twists of its wiring to be fully armed. In the back seat and the trunk police officers found, in addition to a .30-caliber M-1 carbine, a jumbled collection of odd things including parts for other guns, a camera, clothing, shoes, a Bible, a collection of letters from the wife of Jefferson Davis, and a box of blue-and-white antique china that Beckwith would claim he was planning to sell to an antique dealer in New Orleans. Once he was jailed, the bomb squad had time to examine the bomb and estimated that it was "big enough to blow up Botnick's two-story house and take out both next-door neighbors for good measure." And then added "who knows what would have gone up if the bomb had ruptured a gas line."[83]

Why did Beckwith, when asked if he'd ever been arrested before, in effect admit that he had killed Medgar Evers? O'Sullivan's son Arieh, a well-known journalist in Israel, wrote an article for *The Jerusalem Post* in 2005 about his father in which he suggested that Beckwith may have hoped "to win sympathy from a fellow Southerner." Beckwith knew that police officers in Philadelphia, Mississippi, had joined with the Klan in the murder of Chaney, Goodman, and Schwerner and that some police officers in Meridian were Klan members. But in this instance he "picked the wrong white cop." If he had known he was speaking to O'Sullivan, he probably wouldn't have said what he did. "The Klan had [had] my father in their sights for some time," Arieh O'Sullivan wrote.[84]

"B" had been warned several days before Beckwith started driving to New Orleans. "I was advised by friendly law enforcement officials that I was being considered a target for elimination and the guy that was to do it was Byron de la Beckwith [sic]. I considered it to be a joke and didn't give it further notice." He was called a second time and told to leave the house, and again he refused. Up to this point, Fay told me, he hadn't told her of the danger or of the calls from the ADL. Then a third call came from the ADL's Benjamin Epstein in the New York office: "I was told . . . that I had no choice in the matter, that if I wanted employment with the ADL I would have to follow instructions and leave the house. And so we did."[85] They moved to the Fontainebleau Motel for three weeks and remained under the protection of the FBI and the New Orleans police.

Beckwith was tried in a federal court for possession of an unregistered handgun and an unregistered bomb but was found not guilty. He was tried again in a state court, found guilty, and, after losing an appeal, was imprisoned in the state penitentiary in Angola. While in prison he wrote a letter to Richard Butler in Idaho, the founder of a neo-Nazi organization called Aryan Nations, in which he summarized the events in New Orleans in this way: "In 1973 I was accused of coming to New Orleans, La., to put a bomb in the lap of a top Jew of the ADL or B'nai B'rith. In 1974 I was tried and found TOTALLY innocent. . . . In 1975 I was retried before an all nigger jury made up of 5 nigger women and in 5 minutes I was a convict."[86] He served three years of the five-year sentence and in 1980 returned to Mississippi for a short period, then moved to Tennessee. In 1994, more than thirty years after the assassination of Evers, Beckwith was brought back to Jackson to stand trial for his murder, was convicted, and sentenced to life in prison, where he died in 2001.

By the end of this trial and Beckwith's conviction and imprisonment, "B" had been retired for two years. He had been with the ADL for thirty-one years, twenty-eight of them in New Orleans. The years 1964 to 1968 in Mississippi had been the period of his greatest challenge, as well as achievement, something that the Klan's attempted revenge assassination in 1973 seemed to confirm. In 1979 when he received the Milton A. Senn Award, the ADL's top honor for professional excellence, the announcement by the ADL's Advisory Board in New Orleans captured the significance of his role in a single sentence: "During the terrible turmoil of the 1960s, when terrorism became a daily threat to thousands of Southerners, 'B' Botnick's work in counteracting the Ku Klux Klan's programs of violence was so effective that he was marked for assassination."[87] Once, two years before he retired, and perhaps in anticipation of it, he was going through old files and ran across "Rabbi in the Deep South," the essay Mantinband had written for the *ADL Bulletin* in that summer of 1961 when he had gone to its headquarters to personally recommend "B" for a position. On seeing the essay now, "B" decided to send a copy to each of his three children with the brief note, "I have tried to follow the Rabbi's philosophy." Interpreted in the light of the work he did with the ADL for thirty-one years, as "B" himself summarized it in a brief farewell he wrote on the occasion of his retirement, it meant being "moved by the belief that efforts had to be made to deal with . . . the racism, sexism, anti-Semitism, bigotry and the everyday, random hatred one still finds in American life."[88] By the time he retired in 1992, it had been seven years since he'd had triple bypass heart surgery, which, he told me, was expected to last ten years. But the surgery was an experience, he added, he would not be willing to undergo a second time, even if it were possible.

Afterword

At the time Jessica asked me how my parents had come to settle in Mississippi, and even after I'd begun to do the reading and research that I thought would enable me to answer her question, I had no idea that the story would evolve into the larger, more complex one it became and would include the experience of the Jewish community in Hattiesburg during the years of the civil rights movement, as well as the experiences of the communities in Jackson and Meridian. I also hadn't realized the extent to which a local incident such as the Wexler trial, the national economic downturn of the Great Depression, or the civil rights movement had affected Jews in Hattiesburg. But my reading and research showed me how certain individuals in the story—my parents, the elder in the Wexler case, the Jewish businessmen who helped bring Reliance to the city, Rabbis Brodey, Mantinband, and Nussbaum, the Jewish communities in Hattiesburg, Jackson, and Meridian, and "B"—dealt with the issues they faced and in doing so represented what the experience of Jewish life in Mississippi was like over a period of five decades.

Now in this brief afterword, what I need to do is bring the story of my parents and our family up to the present.

The last time I saw my father was in February of 1962 in El Paso, where he and my mother had come to visit Alice and me five months after I had been recalled to active duty in the army and sent to Fort Bliss. Prior to being recalled I had been thinking of going to graduate school and by the time my parents arrived I had already applied but didn't disclose my plans to them. Not knowing if I would be accepted and fearing that I would not be able to answer all the questions my father would ask me, I thought that if I told them we would talk only or mainly about that and ruin the few days we had together. Among his concerns, I knew, would have been how I would afford five years of graduate school, support a family if we had children during that time, and after graduation find a job in the face of the quotas that Jews had often encountered in many fields. I wouldn't have had ready answers to these questions. They would have arisen in my father's mind out of long experience, first as a boy in Russia after his father had left the family, then as a peddler in Hattiesburg, and then as a storeowner during the Depression. I knew he wanted the best for me, but I was of another generation and my experience was very different from his, due in no small measure to what he and my mother had accomplished and been able to give their children, and I felt confident in trusting the encouragement I'd received from professors at Northwestern. Two weeks after my parents left I received word that I'd been accepted at the University of Michigan and I wrote to tell them about my plans.

When my father read my letter, however, he was unable to reply right away, saying only, as Milton told me later, "I'll have to talk to him about it." I would learn later that he had been having prostate problems for several months and had been advised by our family physician, Dr. Ross, to see a specialist in New Orleans. He feared he might have cancer. He was sixty-one and the previous ten years had not been easy for him. He'd had a series of eye surgeries for glaucoma and cataracts that my mother said had taken a severe toll on him. After the cataract operations, very different from today's, he had to lie in a hospital bed for long periods of time with his head kept stationary by sandbags on either side of it. Now he was told he needed prostate surgery. Weighing on his mind must also have been the fact that Uncle Abe had died of prostate cancer four years before. On the morning after the operation he was told that he did not have cancer, but he died in the hospital five days later, presumably from a blood clot.

I learned of his death from Milton, who called me at 6:30 that morning. Rabbi Mantinband presided at the funeral. One or two days later, my mother and I were standing in her kitchen, looking out the windows into the backyard and beyond into the neighborhood, watching the rain come down in a heavy downpour, soaking the earth all around. I thought of my father lying underground in the small Jewish cemetery on the other side of town, as my mother must have, too. "Your father deserved better than this," she said.

She lived on for another twelve years. She took great pleasure in seeing the changes Milton made in the store and she went there most days to wait on customers or work at one of the cash registers. At night, she often played gin rummy with her friends in the Jewish community. She established the educational trust fund for her grandchildren that she and my father had discussed before he died and it helped to fund both undergraduate and graduate education of their grandchildren. In 1965, she went with Fay to visit her sisters and brothers in the Soviet Union, Celia and Lev in Moscow, Klara and Joseph in

Kiev. It was then, as Fay recalled, that one of the tour guides complimented her on how well she still spoke Russian. In the fall of 1973, she learned that she had a tumor the size of a small lemon in the frontal lobe of her brain. She postponed the operation that she had agreed to have in order to be able to enjoy the seventy-fifth birthday party Milton threw for her in November. Then in January, with the same courage she had shown as a young woman in leaving her home and family more than fifty years before, she went to New Orleans for the operation. She stayed with Fay and "B" before the operation and planned to stay with them during the recovery period. Fay wrote me in London, where I was on sabbatical leave, to tell me Mother had successfully undergone the surgery, but on the day her letter arrived she called to tell me Mother had died.

After Fay and "B" moved to New Orleans, Fay began working as assistant to the dean of students at Sophie Newcomb College. From that position she went on to become an assistant to the provost at Tulane University, where she worked until she retired. She and "B" enjoyed traveling to England, France, and Italy, as well as to Israel. After he died, she continued to travel, at times with one of her children. By then, Michael had earned a law degree from Tulane, was practicing in New Orleans, had married, and would eventually become the father of five children. For many years he has been an honorary board member of the ADL's South Central Region and honorary life member of its National Commission. Wendy earned a BA with a major in English and then a degree in nursing. Despite earning a law degree some years later, nursing remained her first love. She married an oncologist, had two children, and moved to Houston where both she and her husband worked at M. D. Anderson Hospital. After retiring from M. D. Anderson, she moved to Austin, Texas, to be near one of her two daughters and continues to practice nursing. Lori earned a BA from Sophie Newcomb, found a job with the ADL in Columbus, Ohio, married, had two daughters, and is now the program coordinator of the Jewish Studies Program at Ohio State. A few years after "B" died, Fay decided to move to Columbus, in part to escape the hurricanes in New Orleans.

In 1956, after four years at the University of Alabama and two in the army, Milton returned to Hattiesburg to join our father and "B" at the store. It hadn't been his first choice. "When I was in college at the University of Alabama," he recalled, "I'd been to New York on buying trips with my Dad and I didn't want to come back to Hattiesburg. I didn't want to be involved in the store, but rather to live in New York."[1] But he soon became very involved in growing the business and he persuaded our father that the store should upgrade the merchandise it offered, transforming it from the working men's and women's store it had been since its founding in the 1920s to one that would appeal to a broader customer base by offering better-known and more fashionable brands and by increasing the budget for advertising to establish the new identity for the store. After our father died in 1962, seven months after "B" had left the business and he and Fay had moved to Atlanta, Milton eventually became its owner. Over the next thirty years, Waldoff's on Pine grew from the original 3,600 square feet to 60,000 in Cloverleaf Mall. During that time, Milton also opened a very successful men's and women's store, Milton's, Ltd., in Hattiesburg. In recognition of his success, he received numerous honors and awards, including Mississippi Man of the Year, Governor's Economic Excellence Award, Mississippi Retailer of the Year, and America's Brand Name Retailer of the Year. Eventually, however, he had to close the stores. "I was trying to do too much," he said, "and was overextended."[2] After a brief period, he founded the Waldoff Group, which specializes in retail consulting (by assisting and advising retail clients about merchandise, inventory con-trol, events, marketing, advertising, and closing sales) and has helped clients in cities across the country. He still lives in Hattiesburg and has two children from his first marriage, a son Paul, who graduated from West Point, did three tours of duty in Iraq and Afghanistan, earned an MBA at Tulane, and now works for Intel in San Diego, and a daughter, Lauren, who earned a degree in nursing at USM and later earned a Master's degree and became an anesthe-tist. She is married, has a daughter, and lives in Atlanta.

I've been retired from the University of Illinois for eighteen years, as has Alice, who had been the Director of Communications in the Business College, where, after she retired, the students in Commerce Council (as it was called then) established an award in her name. Our daughter Jessica earned a BA at Amherst College, won a Mellon Fellowship for graduate study in musicology at Cornell University, became a Mozart scholar, and is an associate professor at the College of Holy Cross in Worcester, MA. She and her husband live in Sherborn.

In the years after Rabbi Mantinband left for the pulpit in Longview, Texas, and after Rabbi Ben-Ami's brief time in Hattiesburg, the congregation had a series of student and fulltime rabbis. Among the latter were two women, one of whom, Judith Bluestein, became the first fulltime female rabbi hired by a con-gregation in Mississippi. The congregation's last fulltime rabbi was Uri Barnea, who served from 2007–14. By the late 1970s, most of the East European Jews who had largely shaped the character of Jewish life in Hattiesburg as

I remember it had died. Of those six Jewish immigrants from Russia or Poland who owned clothing stores on East Pine Street when I was in high school, including my father, four had died and the other two had retired. Now, they are also gone, as are most of the buildings on that entire city block, torn down after years of having been abandoned when most clothing stores either moved to Cloverleaf Mall or closed their doors. The only clothing store left on East Pine Street is at the corner of the next block and is owned by Holocaust survivor David Sackler, who, along with a few other surviving members of his family, was brought to Hattiesburg in 1946 by Sam Sackler. Today, the congregation has a membership of thirty families and among them are a good number of doctors and members of the faculty and staff at USM, as was my cousin Stanley, who, before he retired, was a pianist and professor in the Music Department. According to Stuart Rockoff in the online *Encyclopedia of Southern Jewish Communities*, "while the congregation is not growing, it seems relatively stable" and "will likely continue to be the center of Jewish life in southeast Mississippi for years to come."[3]

Endnotes

CHAPTER 1

1 Paul Waldoff, letter (hereafter abbreviated as PW), April 20, 1922.
2 PW, March 20, 1922.
3 Joseph Stolin, letter, 1974.
4 PW, February 11, 1923.
5 Moishe Stolin, letter, November 3, 1921.
6 Ronald Sanders, *Shores of Refuge: A Hundred Years of Jewish Immigration* (New York: Schocken Books, 1988), 243–45.
7 PW, March 20, 1922.
8 Bernard Marinbach, *Galveston: Ellis Island of the West* (Albany: State University of New York Press, 1983), 10–13.
9 Ibid., 177–78.
10 Barney Auerbach, draft card, 1917, ancestry.com. Accessed August 29, 2012, http://search.ancestry.com. For personal information about Barney Auerbach, I am grateful to his son Maurice.
11 Stephen J. Whitfield, *In Search of American Jewish Culture* (Hanover, NH: University Press of New England, 1999), 22.
12 Howard M. Sachar, *A History of the Jews in America* (New York: Vintage Books, 1992), 125–26, 284–88.
13 Eugene M. Avrutin, *Jews and the Imperial State: Identification Politics in Tsarist Russia* (Ithaca, NY: Cornell University Press, 2010), 138.
14 PW, February 7, 1923.
15 Mary Antin, *From Plotzk to Boston* (Boston: W.B. Clarke & Co., 1899), 12.
16 Nicholas V. Riasanovsky and Mark D. Steinberg, *A History of Russia*, Vol. 2 (New York: Oxford University Press, 2011), 389.
17 Benjamin Nathans, *Beyond the Pale: The Jewish Encounter with Late Imperial Russia* (Berkeley: University of California Press, 2004), 267, 272.
18 Ibid., 181.
19 Marie Waife-Goldberg, *My Father, Sholom Aleichem* (New York: Simon and Schuster, 1968), 160–61, 162; Riasanovsky and Steinberg, *History of Russia*, Vol. 2, 389.
20 Solomon Maimon, *An Autobiography*, trans. J. Clark Murray, with an Introduction by Michael Shapiro (Urbana: University of Illinois Press, 2001), 34.
21 Frederic Cople Jaher, *A Scapegoat in the New Wilderness: The Origins and Rise of Anti-Semitism in America* (Cambridge, MA: Harvard University Press, 1994), 55.
22 Nathans, *Beyond the Pale*, 329, 331.
23 Sanders, *Shores of Refuge*, 289, 293–94.
24 *Encyclopaedia Judaica*, 2nd ed., s.v. "Belaya Tserkov," 150, 178.

25 Zvi Gitelman, *A Century of Ambivalence: The Jews of Russia and the Soviet Union* (New York: Pantheon, 1988), 106.
26 Isaac Babel, *1920 Diary*, ed. Carol J. Avins, trans. H. T. Willetts (New Haven, CT: Yale University Press, 2002), 4.
27 Ibid., 84.
28 Isaac Babel, *Collected Stories*, ed. and trans. W. Morison (Cleveland, OH: World Publishing Company, 1965), 219.
29 Peter later mentioned this in his 2003 memoir, "A Life of Friendship and Service: Tentative Memoirs," trans. Eteri Shvets (unpublished translation), Vols. 1, 4–5.
30 Irving Howe, *World of Our Fathers: The Journey of the East Europeans to America and the Life They Found and Made* (New York: Simon and Schuster, 1976), 179.
31 Sanders, *Shores of Refuge*, 386–87.
32 Hasia Diner, *The Jews of the United States, 1654 to 2000* (Berkeley: University of California Press, 2004), 201.
33 PW, December 6, 1922.
34 PW, January 10, 1923.
35 Ibid.
36 PW, January 17, 1923.
37 PW, January 22, 1923.
38 Ibid.
39 PW, January 23, 1923.
40 Ibid.
41 Ibid.
42 PW, January 24, 1923.
43 PW, January 30, 1923.
44 PW, December 1, 1922.
45 PW, January 29, 1923.
46 PW, January 30, 1923.
47 PW, January 29, 1923.
48 PW, February 7, 1923
49 Ibid.
50 PW, February 11, 1923.
51 PW, February 7, 1923.
52 PW, February 9, 1923.
53 PW, February 11, 1923.
54 Ibid.
55 Ibid.
56 PW, February 14, 1923.
57 PW, February 15, 1923.
58 PW, [between February 20 and February 25, 1923].
59 PW, March 23, 1923.

CHAPTER 2

1 Benjamin Morris, *Hattiesburg, Mississippi: A History of the Hub City* (Charleston, SC: The History Press, 2014), 51–53.
2 Ulysses Grant, *Personal Memoirs*, ed. E. B. Long (New York: De Capo Press, Inc., 1982), 370; Morris, *Hattiesburg, Mississippi*, 88.

3   Mitch Landrieu, *In the Shadow of Statues: A White Southerner Confronts History* (New York: Viking, 2018), 3, 178.
4   *Hattiesburg American* (hereafter abbreviated as HA), "Seen and Heard, Here and There, About the City," August 16, 1933.
5   Morris, *Hattiesburg, Mississippi*, 52–54.
6   HA, "Hardy, Hub City's Founder," January 7, 1929.
7   Nollie Hickman, *Mississippi Harvest: Lumbering in The Longleaf Pinebelt, 1842 to 1915* (Jackson: University of Mississippi Press, 1962), 180–84.
8   *Illinois Central Magazine*, 19 (May 1931): 13.
9   John R. Skates, "Hattiesburg: The Early Years," in *Hattiesburg: A Pictorial History*, ed. Kenneth G. McCarty, Jr. (Jackson: University of Mississippi Press, 1982), 11.
10 Ibid., 6, for the first population figure, and Lee Shai Weissbach, *Jewish Life in Small-Town America: A History* (New Haven: Yale University Press, 2005), 342, for the second.
11 William T. Schmidt, "The Middle Years," in *Hattiesburg: A Pictorial History*, 73, for the Hattiesburg population figure, and Weissbach, *Jewish Life in Small-Town America*, 342, for the Jewish population figure.
12 PW, [fall 1922].
13 Sachar, *A History of the Jews in America*, 340.
14 PW, [fall 1922].
15 PW, April 16, 1922.
16 PW, December 6, 1922.
17 PW, January 29, 1923.
18 PW, December 6, 1922.
19 PW, December 12, 1922.
20 PW, January 10, 1923.
21 PW, dated only 1923.
22 PW. March 5, 1923.
23 PW, March 12, 1923.
24 Hasia Diner, *Roads Taken: The Great Jewish Migrations to the New World and the Peddlers Who Forged the Way* (New Haven, CT: Yale University Press, 2015), 59.
25 Hasia Diner, "Entering the Mainstream of Modern Jewish History: Peddlers and the American Jewish South," in *Jewish Roots in Southern Soil: A New History*, ed. Marcie Cohen Ferris and Mark I. Greenberg (Hanover, NH, and London: University Press of New England, 2006), 93–95.
26 Lu Ann Jones, "Gender, Race, and Itinerant Commerce in the Rural South." *Journal of Southern History* 66, no. 2 (2000): 307.
27 Jaher, *A Scapegoat in the New Wilderness*, 24–32.
28 Richard Wright, *Black Boy (American Hunger)* (New York: Harper Perennial, 1993), 71–72.
29 Ibid., 239.
30 Ibid., 240.
31 Ibid., 241.
32 John Dollard, *Caste and Class in a Southern Town* (New York: Harper, 1937), 130.
33 Arnold Shankman, *Afro-Americans View the Immigrant* (Westport, CT: Greenwood Press, 1982), 137; Aaron Henry, Constance Curry, *Aaron Henry: The Fire Ever Burning* (Jackson: University of Mississippi Press, 2000), 34; and Clive Webb, "Jewish Merchants and Black Customers," *Southern Jewish History* 2 (1999): 75.
34 Eric L. Goldstein, *The Price of Whiteness: Jews, Race, and American Identity* (Princeton, NJ: Princeton University Press, 2006), 149.

35 Louis Schmier, "For Him the Schwarzers Couldn't Do Enough: A Jewish Peddler and His Black Customers Look at Each Other," *American Jewish History* 73, no. 1 (September 1983): 52.
36 Myrlie Evers, *For Us, the Living* (Garden City, NY: Doubleday, 1967), 195.
37 Endesha Ida Mae Holland, *From the Mississippi Delta: A Memoir* (Chicago: Lawrence Hill Books, 1997), 160–61.
38 Bruce Watson, *Freedom Summer: The Savage Season of 1964 That Made Mississippi Burn and Made America a Democracy* (New York: Penguin Group, 2010), 33.
39 Edward Cohen, *The Peddler's Grandson: Growing Up Jewish in Mississippi* (Jackson: University of Mississippi Press, 1999), 146.
40 Arthur Hertzberg, *A Jew in America* (New York: HarperCollins, 2003), 161.
41 Gilbert Mason, *Beaches, Blood, and Ballots: A Black Doctor's Civil Rights Struggle* (Jackson: University of Mississippi Press, 2000), 27.
42 Ella Baker, Marvel Cooke, "The Bronx Slave Market," in *Strangers and Neighbors: Relations between Blacks and Jews in the United States*, ed. Maurianne Adams, John Bracey (Amherst: University of Massachusetts Press, 1999), 369–74.
43 Clive Webb, "A Tangled Web: Black-Jewish Relations in the Twentieth Century South," in *Jewish Roots in Southern Soil*, 195.
44 HA, "B'nai Brith Speaker Talks on Patriotism," December 9, 1929.
45 Eli Evans, *The Provincials: A Personal History of Jews in the South* (Chapel Hill, NC: University of North Carolina Press, 2005), 10, 27.
46 Weissbach, *Jewish Life in Small-Town America*, 342.
47 Stella Suberman, *The Jew Store: A Memoir* (Chapel Hill, NC: Algonquin Books, 2001), 89.
48 Arvarh Strickland "Remembering Hattiesburg: Growing Up Black in Wartime Mississippi," in *Remaking Dixie: The Impact of World War II on the American South*, ed. Neil R. McMillen (Jackson: University of Mississippi Press, 1997), 149.
49 HA, "Harlem Is 'Hot,'" January 1, 1937.
50 Evans, *The Provincials*, 27.
51 HA, "London's: New Store to Open Thursday," January 18, 1939.
52 Evers, *For Us, the Living*, 122.
53 Harry Golden, *The Right Time: An Autobiography* (New York: G. P. Putnam's Sons, 1969), 237.
54 Henry, *The Fire Ever Burning*, 33.
55 HA, "Business Men Hail Theater as Hub Asset," November 27, 1929.
56 HA, "Charming Color Scheme Gives Rich, Restful Air to New Publix Theatre," November 27, 1929.
57 HA, "Fire Insurance Rates Are Cut Down," September 12, 1929.
58 HA, "Midnight Fire Hits Business Area of City," November 25, 1929.
59 Mark Twain, "Concerning the Jews," *Harper's New Monthly Magazine*, 99, September 1899, 529.
60 Patricia Evans, *The Jew in American Cinema* (Bloomington: Indiana University Press, 1984), 30–31.
61 Ida B. Wells, *Crusade for Justice: An Autobiography* (Chicago: University of Chicago Press, 1970), 331.
62 Anthony Julius, *Trials of the Diaspora: A History of Anti-Semitism in England* (Oxford: Oxford University Press, 2010), 246.
63 HA, "Fire Sale Starts Thursday," December 4, 1929.
64 HA, "More Undamaged Fire Bargains," January 10, 1930.

65 Jere Friedman, "A Family Tree and History of the Rubenstein Family" (unpublished), 14.
66 Ibid.
67 HA, "Store Allied with Chicago Retail House," November 21, 1929.
68 HA, "Department Store Head Raps Local Calamity Howlers," February 19, 1930.

CHAPTER 3

1   John Gross, *A Double Thread: Growing Up English and Jewish in London* (Chicago: Ivan R. Dee, 2001), 123.
2   Roger Cohen, *The Girl from Human Street: Ghosts of Memory in a Jewish Family* (New York: Alfred A. Knopf, 2015), 126.
3   HA, "Prince Found Guilty by Jury," January 26, 1932.
4   Neil R. McMillen, *Dark Journey: Black Mississippians in the Age of Jim Crow* (Urbana: University of Illinois Press, 1990), 208.
5   HA, "Sheriff Gray Requests Aid of Citizens," December 12, 1931.
6   HA, "White Man and Negro Held," December 14, 1931.
7   Ibid.
8   McMillen, *Dark Journey*, 229–30.
9   HA, "Lynching Expert Offers Cheap Rate for Hanging Woman," February 19, 1930.
10 HA, "An Impotent Gesture," September 9, 1930.
11 HA, "White Man and Negro Held," December 14, 1931.
12 HA, "Paul Wexler to Face Trial in Court Here," January 22, 1932.
13 For Wexler as "mastermind," see HA, "Prince Found Guilty," January 26, 1932, and for Prince as "black automaton," see "Youth to Die for Slaying of J. L. Odom," HA, January 29, 1932.
14 HA, "Prince Found Guilty."
15 Ibid.
16 Ibid.
17 HA, "Courtroom Proprieties," July 2, 1929.
18 HA, "Judge Pack Fines Jurors for Contempt," July 1, 1929.
19 HA, "Hattiesburg High School Graduates," May 31, 1930.
20 HA, "Prince Found Guilty."
21 State of Mississippi vs Paul Wexler, no. 30024, Mississippi Department of Archives and History (hereafter abbreviated as MDAH), 59, 76, 84, and 109, respectively.
22 Ibid., 167.
23 Ibid., 197.
24 Ibid., 204.
25 Ibid., 211
26 Ibid., 216–17.
27 Ibid., 174–75.
28 Ibid., 178.
29 HA, "Five in Hinds Death Cells," February 2, 1932.
30 Richard H. Luthin, *American Demagogues: Twentieth Century* (Boston: Beacon Press, 1954), 62.
31 HA, "Appeal Move Is Expected," January 30, 1932.
32 "Brief of Appellant to the Supreme Court of the State of Mississippi" in State of Mississippi vs. Paul Wexler, no. 30024, MDAH, 10–13.
33 Ibid., 13.

34 Twain, "Concerning the Jews," 529–30, 534.
35 Weissbach, *Jewish Life in Small-Town America*, 274.
36 Suberman, *The Jew Store*, 116.
37 Jaher, *A Scapegoat in the New Wilderness*, 70.
38 McMillen, "Fighting for What We Didn't Have: How Mississippi's Black Veterans Remember World War II," in *Remaking Dixie*, 97.
39 Westlaw, 167 Miss. 464, 142 So. 501.
40 HA, "Conner Gets Many Letters in Death Case," June 24, 1932.
41 HA, "Conner Talks to Young Man in His Office," July 12, 1932.
42 Ibid.
43 HA, "Sheriff Here Prepared to Execute Two," July 13, 1932.
44 HA, "Interference," July 15, 1932.
45 HA, "Petition for Coram Nobis Is Dismissed," November 19, 1932.
46 HA, "Venue Plea Denied," November 21, 1932.
47 HA, "Wexler Case Will Be Heard Here Friday," November 16, 1932.
48 HA, "Judge Pack Ends Hearing with Ruling," November 22, 1932.
49 Ibid.
50 Ibid.
51 HA, "Venue Change Plea Denied by Judge Pack," November 21, 1932.
52 HA, "Attorneys for Wexler Plan Effort to Obtain New Stay of Execution," July 28, 1932.
53 HA, "Wexler Case Will Be Heard Here Friday," November 16, 1932.
54 HA, "Paul Wexler Dies in Cell; Escapes Rope," April 14, 1933.
55 Ibid.
56 HA, "Paul Wexler Funeral Rites Held Here Friday," April 15, 1933.
57 HA, "Wexler Dies in His Cell," April 14, 1933.
58 HA, "Prince Will Hang Tuesday," April 24, 1933.
59 Rabbi Charles Mantinband, diary entry, January 29, 1939, Mantinband Collection, Goldring / Woldenberg Institute of Southern Jewish Life (hereafter ISJL), Jackson, MS.
60 Evans, *The Provincials*, 140.
61 Steve Oney, *And the Dead Shall Rise: The Murder of Mary Phagan and the Lynching of Leo Frank* (New York: Vintage Books, 2003), 558.
62 *Hattiesburg News*, "Body of Frank an Hour After Lynching" and "Crowd at Undertaker's in Marietta, Ga.," August 23, 1915.
63 C. Vann Woodward, *Tom Watson: Agrarian Rebel* (New York: Macmillan Company, 1988), 443–44.
64 Leonard Dinnerstein, *Antisemitism in America* (New York: Oxford University Press, 1994), 184.
65 McMillen, *Dark Journey*, 244–45.
66 Dinnerstein, *Antisemitism* in America, 81.
67 Neil Baldwin, *Henry Ford and the Jews: The Mass Production of Hate* (New York: Public Affairs, 2001), 146.
68 Ibid., 59.
69 Dinnerstein, *Antisemitism in America*, 107.
70 HA, "Jewish Race Is Favored," November 28, 1936.
71 The Editors of Fortune, "Jews in America," in *The Aliens: A History of Ethnic Americans in America*, ed. Leonard Dinnerstein, Frederic Jaher (New York: Appleton-Century-Crofts, 1970), 120–21.
72 Dinnerstein, *Antisemitism in America*, 127.
73 Ibid., 177.

CHAPTER 4

1. Samuel Rosenblatt, *Yossele Rosenblatt: The Story of His Life as Told by His Son* (New York: Farrar, Straus, Young, 1954), 15.
2. Ibid., 142, 145.
3. *HA*, "Cantor Sings Friday Night," January 19, 1933.
4. *HA*, "Visitor," January 20, 1933.
5. Rosenblatt, *Yossele Rosenblatt*, 337.
6. *HA*, "Cantor Charms Audience Here," January 21, 1933.
7. Rosenblatt, *Yossele Rosenblatt*, 17–18.
8. Eric Goldstein, "Now Is the Time to Show Your True Colors': Southern Jews, Whiteness, and the Rise of Jim Crow," in *Jewish Roots in Southern Soil*, 149.
9. *HA*,"Blackbird Minstrel Will Be Given at YWCA," March 6, 1934.
10. Howe, *The World of Our Fathers*, 562–63; Goldstein, *The Price of Whiteness*, 154–55.
11. Suberman, *The Jew Store*, 251.
12. *HA*, "Hambone's Meditations," February 27, 1932, June 18, 1932, January 5, 1932, and June 14, 1932.
13. Weissbach, *Jewish Life in Small-Town America*, 281.
14. Evans, *The Provincials*, 91.
15. Ernst Klee, Willi Dressen, and Volker Riess, eds. *"The Good Old Days": The Holocaust as Seen by Its Perpetrators and Bystanders* (New York: Konecky & Konecky, 1988), 154. I have also drawn on Saul Friedländer's account of what happened in Belaya Tserkov in his *Nazi Germany and the Jews: The Years of Extermination, 1939-1945* (New York: Harper Perennial, 2008), 215–18.
16. *Encyclopaedia Judaica*, s.v. "Belaya Tserkov," 278–79.
17. Sherwin B. Nuland, *Lost in America: A Journey with My Father* (New York: Vintage Books, 2003), 17
18. Weissbach, *Jewish Life in Small-Town America*, 266.
19. Leo Rosten, *The New Joys of Yiddish*, rev. Lawrence Bush (New York: Three Rivers Press, 2001), 132–33.
20. Antoine Lacassagne, "The Place of Radium in the Treatment of Cancer," *Canadian Medical Association Journal* 38, no 1 (1938): 9–13.

CHAPTER 5

1. *HA*, "Seen and Heard, Here and There, About the City" June 17, 1933.
2. *HA*, "Memphis Negroes Eating Away Mississippi River Banks of Clay," November 1, 1934.
3. Robert S. McElvaine, ed., *Down and Out in the Great Depression: Letters from the Forgotten Man* (Chapel Hill: University of North Carolina Press, 1983), 88.
4. *HA*, "Employment Gains in Hattiesburg," March 12, 1935.
5. *HA*, "Beck Praised for Pay Raise," May 25, 1933.
6. *HA*, "We Have Accepted Roosevelt's Program," July 28, 1933.
7. *HA*, "You Should Be Willing to Pay Higher Taxes," September 10, 1933.
8. Robert S. McElvaine, *The Great Depression: America, 1929-1941* (New York: Times Books, 1984), 161.
9. *HA*, "Foote Analyzes Taxation Problem," February 14, 1935.
10. *HA*, "Big Factory at Columbia Is Dedicated," June 17, 1933.

11   James C. Cobb, *The Selling of the South: The Southern Crusade for Industrial Development, 1936–1980* (Baton Rouge: Louisiana State University Press, 1982), 8.
12   Ernest J. Hopkins, *Mississippi's BAWI Plan: An Experiment in Industrial Subsidization* (Atlanta: Federal Reserve Bank of Atlanta, 1944), 11.
13   HA, "Hub Citizens Cooperate in Campaign," October 19, 1933.
14   HA, "Jacob London an Immigrant," September 2, 1929.
15   HA, "New Reliance Plan Signals City Monument," October 19, 1933.
16   Milton Gordon, *Assimilation in American Life: The Role of Race, Religion, and National Origins* (Oxford: Oxford University Press, 1964), 80–81.
17   Hodding Carter, *Where Main Street Meets the River* (New York: Rinehart, 1953), 185.
18   Stephen S. Wise, *Challenging Years: The Autobiography of Stephen Wise* (New York: G. P. Putnam's Sons, 1949), 82.
19   Rabbi Stephen S. Wise to Rabbi Arthur Brodey, October 11, 1935, SC-1390, Jacob Rader Marcus Center of the American Jewish Archives, Cincinnati, Ohio (hereafter AJA).
20   HA, "Brodey Will Preach in New Orleans," April 6, 1938.
21   HA, "Brodey Speaks at College," October 14, 1935.
22   Ibid.
23   HA, "New Armistice," November 9, 1935.
24   HA, "Jewish New Year Holiday's End," September 8, 1937.
25   HA, "Brodey Guest Speaker at Walthall PTA," November 2, 1937.
26   HA, "Need for Rededication," December 7, 1937.
27   HA, "Brodey Speaker at Review Club," March 17, 1938.
28   HA, "Exchange Club Hears Address on Current Events," November 9, 1938.
29   HA, "Rabbi Pleads for United Front," December 31, 1938.
30   HA, February 17, 1939.
31   Saul Friedländer, *Pius XI and the Third Reich*, trans. Charles Fullman (New York: Alfred A. Knopf, 1966), 6, and *Nazi Germany and the Jews: The Years of Persecution* (New York: HarperCollins, 1997), 251.
32   Emma Fattorini, *Hitler, Mussolini, and the Vatican: Pope Pius XI and the Speech That Was Never Made* (Malden, MA: Polity Press, 2011), 16, 152–57.
33   HA, "German Jews Given Help," August 23, 1933.
34   HA, "Jewish Appeal: $1000 Sought in Hattiesburg," June 12, 1935.
35   HA, "Atrocities," November 12, 1938; "Refuge," March 30, 1938.
36   HA, "Assail Jews: Nazis Continue Anti-Semitic Drive," July 18, 1935.
37   HA, "Nazis Deprive Jews of All Political Rights," November 15, 1935.
38   HA, "Atrocities," November 12, 1938.
39   HA, "Refuge," March 30, 1938.
40   Pierre Van Paassen, *Days of Our Years* (New York: Hillman-Curl, 1939), 165, 167.
41   HA, "Van Paassen Pictures World Catastrophe," April 8, 1937.
42   HA, "Zionist Will Address Jews, Gentiles," April 1, 1938.
43   Morris, *Hattiesburg, Mississippi*, 133.
44   HA, "First Conscripts Report in November," September 12, 1940.
45   HA, "Job-Hunters Swarm into Hattiesburg," September 16, 1940.
46   HA, "Army of Job-Seekers Lay Siege to Shelby," September 17, 1940.
47   HA, "Seen and Heard," November 15, 1940.
48   HA, "German-American Bund Bares Fight on Jews in U.S.," June 23, 1938.
49   Richard Lingeman, *Sinclair Lewis: Rebel from Main Street* (New York: Random House, 2002), 398–402. For calling my attention to Mussolini's fascism in the conception of the novel, I am indebted to Stephen J. Whitfield.

50 *HA*, "Violence Flares at Nazi Meeting," February 21, 1939.
51 Strickland, "Remembering Hattiesburg," 154.
52 Julian Feibelman, *The Making of a Rabbi* (New York: Vantage Press, 1980), 97.
53 *HA*, "Passover Services," April 6, 1942.
54 *HA*, "Rabbi Discusses Patriotism of Jews," December 1, 1942.

CHAPTER 6

1   Morris, *Hattiesburg, Mississippi*, 159–60.
2   David McCullough, *Truman* (New York: Simon & Schuster, 1992), 588.
3   McMillen, "Fighting for What We Didn't Have," in *Remaking Dixie*, 98–99.
4   Ibid., 187n41.
5   Ibid., 108, 110.
6   Mantinband, "Is Religion Necessary?", typed manuscript, Mantinband Collection, ISJL, 1.
7   Clarence Darrow to Rabbi Charles Mantinband, October 22, 1932, Mantinband Collection, ISJL; *The Williamsport Sun*, "Large Audience Present at Debate," December 1, 1932.
8   Yosef Hayim Yerushalmi, *Freud's Moses: Judaism Terminable and Interminable* (New Haven: Yale University Press, 1991), 31.
9   Joseph Lelyveld, *Omaha Blues: A Memory Loop* (New York: Farrar, Straus, and Geroux, 2005), 95.
10 Gary Philip Zola, "What Price Amos? Perry Nussbaum's Career in Jackson, Mississippi," in *The Quiet Voices: Southern Rabbis and Black Civil Rights, 1880s to 1990s*, ed. Mark K. Bauman, Berkley Kalin (Tuscaloosa: University of Alabama Press, 1997), 237.
11 P. Allen Krause, *To Stand Aside or Stand Alone: Oral Histories of Southern Rabbis and the Civil Rights Movement*, ed. Mark K. Bauman, Stephen Krause (Tuscaloosa: University of Alabama Press, 2016), 370n27.
12 Anna K. Mantinband, "A Time for Remembering," 1979, typed manuscript, SC-7732, AJA, 73.
13 "Jewish Communities in the South and the Desegregation Issue," Atlantic City, NJ: National Community Relations Advisory Council, June 1956, collection 563, AJA, 33–34.
14 Clive Webb, *Fight against Fear: Southern Jews and Black Civil Rights* (Athens: University of Georgia Press, 2001), 46.
15 Mark Cowett, "Morris Newfield, Alabama, and Blacks, 1895–1940," in *The Quiet Voices*, 46–47.
16 Berkley Kalin, "A Plea for Tolerance: Fineshriber in Memphis," in *The Quiet Voices*, 56–58.
17 Hollace Ava Weiner, "Rabbi Sidney Wolf: Harmonizing in Texas," in *The Quiet Voices*, 130–31.
18 Janice Rothschild Blumberg, "Jacob M. Rothschild: His Legacy Twenty Years After," in *The Quiet Voices*, 271.
19 Mantinband, "Rabbi in the Deep South," *ADL Bulletin*, 19 (May 1962): 3.
20 Mantinband, "From the Diary of a Mississippi Rabbi," *American Judaism*, 12, no. 2 (Winter 1962–63): 9. The extracts from his diary in this essay are the only ones I know of to have been published in his lifetime.
21 Mantinband, "In Dixieland I Take My Stand," collection 563, AJA, 7.

22 Mantinband, "The Horns of a Dilemma," speech for Central Conference of American Rabbis Convention, 1964, collection 563, AJA, 242.
23 Mantinband, "Our Sages Teach Us" (untitled and undated three pages), Mantinband Collection, ISJL.
24 Ibid.
25 Ibid.
26 Mantinband, "In Dixieland I Take My Stand," 5.
27 Mantinband, address to graduating seniors of Sterling Negro High School in Sheffield, Al, 1951, Mantinband collection 563, AJA, 3.
28 Krause, *To Stand Aside or Stand Alone*, 283.
29 *Montgomery Advertiser—Alabama Journal*, "Inter-Racial Unit on Human Relations Calls on Leaders for Peaceful Mixing," February 12, 1956.
30 *HA*, "Local Rabbi Says Race Problems Stink," February 13, 1956.
31 Mantinband to Editor of *HA*, February 13, 1956, Mantinband Collection, ISJL.
32 Anna Mantinband, "A Time for Remembering," 61; Mantinband refers to the sermon in "Rabbi in the Deep South," 3.
33 Francesca DeRosa, "Finding Hellen Keller's Thank You Note to a Southern Rabbi." Accessed September 15, 2015, http://www.myjewishlearning.com.
34 Mantinband, diary entry, February 13, 1956.
35 Ibid., February 14, 1956.
36 Ibid., February 15, 1956.
37 Ibid., February 16, 1956.
38 Rabbi Julius Rosenthal, "Mezuzahs and Magnolias," collection 563, AJA, 4.
39 John D. Mangram to Mantinband, February 20, 1956, Mantinband Collection, ISJL.
40 Rosenthal, "Mezuzahs and Magnolias," 12.
41 Virgil, *The Aeneid of Virgil: A Verse Translation by Rolfe Humphries*, ed. Brian Wilkie (New York: Macmillan Publishing Co., 1987), 29, line 58.
42 Mantinband, diary entry, February 17, 1956.
43 Ibid.
44 Ibid., February 19, 1956.
45 Francis Harmon to Herman Katz, February 24, 1956, Mantinband Collection, ISJL.
46 Mantinband, diary entry, February 18, 1956.
47 Ibid.
48 Ibid., February 19, 1956.
49 Rosa Lynn Hemeter, et al. to Mantinband, February 19, 1956, Mantinband Collection, ISJL.
50 Krause, *To Stand Aside or Stand Alone*, 282.
51 Mantinband, "Rabbi in the Deep South," 3–4.
52 Anna Mantinband, "A Time for Remembering," 69.
53 Krause, *To Stand Aside or Stand Alone*, 270–71.
54 *HA*, "Letter to Editor," December 6, 1958.
55 *To Stand Aside or Stand Alone*, 279; and Anna Mantinband, "A Time for Remembering," 70–71.
56 Anna Mantinband, "A Time for Remembering," 70.
57 Zack J. Van Landingham, "Clyde Kennard," Report to Mississippi State Sovereignty Commission, September 14, 1959, MDAH. Accessed February 14, 2016, http://mdah.state.ms.us/arrec/digitalarchives.

58 Anna Mantinband, "Time for Remembering," 71–72.
59 Mantinband, diary entries, November 19 and November 21, 1960.
60 Webb, "Big Struggle in a Small Town," 222.
61 Anna Mantinband, "A Time for Remembering," 71.
62 Taylor Branch, *Parting the Waters: America in the King Years, 1954–63* (New York: Simon & Schuster, 1988), 745.
63 Mantinband, "Reflections of a Rabbi" (early draft of "Rabbi in the Deep South"), 1961, collection 563, AJA, 2.
64 Zack J. Van Landingham, "Memorandum," December 5, 1958, MDAH. Accessed February 15, 2016, http://mdah.state.ms.us/arrec/digital archives
65 Mantinband, "Rabbi in the Deep South," 4.
66 Ibid.
67 John Dittmer, *Local People: The Struggle for Civil Rights in Mississippi* (Urbana: University of Illinois Press, 1994), 69.
68 Terri Barr, "Milton Grafman and Birmingham's Civil Rights Era," in *The Quiet Voices*, 178.
69 Ibid., 173.
70 Mantinband, "The Horns of a Dilemma," 245.
71 Joseph K. Gumbiner, "Taking a Stand in Dixie," SC-2854, AJA, 5.
72 Gumbiner to Mantinband, March 13, 1962, Mantinband Collection, ISJL.
73 Mantinband, "A Message for Race Relations Sabbath, 1962," issued by the Committee on Justice and Peace of the CCAR Journal, XXIX (1962), collection 563, AJA, 108.
74 Blumberg, "Jacob Rothschild," 279.
75 In a roundtable discussion of the topic "Liberalism and the Negro" (including James Baldwin, Nathan Glazer, Sidney Hook, Gunnar Myrdal, and Norman Podhoretz) that appeared in the March 1964 issue of *Commentary* magazine, Baldwin had called white liberals "a kind of affliction" in the sense that "there is something impertinent in the assumptions they make about me," using himself, the only black present, as representative of others.
76 Mantinband, "Horns of Dilemma," 245.
77 Minutes of a special meeting of Congregation B'nai Israel, December 3, 1962 McCain Library, USM.
78 Mantinband, diary entry, January 3, 1963.
79 Mantinband, diary entries, February 19 and February 20, 1963.
80 President John F. Kennedy to Mantinband, telegram, June 12, 1963, Mantinband Collection, ISJL.
81 Mantinband, "From the Diary of a Mississippi Rabbi," 8–9.
82 Webb, "Big Struggle in a Small Town," 224.
83 Shemper and Ginsburg quoted in Webb, "Big Struggle in a Small Town," 225, 228.
84 Mantinband, diary entry, February 14, 1963.
85 Rosenthal, "Mezuzahs and Magnolias," 4.
86 Krause, *To Stand Aside or Stand Alone*, 274.
87 Krause, "The Southern Rabbi and Civil Rights," master's thesis, AJA, 162.
88 Webb, *Fight against Fear*, 199; Adam Mendelsohn, "Two Far South: Rabbinical Responses to Apartheid and Segregation in South Africa and the American South" in *Southern Jewish History* 6 (2003): 96–98.
89 Mantinband, diary entries, September 18, 1960, November 18, 1960, and January 27, 1963, respectively.
90 Mantinband, diary entry, January 28, 1963.

91 Adam Mendelsohn, "Two Far South, 108–109.
92 *The National Jewish Post and Opinion*, "Was Not Ousted: Mississippi Rabbi," January 29, 1965.
93 Ibid.
94 Ibid.
95 Leonard Baker, *Days of Sorrow and Pain: Leo Baeck and the Berlin Jews* (New York: Oxford University Press, 1980), 247.
96 Mendelsohn, "Two Far South," 76.
97 Cohen, *The Girl from Human Street*, 127–28.
98 Mantinband, "Factual Data," collection 563, AJA, 13.

CHAPTER 7

1 "Resolution" of B'nai Israel Congregation, October 30, 1945, SC-1390, AJA.
2 Mantinband, "Mississippi, the Magnolia State" (unpublished manuscript, 1961), Mantinband Collection, ISJL, 3.
3 Bruce Watson, *Freedom Summer*, 143.
4 Ibid., 181.
5 Marc Fisher, "When Freedom Summer Came to Town," *Moment Magazine* (July/August, 2014), 2.
6 Ibid., 4.
7 Mantinband to Arthur Lelyveld, July 22, 1964, Amistad Research Center, Mantinband papers; Mantinband to Perry Nussbaum, October 3, 1962, collection 430, AJA.
8 ADL Oral Memoirs of Bernard Mintz, 27–28.
9 ADL Oral Memoirs of A. I. Botnick, 130, unbound copy given to me by Lori Botnick Fireman, hereafter cited as "Botnick," 1984.
10 Rabbi M. M. Landau to Rabbi Perry Nussbaum, August 3, 1961, collection 430, AJA.
11 Botnick, 130; Botnick to Label A. Katz, June 13, 1958, collection 430, AJA.
12 Botnick, 131.
13 McMillen, *The Citizens' Council: Organized Resistance to the Second Reconstruction, 1954–64* (Urbana: University of Illinois Press, 1971), 22.
14 Zola, "What Price Amos," 245.
15 Mantinband, "Factual Data," collection 563, AJA, 11.
16 "A Jewish View on Segregation" (Greenwood, MS: Association of Citizens' Councils in Mississippi, 1956), 4–5.
17 McMillen, *The Citizens' Council*, 23n.
18 Botnick, 131.
19 Botnick, "The Business of Bigotry," *ADL Bulletin* 26 (March 1969), 3.
20 Ibid.
21 Botnick, 131–32.
22 Rabbi Perry Nussbaum to Mantinband, April 17, 1964, collection 430, AJA, 2–3.
23 *New York Times*, "Mississippi Rabbi Sees Rise in Bias," September 20, 1967.
24 Botnick, 132.
25 Zola, "What Price Amos,", 234.
26 Krause, *To Stand Aside or Stand Alone*, 72.
27 Ibid., 55.
28 Ibid., 273.

29   Zola, "What Price Amos," 236.
30   Ibid.
31   A. I. Botnick to Perry Nussbaum, November 13, 1964, collection 430, AJA.
32   *To Stand Aside or Stand Alone*, 285–86.
33   Botnick, 132.
34   *To Stand Aside or Stand Alone*, 113.
35   Botnick, 132.
36   Quoted in Watson, *Freedom Summer*, 183.
37   Jack Nelson, *Terror in the Night: The Klan's Campaign against the Jews* (New York: Simon and Schuster, 1993), 55.
38   Ibid.
39   Ibid., 56.
40   *Jackson Daily News*, "Nussbaum Home Ripped by Bomb," November 22, 1967.
41   Ibid.
42   Zola, "What Price Amos," 239, 242.
43   Ibid., 249.
44   William M. Kunstler, *Deep in My Heart* (New York: William Morrow and Company, 1966), 58.
45   Botnick, 130.
46   Kunstler, *Deep in My Heart*, 58–59.
47   Nelson, *Terror in the Night*, 41
48   Ibid., 71–72.
49   Jim Ingram, James L. Dickerson, *The Hero among Us: Memoirs of an FBI Witness Hunter* (Brandon, MS: Sartoris Literary Group, 2013), 100–101.
50   Nelson, *Terror in the Night*, 76
51   Dinnerstein, *Antisemitism in America*, 194.
52   Ingram, *The Hero among Us*, 101.
53   Nelson, *Terror in the Night*, 74–75.
54   Zola, "What Price Amos," 254.
55   Ibid., 256.
56   Ibid., 133.
57   Ingram, *The Hero among Us*, 95.
58   Leo E. and Evelyn Turitz, *Jews in Early Mississippi* (Jackson: University of Mississippi Press, 1983), 94–95, 100.
59   Nelson, *Terror in the Night*, 125–26.
60   Ibid., 136.
61   For the different accounts of who shot first, see Nelson, *Terror in the Night*, 179; Ingram, *The Hero among Us*, 106; and Thomas A. Tarrants, III, *The Conversion of a Klansman: The Story of a Former Ku Klux Klan Terrorist* (New York: Doubleday & Company, 1979), 126.
62   Tarrants, *Conversion of a Klansman*, 126.
63   Nelson, *Terror in the Night*, 219.
64   Ibid., 224.
65   Ibid., 237.
66   Tarrants, *The Conversion of a Klansman*, 125–26.
67   Botnick, 133.
68   ADL "Statement Concerning Jack Nelson's *Terror in the Night*, December 1992, for responding to press inquiries," quoted from copy given to me by Fay Botnick.

69 Maryanne Vollers, *Ghosts of Mississippi: The Murder of Medgar Evers, the Trials of Byron De La Beckwith, and the Haunting of the New South* (New York: Little Brown and Company, 1995), 230.
70 Nelson, *Terror in the Night*, 265.
71 Jack Nelson, *Scoop: The Evolution of a Southern Reporter* (Jackson: University Press of Mississippi, 2013), 150–52.
72 Ingram, *The Hero among Us*, 106.
73 Botnick, 134.
74 Ingram, *The Hero among Us*, 97.
75 Vollers, *Ghosts of Mississippi*, 163–64.
76 Reed Massengill, *Portrait of a Racist: The Man Who Killed Medgar Evers* (New York: St. Martin's Press, 1994), 163.
77 Vollers, *Ghosts of Mississippi*, 52, 55, 223–24, 228.
78 Ibid., 231.
79 Massengill, *Portrait of a Racist*, 267.
80 Dina Kraft, "The JFK Files: How Oswald's Childhood Friend Found Himself in Israel and Ended Up 'Helping the Mossad,'" *Haaretz*, October 29, 2017, 1–2. Accessed October 29, 2017. https://www.haaretz.com/us-news/1.819219.
81 Ibid., 3.
82 Ibid., 8–9; Massengill, Portrait of a Racist, 267.
83 Vollers, *Ghosts of Mississippi*, 231–37.
84 Arieh O'Sullivan, "A Jewish Cop in Burning Mississippi," *The Jerusalem Post*, July 3, 2005.
85 Botnick, 134.
86 Vollers, *Ghosts of Mississippi*, 242.
87 "Memorandum to 'Friends of ADL,'" from Allan L. Katz, July, 1979, a copy of which was given to me by Fay Botnick.
88 Botnick, "'B' Botnick Says Goodbye,"*ADL Frontline Newsletter*, April/May 1992, 13.

AFTERWORD

1 *Signature Magazine*, "A Class Act: Waldoff's Dept. Store," September, 2017, 70.
2 Ibid., 71.
3 Stuart Rockoff, "B'nai Israel, Hattiesburg," In *Encyclopedia of Southern Jewish Communities*. ISJL, 2017. Accessed September 25, 2017, http://www.isjl.org/mississippi-hattiesburg-bnai-israel-encyclopedia.html.

Acknowledgments

This book owes a great deal to a few people who, without knowing they were doing so, helped me bring it into being. Long before I began to think of writing it, I benefitted from conversations with my sister and brother, Fay Botnick and Milton Waldoff, about our family's history. Their memories and their sharing copies of family letters, photos, documents, and other materials went a long way toward making this book possible. My conversations with my late cousin Melvin (Buddy) Stein, as well as with cousins Jere Friedman, Maurice Auerbach, and Stanley Waldoff, helped me with their knowledge of different branches of our extended family. My nephew Michael Botnick and niece Lori Botnick Fireman provided me with information about their father's work with the ADL, and my daughter Jessica's and my niece Wendy Botnick's memories of their separate conversations with Aunt Rose provided confirmation of an important episode in our family history.

In Urbana, I am indebted to my colleagues and friends Jack Stillinger and the late Nina Baym for their encouraging comments on an early draft of the book and to Karl-Heinz Schoeps for his comments on Chapter 3. I am especially indebted to Eugene M. Avrutin and Mark D. Steinberg for their advice and suggested readings in Russian history, which provided me with a far better understanding of my parents' early experience than I would otherwise have had. I am grateful to Veronica Shapovalov for her translations of letters in Russian and Chana Bursztyn for those in Yiddish. Others whose help along the way enabled me to better understand parts of the story I tell in this book are P. Irving Bloom, Fanny Bryan, Jan Hillegas, Robert D. King, Aili Monahan, and Arieh O'Sullivan.

I want to thank Gary Zola and Dana Herman for their help at the American Jewish Archives in Cincinnati and Mark K. Bauman for providing me with a prepublication electronic copy of *To Stand Aside or Stand Alone*. Macy Hart and Rachel Meyer gave me ready and welcoming access to the Mantinband collection at the Institute of Southern Jewish Life in Jackson, Mississippi. Jennifer

Brannock provided help with the Mantinband and Congregation B'nai Israel papers at the Rare Books Library of the University of Southern Mississippi in Hattiesburg.

At Academic Studies Press, Daria Pokholkova and Kira Nemirovsky were very helpful during the copyediting process and Alessandra Anzani was wonderfully prompt and obliging in response to my many questions and requests in the course of seeing the manuscript through the press.

I am particularly grateful to Michael Shapiro, my colleague and friend of many years, for his early interest in the project, his extensive comments on the manuscript, and his unfailing support throughout.

My greatest debt is to my wife Alice. She read successive drafts of each chapter and brought to her readings the discerning eye of an experienced editor, helping me to sharpen the focus of the narrative. Her confidence in the book, her continuing support during the years I worked on it, her travelling with me to several libraries and often sorting through and reading the primary materials with me, were crucial to its completion.

www.ingramcontent.com/pod-product-compliance
Lightning Source LLC
Chambersburg PA
CBHW050525170426
43201CB00013B/2088